AF521819

Disneyana Collectors Guide To California Pottery

Brayton's Laguna, Vernon Kilns, American/Shaw, Hagen-Renaker

Devin Frick
Tamara Hodge

Park Place Press
Orange County, California

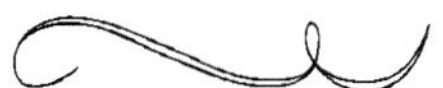

Printed in the United States of America
First Edition

Library of Congress Catalog Card Number: #98-091349

ISBN 0-9663493-0-X

The current values in the book should be used only as a guide. They are not intended to set prices, which vary from one section of the country to another. Auction prices as well as dealer prices vary greatly and are affected by condition and demand. Neither the Authors nor the Publisher assume responsibility for any losses which might be incurred as a result of consulting this guide.

Table of Contents

Foreword 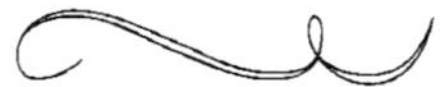

Since the early 1930s, the history of Southern California has been closely aligned with that of the Walt Disney Studios. It has been both an auspicious and celebrated history. Especially colorful has been the array of ceramic products resulting from the release of the classic animated features the Disney Studios produced in their early history. Today these enduring byproducts are avidly collected by two major groups: Disneyana collectors and collectors of California Pottery.

This new book fills a major void known to both groups by providing a comprehensive catalog of the wares produced by the Southern California ceramic industry between 1938 and 1960 under direct license from the Walt Disney Company. The book benefits dealers, as well as collectors, in the field by assigning current values to these sought-after items.

Devin Frick, author of the recently published Collectible Kay Finch, has profiled the early California companies that manufactured some of the best figurines and tableware to ever bear the Disney trademark. He, in collaboration with Disneyana & California Pottery collector Tamara Hodge, have documented nearly all the individual items produced by the Disney-California big 4: Brayton Laguna, Vernon Kilns, Hagen-Renaker, and the the Evan K. Shaw Company. Lastly, we are treated to the superb documentary photography of Victoria Damrel. Ms. Damrel has assisted on some of my own book projects so I know full well what a refined sensibility she supplied.

Every so often a new reference book appears that has been so acutely needed that it requires no introduction or fanfare. I believe this is one of those instances. Accordingly, nothing more need be said except, "The wait is over!"

Jack Chipman

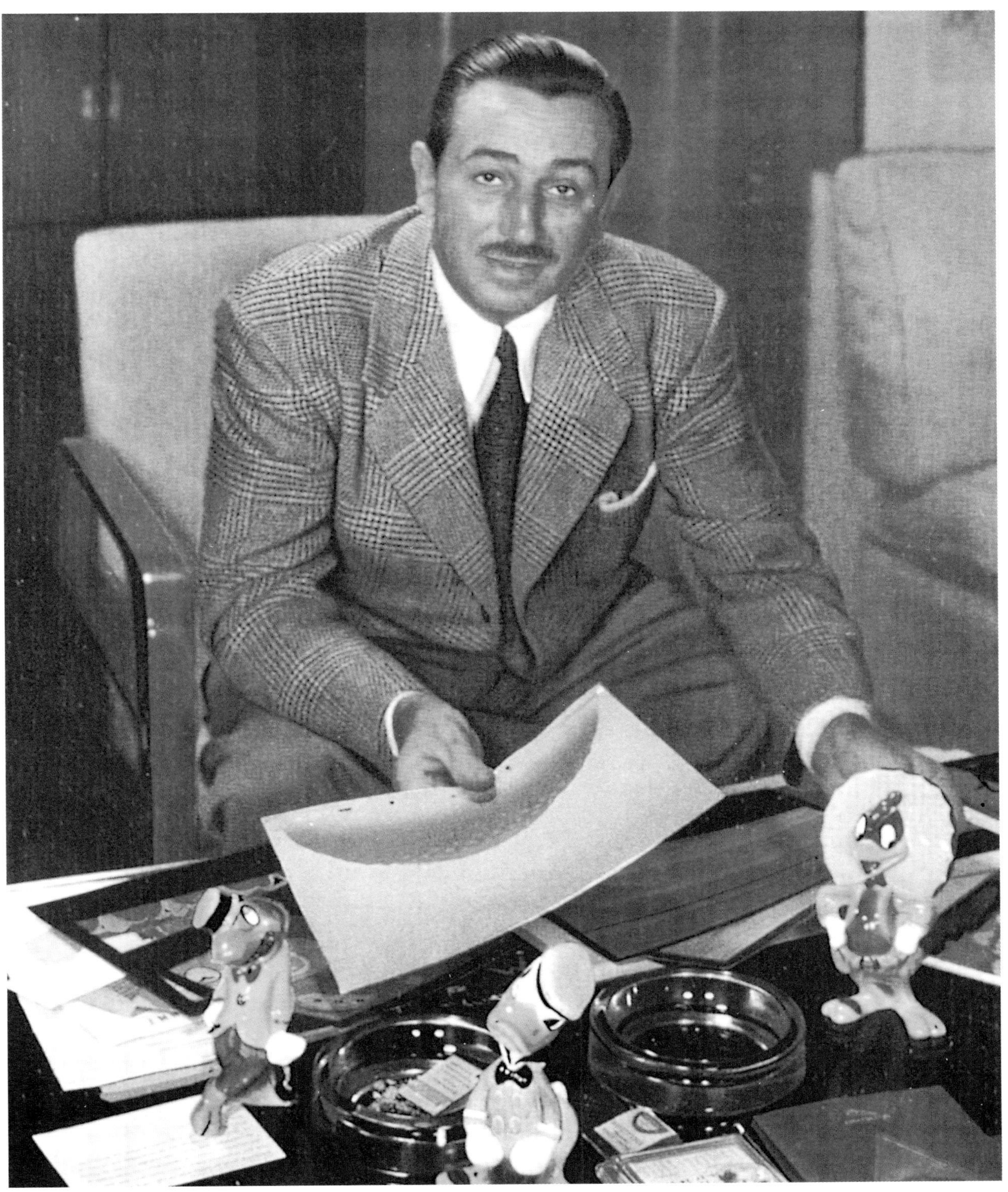

Walt Disney at his desk with American Pottery's "Three Caballeros".

Introduction & Acknowledgements

This book would not have been possible without the help and encouragement of many individuals. The authors want to particularly thank the numerous Disneyana and California pottery collectors who lent their collections to be compiled and photographed in this publication. Thanks to Greg Abbott, Jim, Joanne and John Barrett, George and Bonnie Beckerson, Matt Crandall, Stephen and Kathleen Mutrynowski, and Fred and Margaret Wilhelm. We wish to thank the many Disney and pottery collectors and innovators who lent their time, knowledge and insight. Thanks to Stacia Martin, Don Winton, Mike Ellis, Susan Renaker of Hagen-Renaker, Jack Chipman, Peter Eastment, Scott and Shani Wolf, Barbara Murphy, Tom Tumbusch, Richard Martinez, Jean Frick, Carl Gibbs Jr., Michael Brayton, Stan Skee, Steve Stuart, Bob Molinari, Maxine Nelson, and Blue Bauer. Professional photography was provided by Victoria Damrel. We particularly wish to thank Margaret Adamic from Disney Publishing and Dave Smith and staff from the Walt Disney Archives for their dedication to the project and to the Los Angeles Public Library, the Manhattan Beach Historical Society, and the Laguna Beach Historical Society for research information on these potteries.

This book was written and photographed as a guide for both Disneyana and California pottery collectors and admirers. It is a testimony to the state's golden era of ceramics art production concurrent with The Walt Disney Studios golden era of animation. This publication is not intended to be an exact historical representation of the Walt Disney Company or the other ceramics manufacturers featured in the book.

Hollywood's Arts and Crafts

In the 1920s two brothers came to California from Kansas City to strike their fame in the world of animated entertainment. Like many artistic creators and businessmen before and after them, Walt and Roy Disney had come to the state seeking something grander. Over the decades, the name Walt Disney became renowned for quality entertainment with his many extraordinary characters becoming instant icons in the hearts of millions of Americans and people the world over.

It was fortuitous that some of these characters would be cast in their charming poise and style by some of California's most famous ceramic operations of that day. Disney's artists personally created or oversaw the creation of each sculpture to be reproduced in ceramic to be authentic in every detail that fully represented their creation in order that the child in all of us could have a piece of true motion picture Americana.

Yesterday the ceramics were given as presents to children to display on their bedroom shelf. Today many adult collectors eagerly search on the second hand market for that Vernon Hippo or a Hagen Renaker Scrooge McDuck figure to add to their increasing collection.

The true collector is seeking not only a well-rounded character representation from an earlier time but the quality and originality found in California ceramics design. Is it by chance that the majority of these California pottery concern products just complemented Disney's succeed in films perfectly? Or can one only imagine what a unique Brayton Laguna Centaur from Fantasia might have appeared had the firms license continued for another year or a Vernon Kilns Snow White figurine in their quality ceramic base and finishing had the company produced one?

Brayton Laguna employed its warm, earthy clays and vivid colors that suited perfectly to a little wooden boy. Vernon with its dreamy pastels and museum-quality clays couldn't be more adept in representing a shy cupid or "graceful" dancing ostrich from a ground breaking film. Evan K. Shaw's American and later Metlox ceramic operations produced figures that captured in each clay sculpture the colors and spirit of the brilliant studio artwork utilized in the creation of fine animation. And Hagen-Renaker developed its masterful miniatures of the 1950s with each piece precise to the smallest and slightest detail.

As an art medium, ceramics have been used for thousands of years. Histories of early cultures have been compiled from the many pottery shards found in excavations of ancient ruins. Many of these ancient shapes and designs represented a god or an idealized image respected in their daily life. Figurines were first made as long ago as 5000 B. C. Both serious and humorous creations have been unearthed in the worlds of the Aztecs and the Incas.

The Egyptians created the forerunners of our modern figurines. Several of these earlier pieces displayed a definite sense of humor such as the turquoise hippopotamus decorated with lotus blos soms or a bowl with "feet". Humor has played a role in ceramics in this century from fabled English character jugs to whimsical mugs from Germany to funny-in-appearance but very important good luck figurines made in the orient.

California's own arts and crafts movement had begun in the early 1900s and with the presence of Hollywood's burgeoning motion picture industry, much of the area's movement and output grew commercial. Production of the state's earlier ceramic creations had tended to be purely functional with such items as bathroom plumbing, pipes, roofing and decorative architectural tiles. In the 1920's and 30's as Southern California's population began to bloom, a need arose for functional, decorative and inexpensive dinnerware, bowls, vases and figurines to fill the area's swath of new houses. Some of the region's fine pottery operations began to emulate the architectural elements of the state's own earthy Spanish and Mexican historical eras in colorful tiles and pots, while many artists, often transplants to the region, simulated the established and proven European silhouette, decoration and designs long popular in other pottery manufacturing centers in the country.

But certain California manufacturers chose not to follow these recommended routes. By pursuing their own instincts and establishing local artists living in California to their lines, these ceramic houses achieved a greater level of intelligence and outright courage.

The animated character reproductions proved to be a bonanza in that they continued to feed the country's popular culture inside as well as outside the crowded movie theater. The state realized it had its own creative outlet in Hollywood that fortunately made millions of people smile and laugh. This commercialism should be looked on favorably as what was produced was socially popular with America's booming populace of the 1940s and 50s and economically stupendous. In further defense, what was being produced ceramically was a product of the state's homegrown Hollywood art studio. It was original popular art.

Hunting and Gathering

Much of the ceramic art pictured in this book originally sold in gift shops, department stores and florist shops across the United States from 1938 to about 1964. Disney California ceramics today can be found on the second-hand collectors market if one truly wishes to pursue them. Check in early at your local reputable Flea Markets, and be the first one at garage sales or tag sales, antique shops, malls and shows, Disneyana shows, pottery shows, auctions and check out mail order catalogs. Please be advised that numerous ceramics were and still are produced by various companies across this country as well as in Europe and the Orient. Check Disneyana guides and books for more resources.

While some of the more rare figures pictured in this book are very hard to find and, when found, very expensive, don't get discouraged. Remember most of these ceramics were produced for a short time fifty some years ago in an earthquake-prone region. Most were given as gifts to children, therefore these pieces are rare. It is a good idea to make contacts with collectors and collectible dealers to find what you are looking for.

Occasionally a collector will find a duplicate that they do not want and a "find" is infrequently out there. Some of the ceramics pictured in this book were hunted down for $20 and $30 and in the most unusual places while many others were tagged in the hundreds. Remember the thrill is always in the hunt. In the production and development of this book not all ceramics were available for photography. A few ceramics depicted in past Disney merchandise catalogs the authors of this book have never even seen.

Care and Display of your Collection

What all pieces of ceramic art need are an occasional dusting, however sometimes a piece just purchased needs some tender loving care with a soft, slightly damp cloth. It is advisable not to use any detergents as they can strip away the original decoration. While cleaning, be careful to avoid paint over-glaze that can very easily flake off the glaze. Also beware of glaze crazing as water and detergents can seep in through the cracks and permanently discolor the bisque clay body.

The display of your collection has hard and fast rules and rules that are meant to be broken. The hard and fast: Never display your figures in direct sun light. As with any fine art, the sun's rays will fade the paint decoration and increase the likelihood of glaze crazing. Never display your collection without a museum putty hold. The hold will guard against accidents both natural and man-made. Always keep your ceramics out of the reach of children and animals to avoid loss and even worse injury. Rules that can be broken: Most collectors like to fill their shelves to overflowing with colorful ceramics while others develop small groupings and individual settings in order that each sculpture may be appreciated fully. One collector specialized in miniatures, placing them in shadow boxes while others display corresponding animation art as a backdrop behind the figures.

Ceramic Restoration

Professional restoration does not necessarily lower the value of a piece. Most long-time collectors have at least one restored piece in their collection, whether they know it or not. Museums have been restoring works of art for years, insuring that the piece will be preserved to be enjoyed for years to come. Some of the ceramics pictured in this book are extremely rare! Without restoration they would not be pictured herein at all.

Many of the Disney figures were created from the actual character sculptures used in the development of an animated film. When originally created these sculptures (maquette) were used as three dimensional guides for the animators and were not intended as merchandise for the marketplace. Therefore many of the sculptures produced in ceramic form are top-heavy with large heads and hats that tend to easily topple and break. If one of your figures breaks, do not glue it back together. Place all of the pieces in a sealed plastic bag. Ask fellow collectors and dealers for a good restorer and ask to see an example restored piece. When selling or trading a restored piece, always let the buyer know its current condition. Restoration is a very difficult art and takes a great deal of time, care and patience. Always beware of quick-fix techniques in any restoration as it takes years and a great love of pottery to fully master this art.

Price Note

Prices listed in this book are only meant to be a guide. This is only a guide! Prices can be higher or lower depending on various circumstances such as condition, decoration, high and low demand and other factors. Prices also fluctuate throughout the United States and around the world. The publisher and authors do not take responsibility on any losses incurred due to consulting this book.

NPA = No Price Available

The Authors

Devin Frick has been a California pottery collector and historian since 1978. He has produced museum exhibits, catalogs and lectured on art pottery. Tamara Hodge has been an avid Disney and pottery collector since 1984. She is a professional pottery/ceramics restorer and operates Ceramics Care Unit in Long Beach, California.

Book and cover designed by Devin Frick, Tamara Hodge, Victoria Damrel, Bobbi Murphy and Richard Martinez.

From the publisher to Kasie and Garrett and any furture grandchildren.

Bibliography

Chipman, Jack. *Collectors Encyclopedia of California Pottery.* 1992 Collector Books.

Frick, Devin. *California Kilns* exhibit catalog, 1994 Anaheim Museum, Anaheim California.

Gibbs, Carl Jr. *Metlox Potteries*, 1995 Collector Books. Paducah, Kentucky.

Henzke, Lucile. *Art Pottery of America*, 1982 Schiffer Publishing Exton, Pa.

Maltin, Leonard. *The Disney Films*. 1973 Crown Publishers, New York.

Munsey, Cecil. *Disneyana: Walt Disney Collectibles*. 1974 Hawthorn Books, New York.

Nelson, Maxine. *Collectible Vernon Kilns,* 1994 Collector Books. Paducah, Kentucky.

Roller, Gayle, Kathleen Rose, Joan Berkwitz. *The Hagen-Renaker Handbook*, 1989.

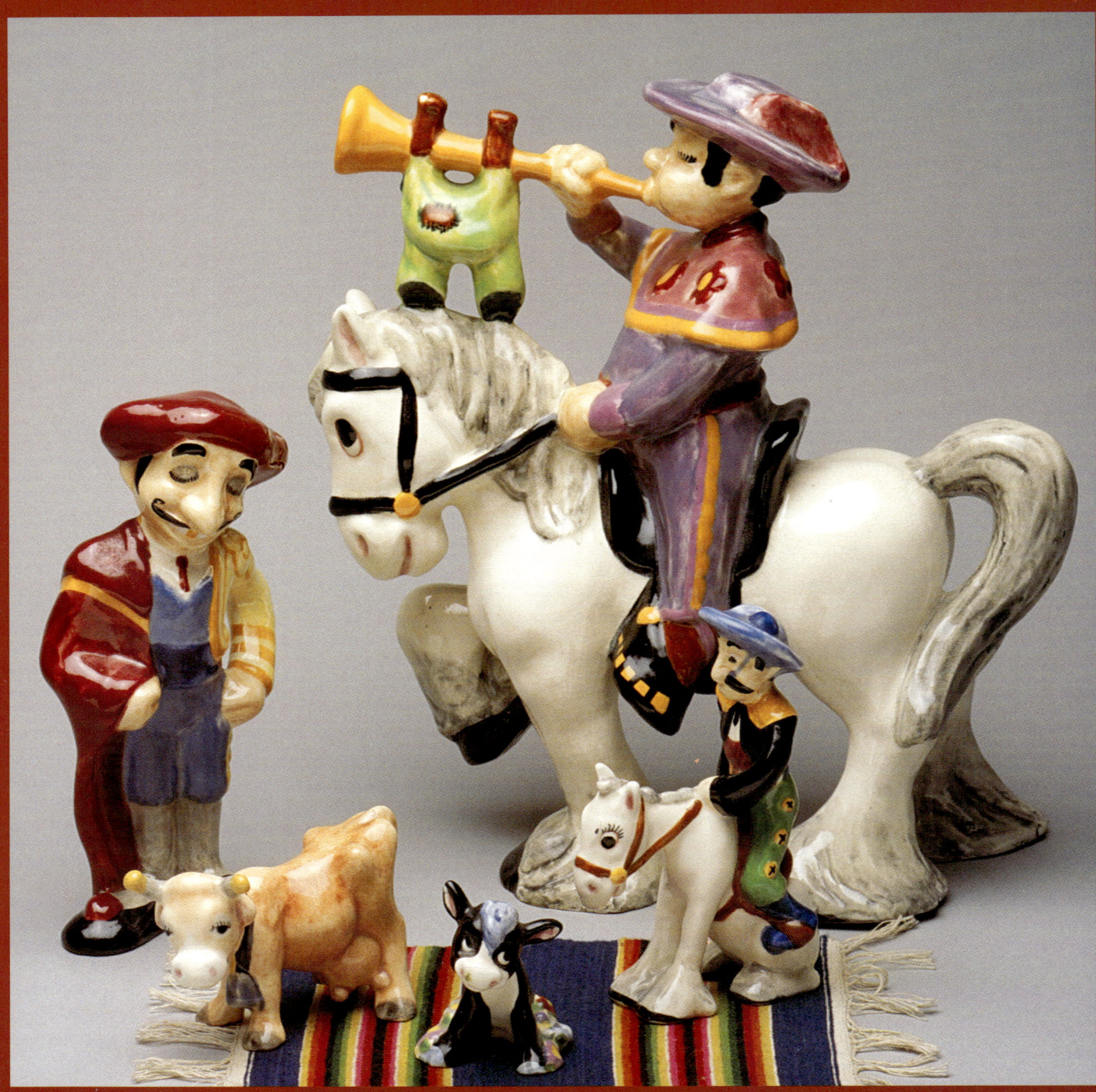

Brayton's Laguna Pottery
1938-1939

Brayton's Laguna Pottery of Laguna Beach, California was licensed to produce ceramic figurines of select Walt Disney characters for only seventeen months. The work produced by Brayton artisans over this short span of time ranged dramatically from charmingly unrefined to beautifully detailed in its final efforts. These unique creations were produced during Hollywood's golden era of film and simultaneous with the peak of the state's arts and crafts movement.

Brayton's Laguna Pottery was a pioneer and trendsetter in Southern California ceramics production. Historically the concern led the way in ceramic firsts in pottery production. The small studio was founded in 1926 by artist Durlin Eugene Brayton. Brayton was a California native and after graduating from Hollywood High, he traveled to Chicago to advance his studies in art and sculpture at the Chicago Art Institute. For their involvement in the first World War, Brayton's family had been given land in the small village/artist community of Laguna Beach and upon his return to the state, Brayton resided in a modest home he had built for himself on this property along Coast Highway. Brayton dabbled in many eclectic artistic projects and ventures including oil and watercolor painting, carpentry work and the development of unique furniture designs. One of his unusual medieval style seats made from pine and rope was featured in the June, 1935 issue of Popular Science. He even delivered the morning newspaper to the town residents for some time. Brayton's fascination with art, gadgets and artists in general would continue over the length of his life.

As most artists do, Brayton occasionally dabbled in clay and found he had a knack for it. He began designing hand-formed one-of-a-kind bowls, vases and place settings that he hand dipped in bright, vibrant and unique color glazes and then had fired in a local kiln. Placing the product for sale in his front yard, the ceramics quickly sold as their unique form and strong colors had caught the attention of the many travelers to the village, citizens passing by. Prior to this time, dinnerware was white or cream china with limited flower or decal color decoration.

Other larger area ceramics manufacturers would soon begin duplicating Brayton's unrivaled work. With this business success, Brayton soon borrowed $300.00 from his father to purchase his own kiln and Brayton's full pottery production began in 1927.

Word spread about the little ceramics studio by the beach that made and sold this unusual pottery. Jugs, jars and pitchers were added to the line and soon vibrant detailed tiles derived from the area's provincial landscape appeared. Locals and summer tourists proved to be the firm's first and best publicity by spreading the product and name Brayton across the country.

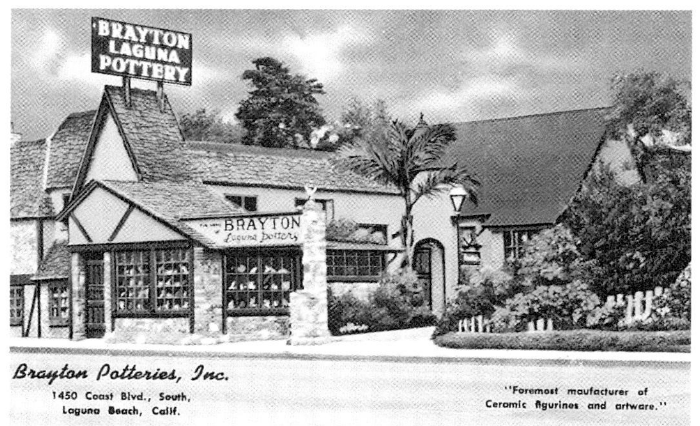

Throughout the 1930's, the cottage company at 1450 Coast Highway expanded its facility and production output and was the first to include not only Durlin's work but his wive's and many other well-schooled designers living in and around Laguna Beach. By the mid 30's, Brayton's Pottery had grown into a charming English cottage structure of 14,000 square feet and its employee work force peaked in the mid 1940's at close to 70.

The staff itself was a close knit family with many socializing after work and the company Christmas parties were wonderfully wild with police being called in not to break up the party but safely escort the guests home at night's end.

The company's product now included mostly decorative figurines, planters and household items and they all could be found in many fine department stores and gift shops around the country. Brayton developed their own paint colors and lead-less glazes that retained paint colors. The pottery continued to encourage other outstanding artists and organizations to contribute to the growing line.

In the late 1930's, the firm produced many beautifully decorated, richly detailed and humorous storybook inspired ceramic sets. Literary characters from Alice in Wonderland, Old King Cole, Little Bo Peep and Miss Muffett among others were popular sellers. A trio consisting of a purple bull, cow and calf inspired by the famous poem by Gelett Burgess found a home at Brayton's. So favored by the public were the unusually hued bovines, that more than 45,000 sets originally designed by wood carving artist Andy Anderson were produced and sold over the years.

Other characters included the Ginghan Dog and Calico Cat and an English fox hunting set. At this time representatives from Kay Kamen Ltd., under contract from Walt Disney Enterprises for the licensing of its character merchandise, were seeking quality ceramic representations of their characters.

With Brayton's renowned reputation and cross-country sales, a standard one year contract was drawn up on May 16, 1938 and Brayton's became the first California ceramic company to began producing authorized Disney ceramics in their standard colors and glazes. Before and during this time, most of Disney's character ceramics were licensed through the George Borgfelt Company. The Borgfelt un-glazed and rough textured bisques of the 1930's and early 40's have a crude appearance and were produced in the thousands in Japan and have been found in various sizes. *Snow White and The Seven Dwarfs* had its world premiere in Los Angeles at the Carthay Circle Theater on December 21, 1937. The film's critical and financial reaction was enormous for the first feature length animated motion picture with a box office take totaling over four million dollars in its first issue in the United States and Canada. The film was also a post depression licensing bonanza with hundreds of toys, dolls and tie-in products. At this point in history, no other film had achieved this type of box office and lucrative merchandise success.

Brayton produced a full Snow White set with all the Seven Dwarfs and the forest animals including a large and small fawn, rabbits, squirrels, raccoons and chipmunks. A large version of Snow White herself was the most expensive, originally retailing for around $3.50. The milky glazed figures are unpolished in appearance but capably finished in Brayton's unique style.

Truthfully these ceramic figures do not look as the characters appear in the film or even how they are depicted in Disney illustrations on the printed page. Liberties have been taken mostly in the ceramics decoration. For example Snow White's dress is painted blue rather than yellow and her cape is of an intricate cross-hatch design unlike the film version. In their defense, pottery decoration and glazing in the 1930s could not exactly duplicate the specially mixed paints employed in the animated motion picture in their finished product. Therefore the ceramics could be considered artful artist's representations of Disney's motion picture representation of the Brothers' Grimm characters. As individual ceramic art they are more than able to stand on their own and characteristically represent Brayton's fine craft at this time. Most of the Snow White figures were impressed with a W. D. E. mark in the unglazed base or inside the body cavity. A small dated gold paper label, "1938 Walt Disney Enterprises Brayton Laguna Pottery", is also found on many examples. All of the Disney ceramics were originally given wholesale order numbers but these do not appear on the actual figures.

Ferdinand the Bull was Walt Disney's 1938 Academy Award® winning animated short adaptation of Munro Leaf's popular book. As with Snow White, the cartoon was a licensing bonanza and Brayton had much

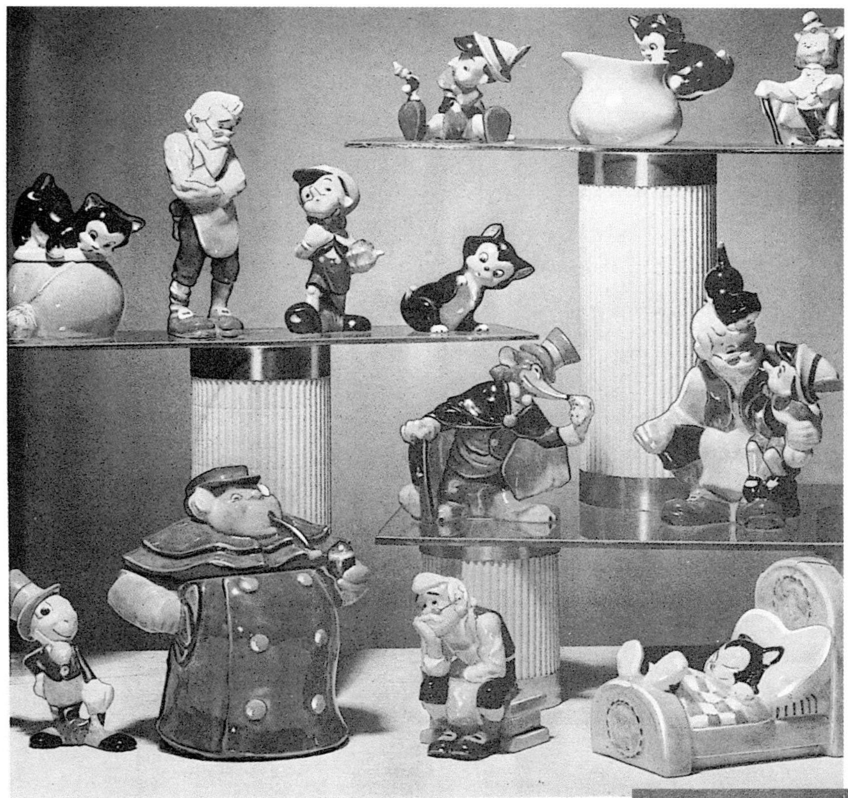

Pottery figures based upon characters from Walt Disney's PINOCCHIO in a new and irresistible collection. California clays, delicately colored and beautifully glazed, are modelled by native artists into faithful reproductions of the motion picture characters.

RETAIL PRICES

PINOCCHIO figures (4 poses)	$2.00 to $3.00	FOX	2.50
GEPPETTO (standing or sitting)	2.50	GIDDY THE CAT	1.50
GEPPETTO GROUP	7.50	COACHMAN (candy jar)	6.00
		FIGARO IN BED	3.50
		FIGARO SUGAR & CREAMER	$3.50 per set

BRAYTON'S LAGUNA POTTERY
1450 Coast Boulevard South
Laguna Beach, California

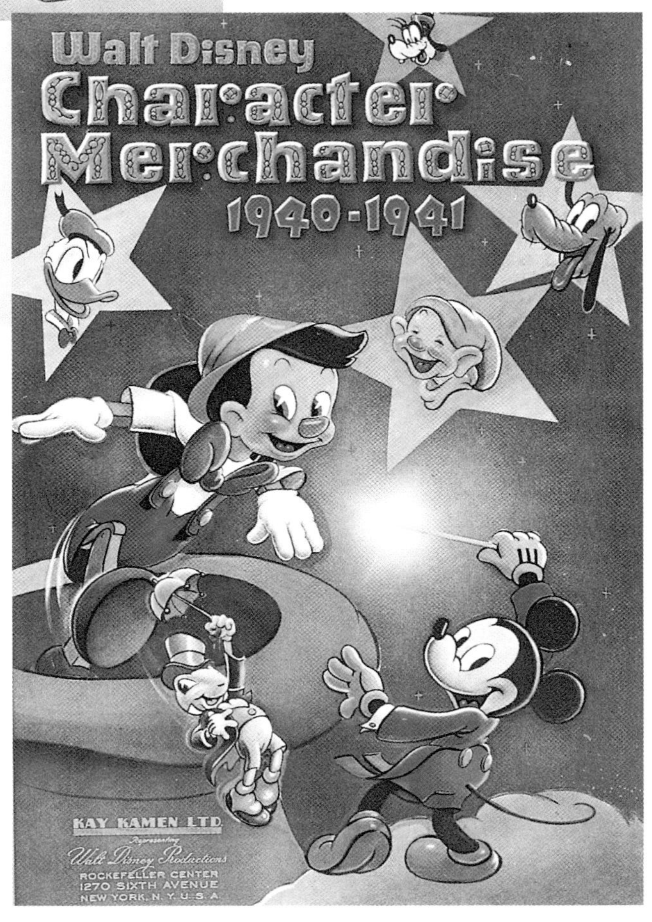

Brayton Laguna's Disney line was promoted through Kay Kamen's 1940 merchandise catalog

better fortune aesthetically with these figures inspired by the famed but tame flower-sniffing bull of the Spanish arena.

Ferdinand was produced in ceramic in both young and old poses and for reasons unknown to the authors, the complete set was produced in two sizes, regular and miniature. Ferdinand's Ma, the cow and a fabulous and beautifully decorated band of five comical Men in Funny Hats, a Trumpeter on horse, spectators, horses, and the Matador rounded out this beautiful set. The company also produced several mainstay Disney characters such as the howling Pluto, crouching Pluto and a companion worm, a squawking Donald Duck, Donald pondering and the very rare ceramic blushing Princess Minnie Mouse with a proposing Mickey Mouse. Mickey and Minnie are believed to be inspired from the cartoon short "Brave Little Tailor", 1938 and few examples are known (if any) to be in existence. A Goofy casting was sent to Brayton's in October 1939 but as the authors suspect, it probably never made it to the production process.

These pieces and the Ferdinand set were generally not marked in lieu of a paper label although collectors will notice most pieces have an initial on the underside. It was a common practice for the pottery cleaner or mold line trimmer to initial the pieces they had cleaned, while the piece was still moist in the production process.

For Brayton's last Disney set produced in the fall of 1939, the company introduced an exquisitely decorated Pinocchio line. Like some of the other pieces, these exceptionally done figures were cast from original sculptures created by Disney artists for the production of the animated films. One of the set's exclusivities was that it was specially named, marketed, and ink stamped "Geppetto Pottery", some figures with small bases being left unmarked. The film *Pinocchio* was released on February 7, 1940 and was based on the famous story by Carlo Collodi.

The story of the little wooden puppet come to life was indeed one of the Walt Disney Studios greatest artistic achievements. Because of World War II, the film did not receive the same European release that *Snow White and the Seven Dwafts* had been given and therefore its box office did not equal its predecessor.

The cast of characters represented from the several active figures of Pinocchio, Geppetto, Figaro the kitten, Jiminy Cricket, Honest John, Gideon, and the Pleasure Island Coachman as a candy jar. A Figaro sugar and creamery set along with the same sly kitten in his kitty bed are also considered rare and hard-to-find by many collectors.

Most of the ceramics were cast in color oxide-tinted clays giving them a feeling of reality and warmth and were beautifully detailed by Brayton's skilled decorators. Some of the larger figures required an hour or more to decorate.

Because the molds were made from actual detailed Disney sculpted figures, the charming ceramics were very successful in retail sales especially the numerous Figaro models. They were heavily promoted being featured after their actual production run at Brayton had ended in the 1940 merchandise catalog, but unfortunately the pottery group were made for less than six months only due to the contract expiration.

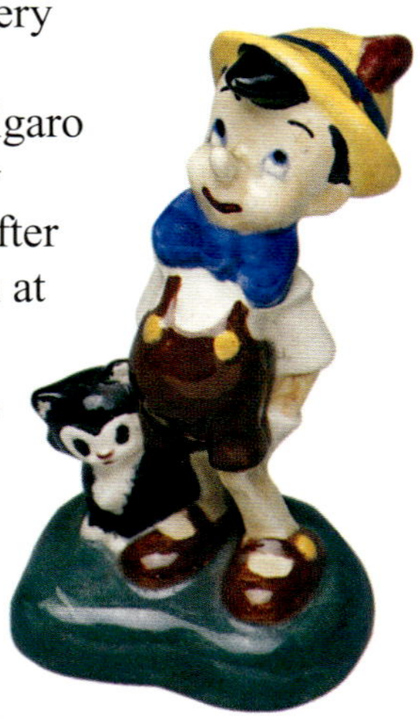

Pinocchio and Figaro
4 1/4" $200-400

In records from the studio, the castings for some of the Pinocchio ceramics were sent to Brayton's in July and August, 1939.

Brayton's production methods changed from the time consuming hand-thrown and hand-pressed pieces of the 1920's and 30's to a more effective modern slip casting process, one process that was similar to most ceramics outfits of the day. The Disney ceramics were made in this manner. After the two-piece plaster molds were produced from the original sculpture, the plaster parts would be cleaned and clamped together. Aged clays from Kentucky and Tennessee would be mixed with

California talc to give the clay flexibility and then finely ground in mills before being mixed with water to a creamy consistency. A coloring oxide would be added at this time if a color tint was desired in the base. The clay slip would be poured into the plaster mold, filling the cavity completely. The dry plaster mold causes the clay to draw in and thicken on the inside of the mold. After a designated time period, the excess clay slip is poured out the block mold case and then the moist figure is carefully removed from the mold, before a cleaner or trimmer removes all mold lines with a small dull knife. The figures are then ready for air drying for firmness and their first bisque firing. During this tunnel kiln firing, all chemically combined water and carbon dioxide evaporates with the ceramic piece shrinking and hardening to a stone-like finish. The Disney Studio model department produced most if not all of the Disney molds for Brayton as the pottery was charged a nominal casting and labor fee.

The decorating department was one of the largest sections in the company as it was the most time-consuming. Fifteen to twenty girls would sit painting the many figures. Some pieces such as the Pluto figures required only minimal painting with just a few paint colors and details, while other more complex ceramics such as most of the Pinocchio pieces took a great deal of care and patience. Some of the specially mixed paints had to fully dry on the surface of the bisque figure before another color was applied, for fear that the colors would run together in the glazing and final firing. Bright reds and certain yellow paints could not be used as they would turn brown and muddy when glazed and fired. The next step in production was glazing. The ceramics were finely and completely sprayed with a glass-like silica mixture. The pieces were fired once more at their exact temperature to meld the glaze to the ceramic and bring out the maximum enhancement of the figure's various colors.

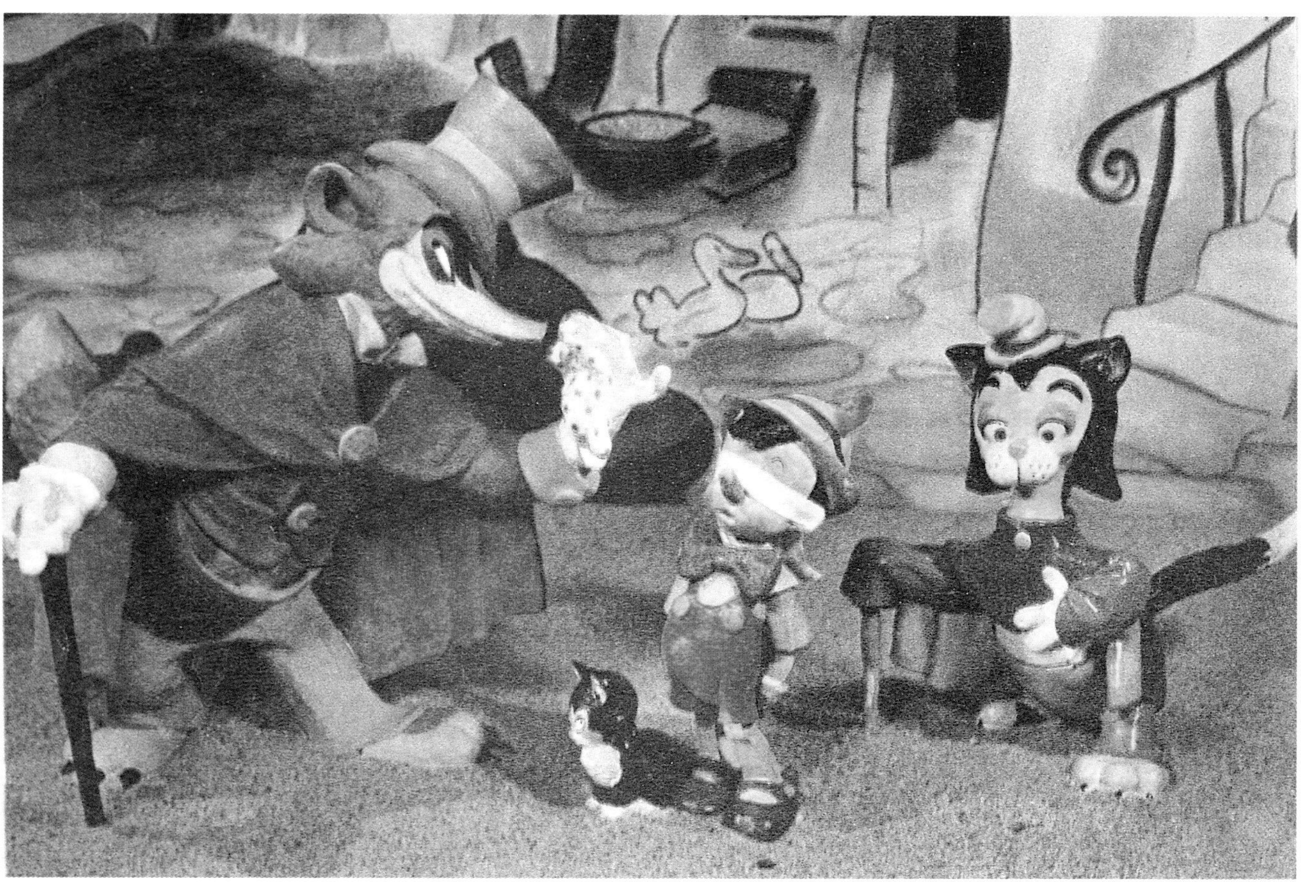

1939 storybook showing original animators models used to cast Brayton figurines

Brayton Laguna

After the Disney contract had expired in December 1939, Brayton continued its profitable operation producing quality ceramics throughout the war years and through the late 1960's. Several of the Snow White forest animal models were made through the first half of the 1940's. The figures were sold separately and as part of a Forest Knome set. These figures were generally decorated in different color schemes and should not be confused with the Disney ones.

Many lackluster copies and close imitations of Brayton's work produced in California and in overseas countries during the 1940's and 50's have been seen on the collector's market. A cookie jar in the shape of a ball of yarn with two Figaro type kittens at play as well as numerous copies of Pluto and Ferdinand the Bull can be found. Other foreign imitations of the forest fawn and rabbits have also been seen.

About the same time, the Brayton pottery produced a large selection of charming sets of American children at play and couples in native costume sculpted by local artists Letitia Ann Dowd and Frances Robinson. A hillbilly orchestra and shotgun wedding set and various animal groupings as well as kitchen items including cookie jars, shakers and an extensive line of Mammy collectibles were also very popular.

Durlin Brayton passed away in 1952 but his company continued to prosper through the 50's producing cast sculpture, artwear, bowls, vases and various home decorative items. Brayton's Laguna closed their doors forever in 1968.

Many collectors believe Brayton produced its most colorful, inspiring and vivid work before and during the second World War. The 1920's, 30's and early 40's were the beginning of the end of the state's many arts and decorative movements, an era not destined to reoccur.

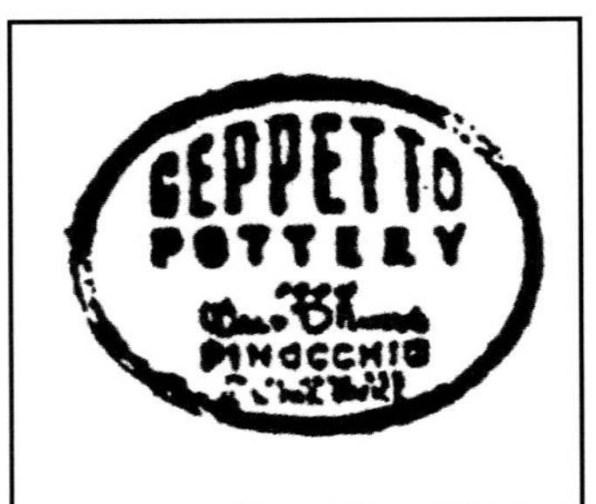

Geppetto Stamp

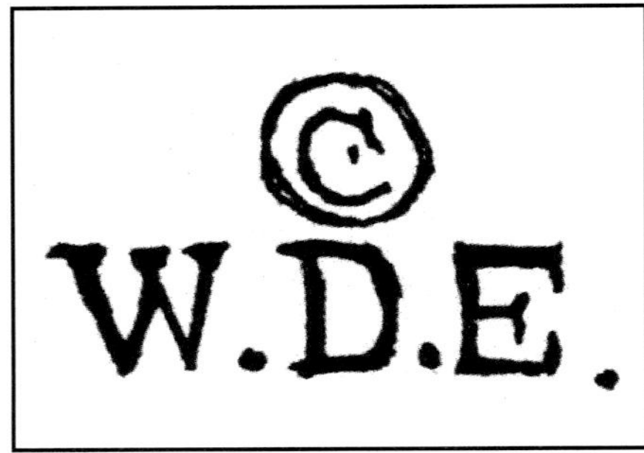

Incised mark

Gold Foil

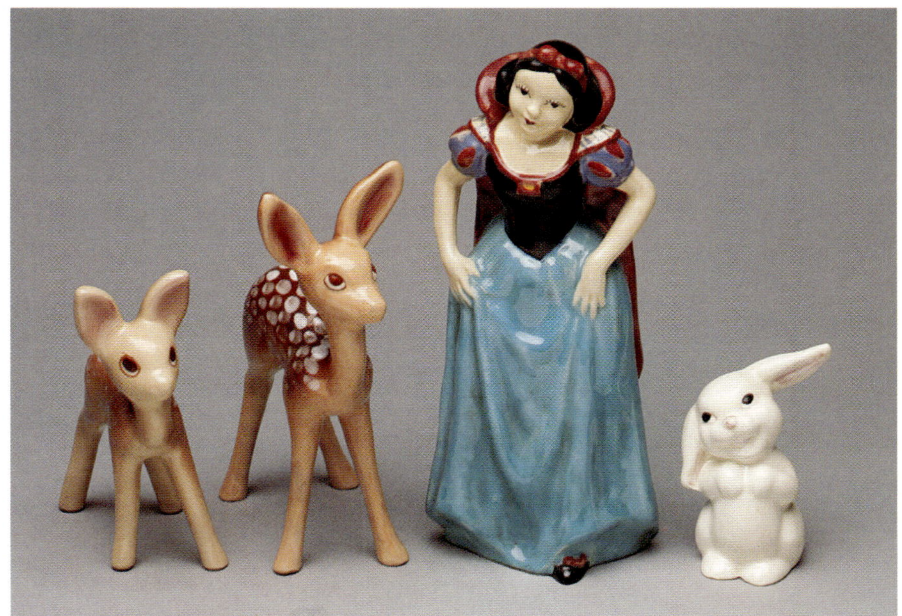

Baby fawn 7" $100-200, mama fawn 9" $175-275, Snow White 11" $400-600, rabbit with 1 ear down 5" $150-250.

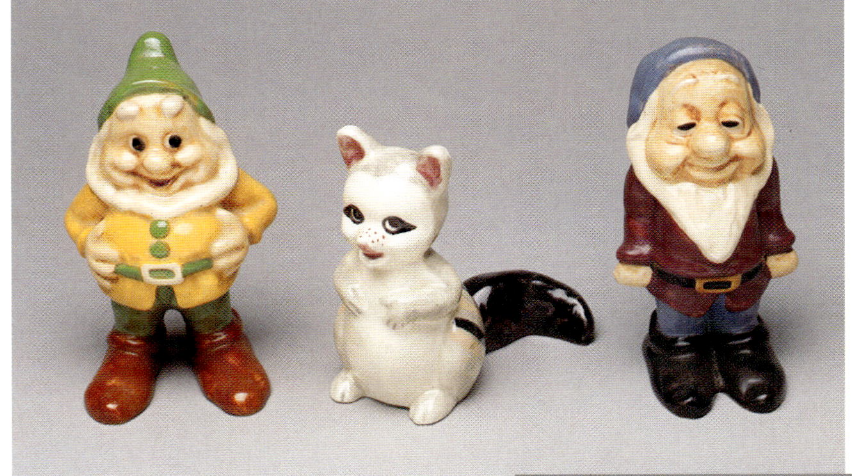

Happy 6" $200-375, raccoon 5" $200-300, Sleepy 5 " $200-375.

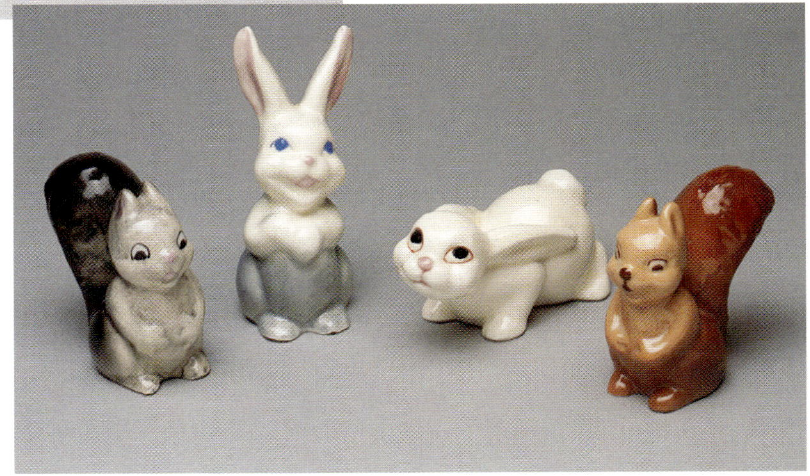

Squirrel 3 " $200-300, rabbit with ears up 4 °" $150-250, rabbit on all fours 2 " $150-250, squirrel color variant.

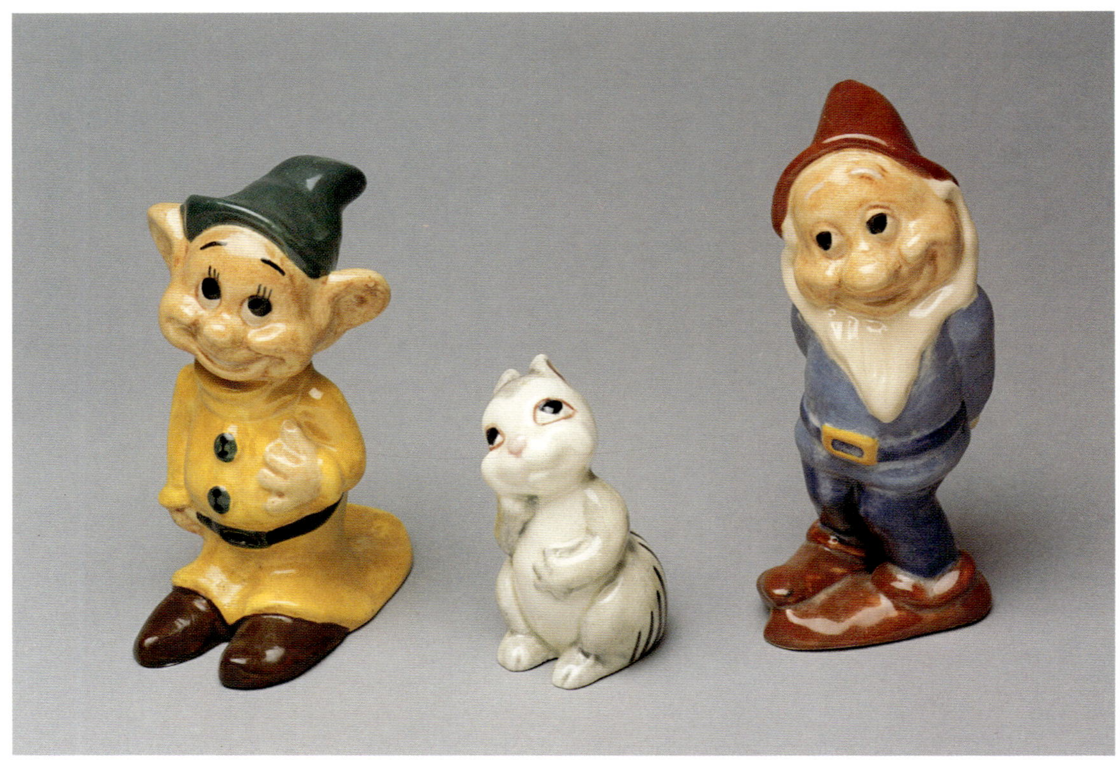

Dopey 5 " $200-375, chipmunk 3 °" $200-300, Bashful 6" $250-400.

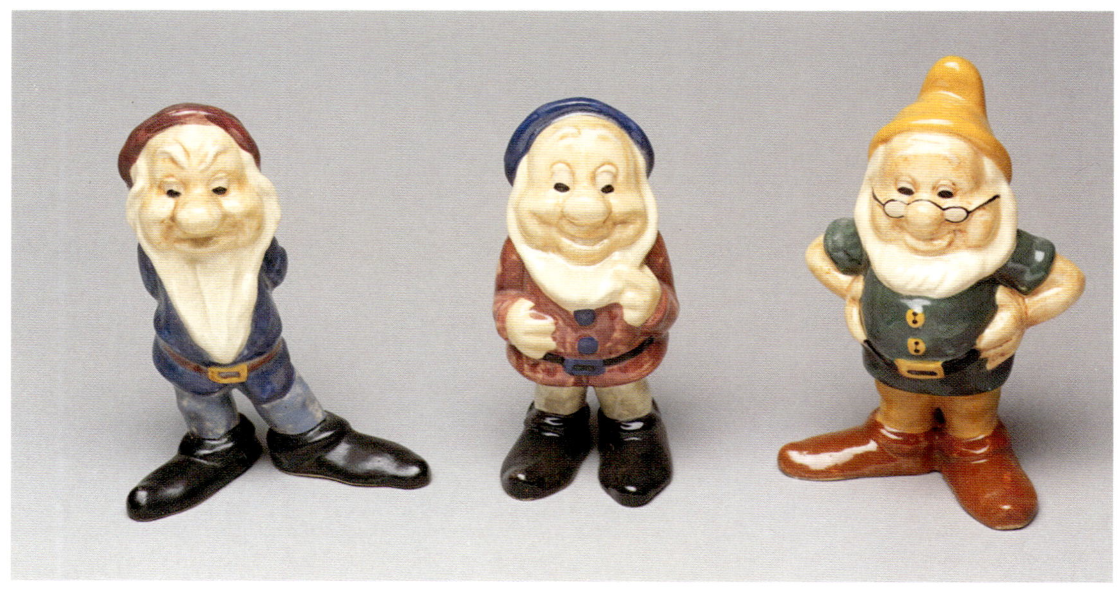

Grumpy 6" $250-400, Sneezy 5 " $200-375, Doc 6" $250-400.

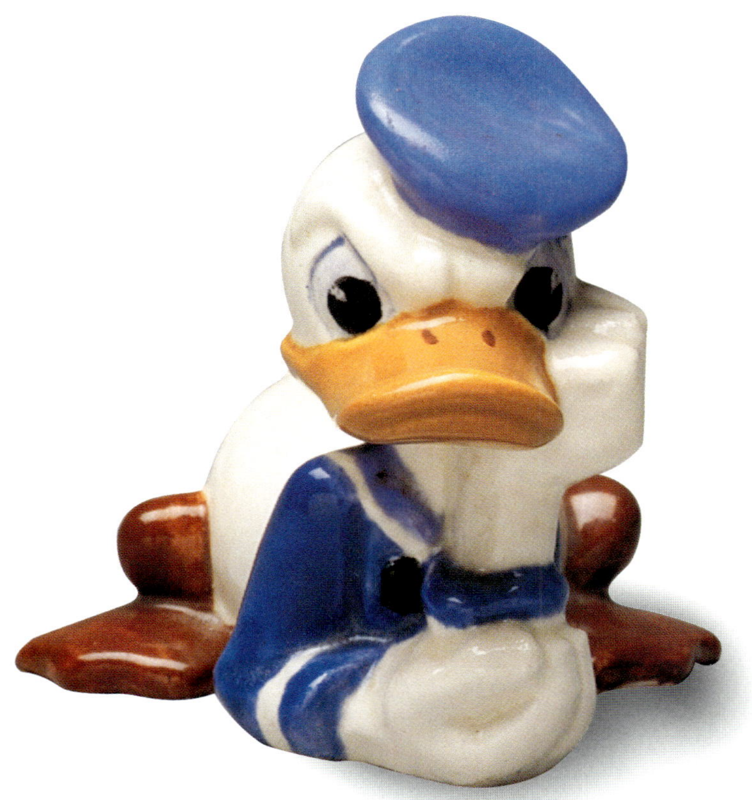

Donald pondering 3 " $250-350.

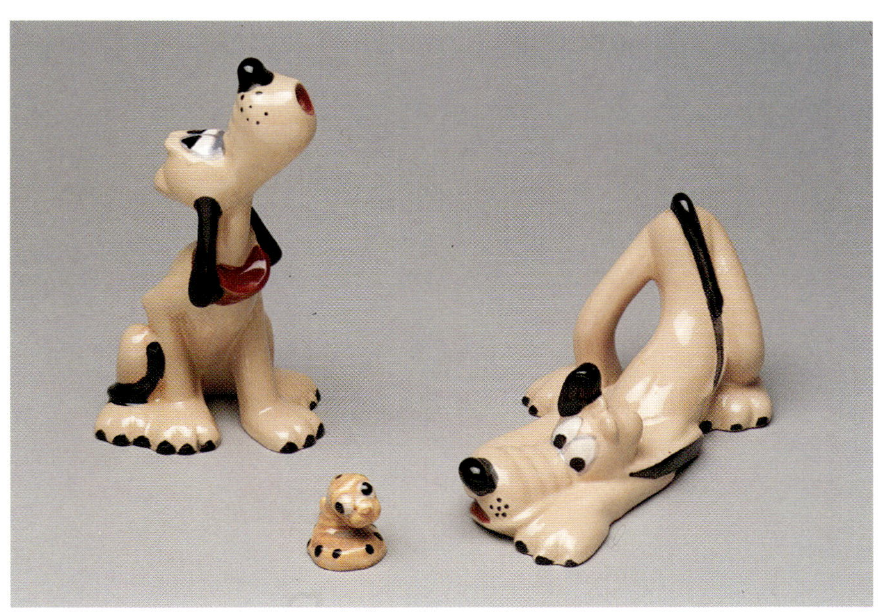

Pluto howling 6" $100-150, Pluto sniffing 3" $95-125 and the worm 1" NPA.

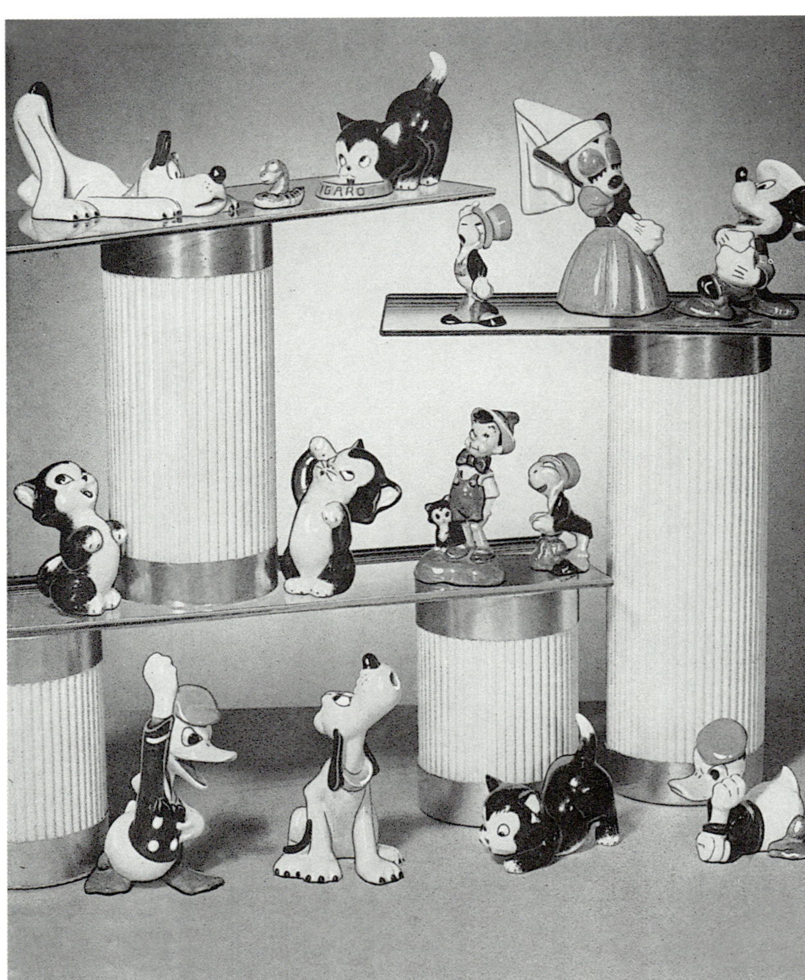

From the Kay Kamen merchandise catalog, 1940
Rare Mickey and Minnie in upper right hand corner
$NPA

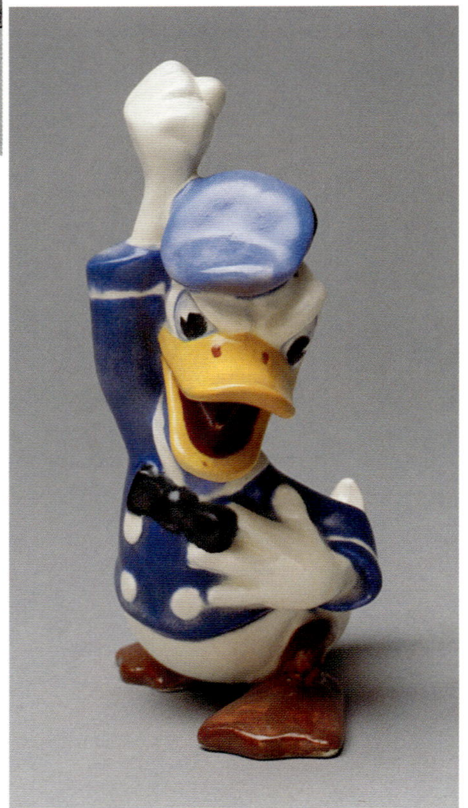

Angry Donald 6" $350-500.

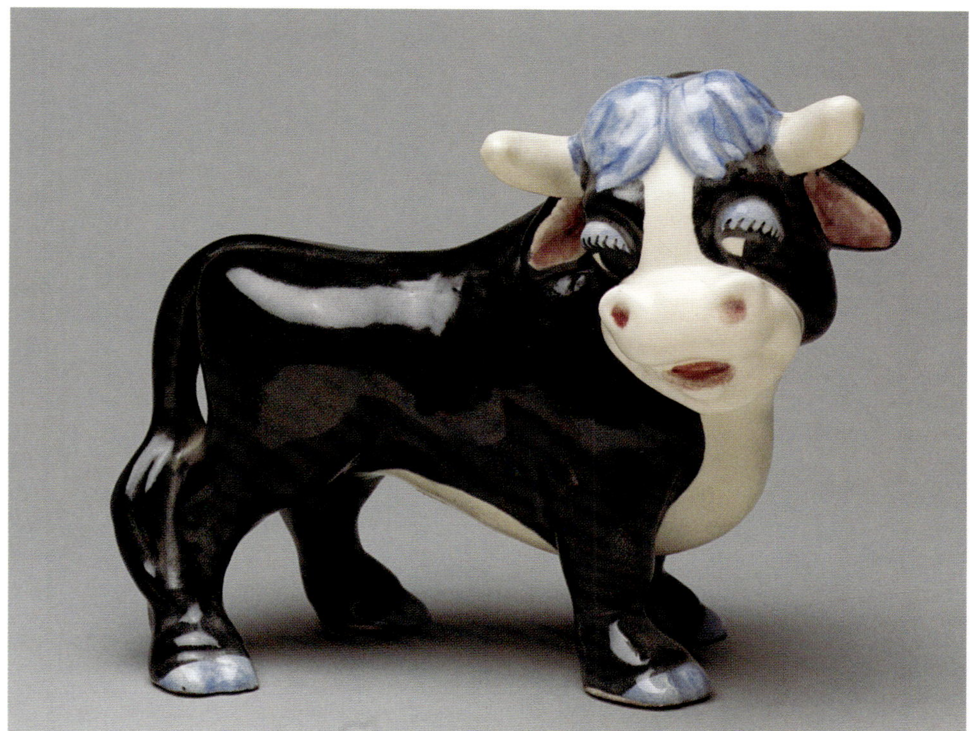

Ferdinand the Bull 7 1/2"$500+

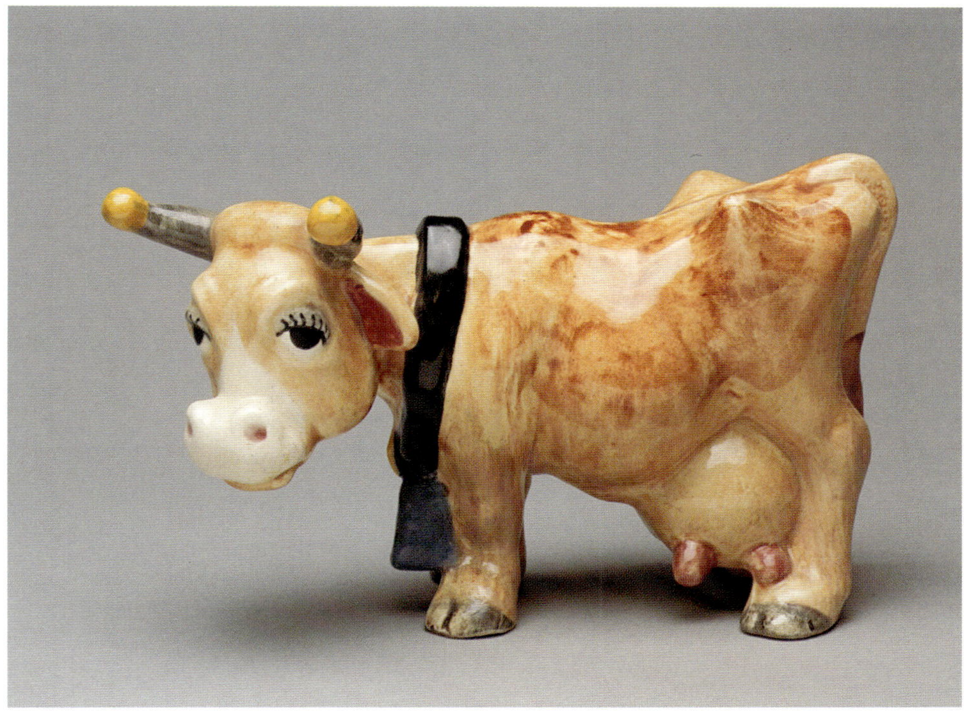

Ferdinand's Ma 6" $500+.

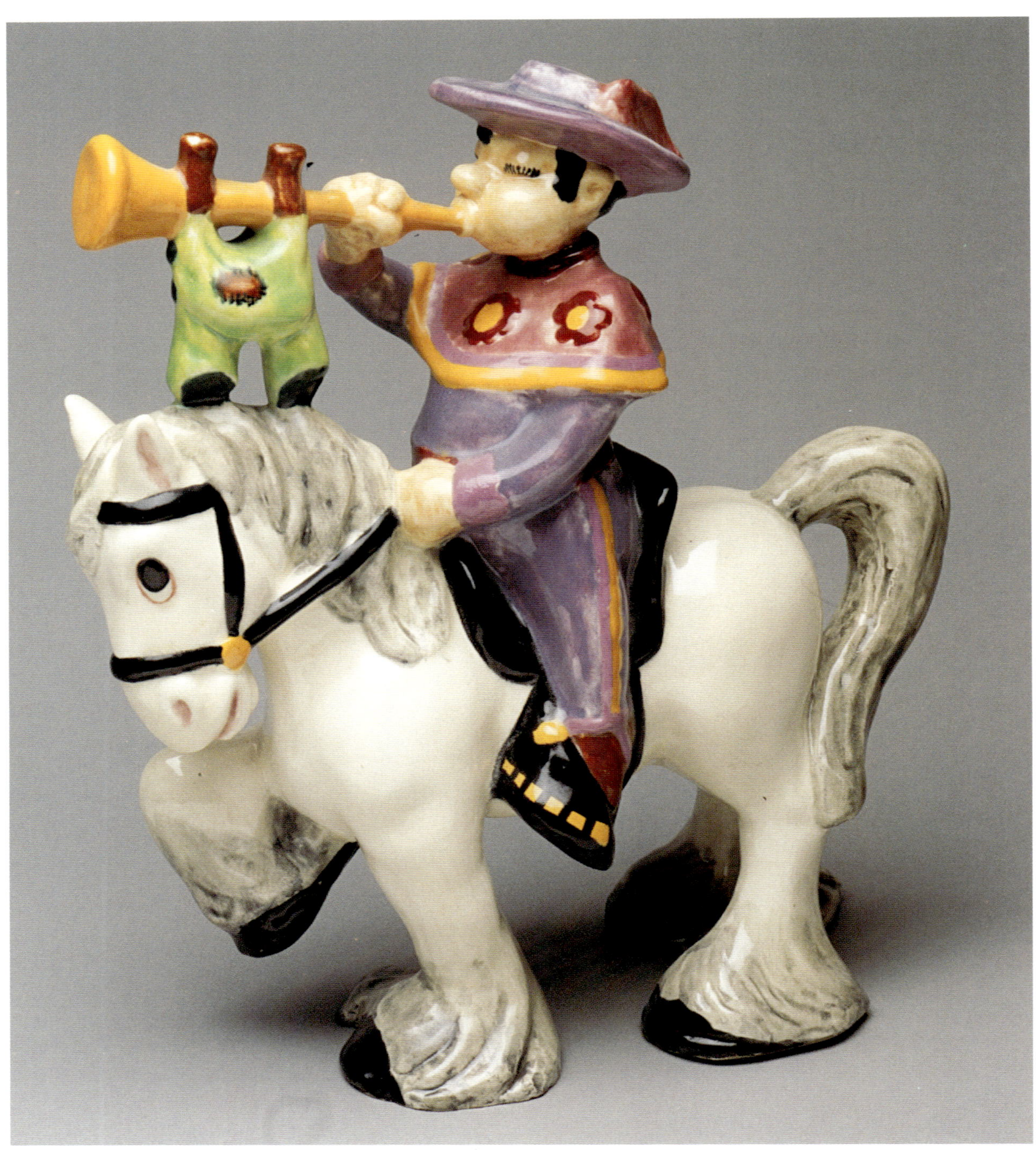

Trumpeteer on horse 13" $1000+.

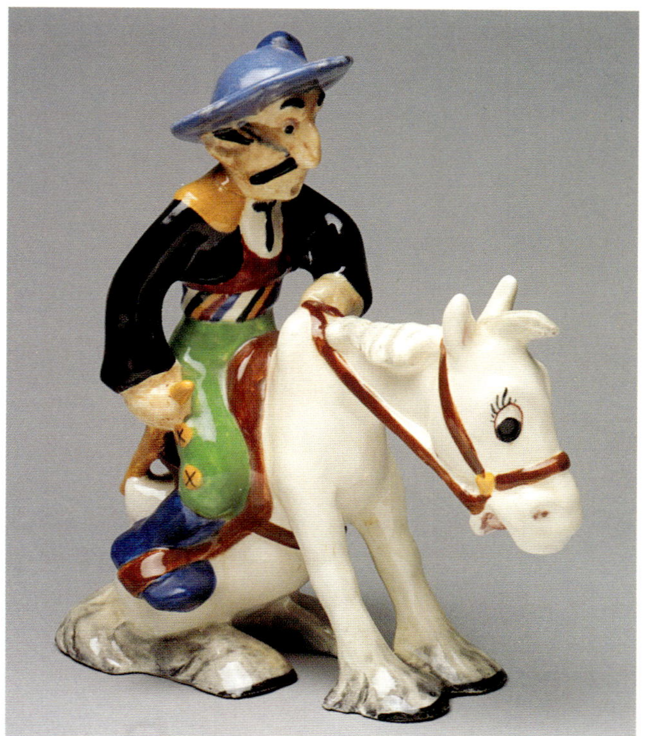

Horse sitting down 11 °” $800+.

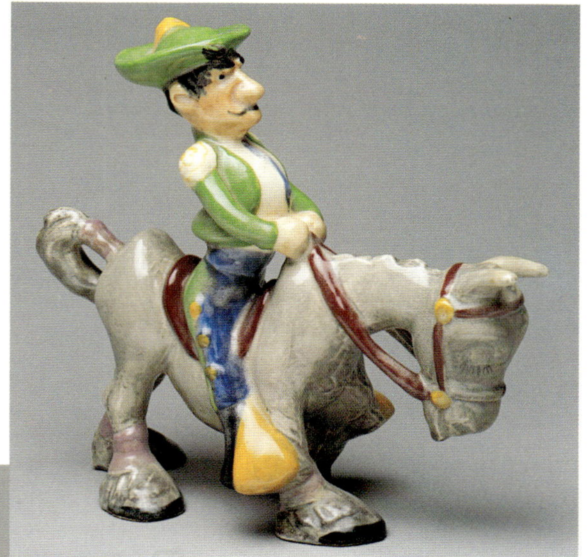

Horse swayback 11" $800+. This character was modeled after animator Bill Tytla

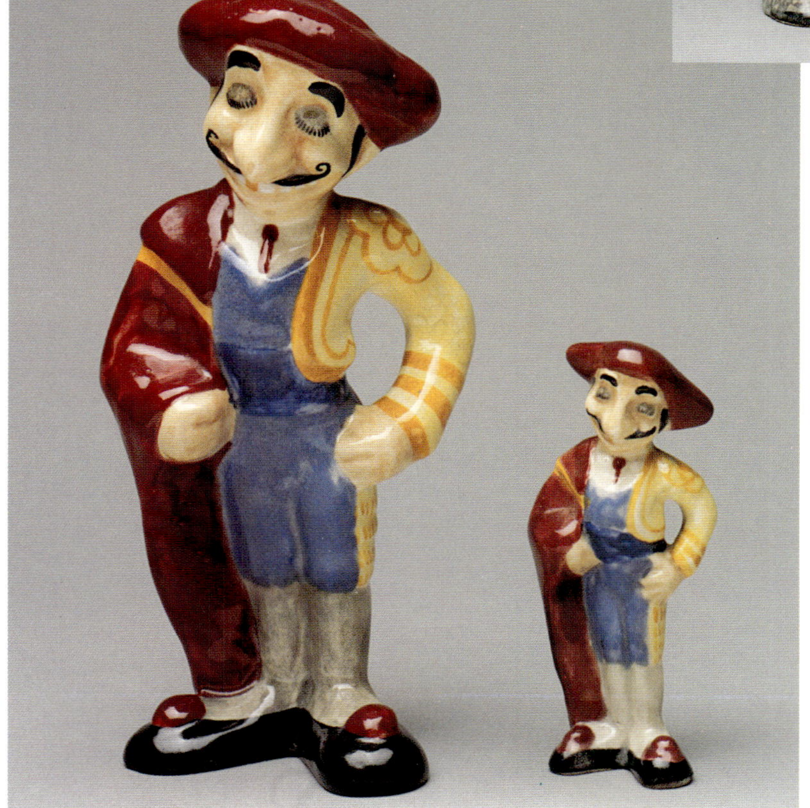

Matador regular, 9" $800+, Matador miniature, 5" $600+. Walt Disney himself was caricatured as the Matador.

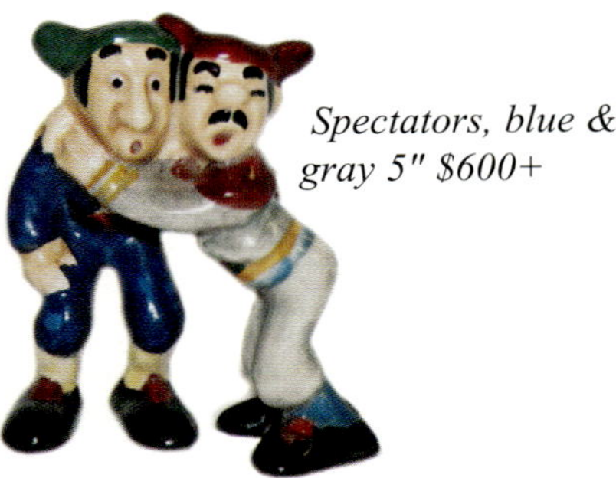

Spectators, blue & gray 5" $600+

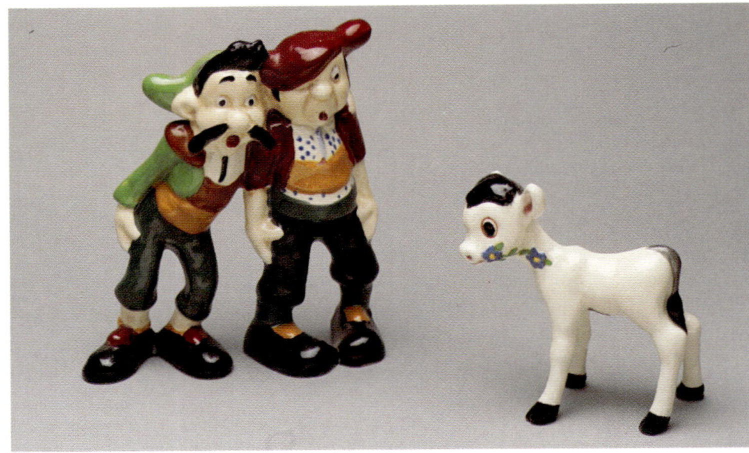

Spectators, green & black, 9" $800+, baby Ferdinand 3" $300+.

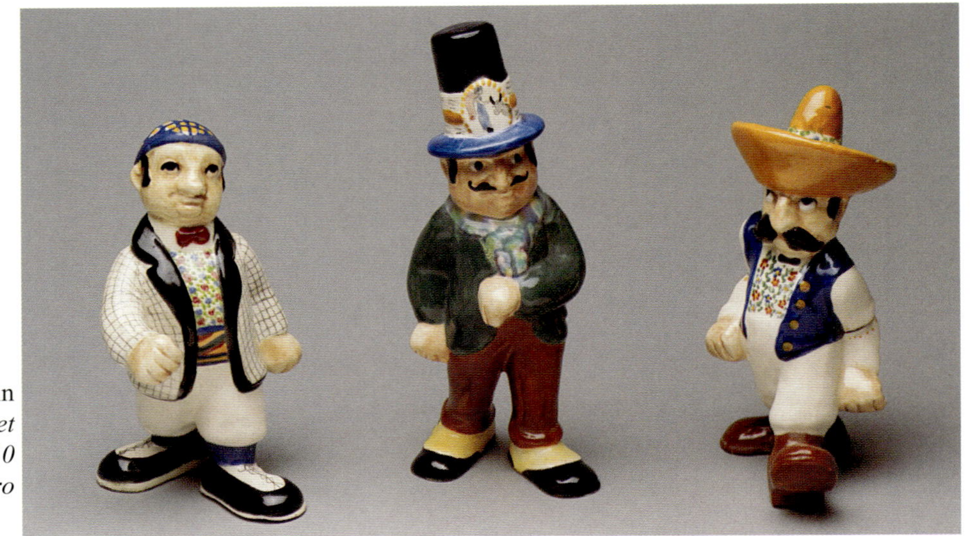

Three of the "Five men in funny hats". *Man with beret 8 1/4", man with high hat 10 1/4" and man with sombrero 8 3/4", $600+ each.*

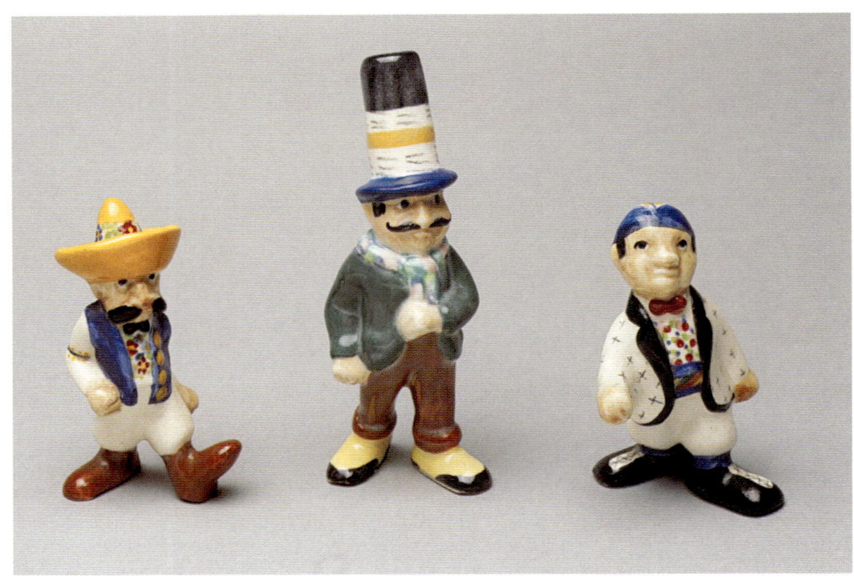

Same men in miniature. *Man with sombrero 4", man with high hat 5 1/4", man with beret 4", $400+ each. Not pictured; man with Patch on eye and man with Serape.*

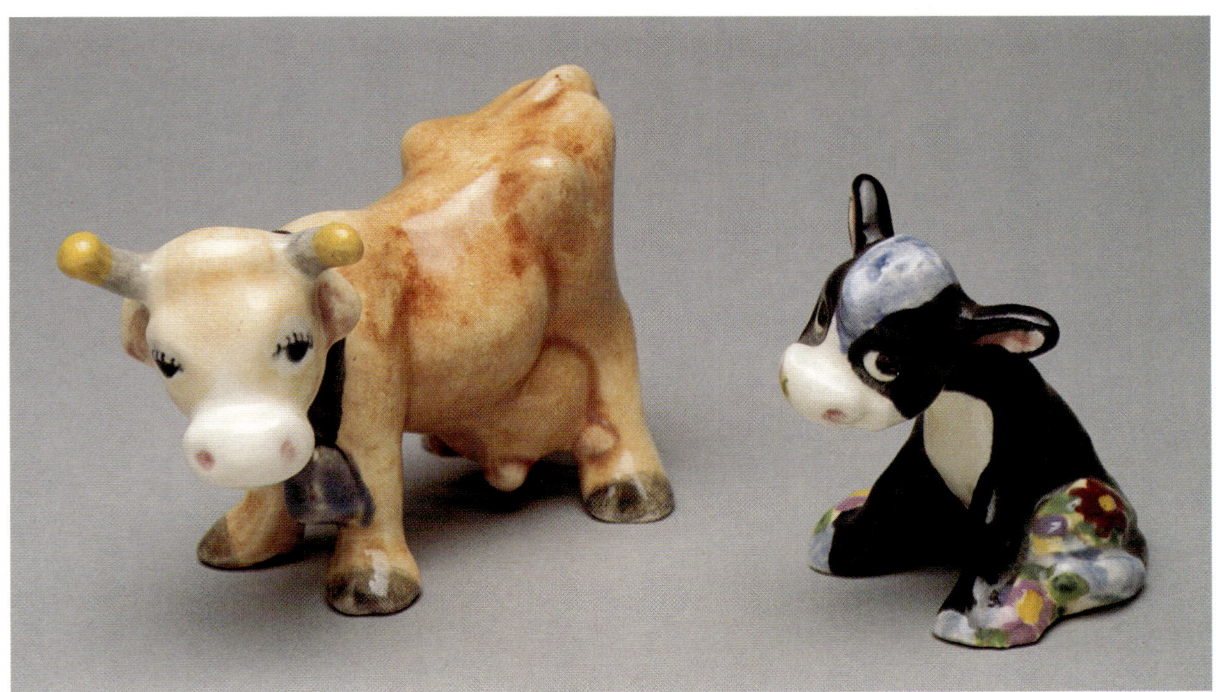

Ferdinand's Ma in miniature 3" $300+ and baby Ferdinand in flowers $300+

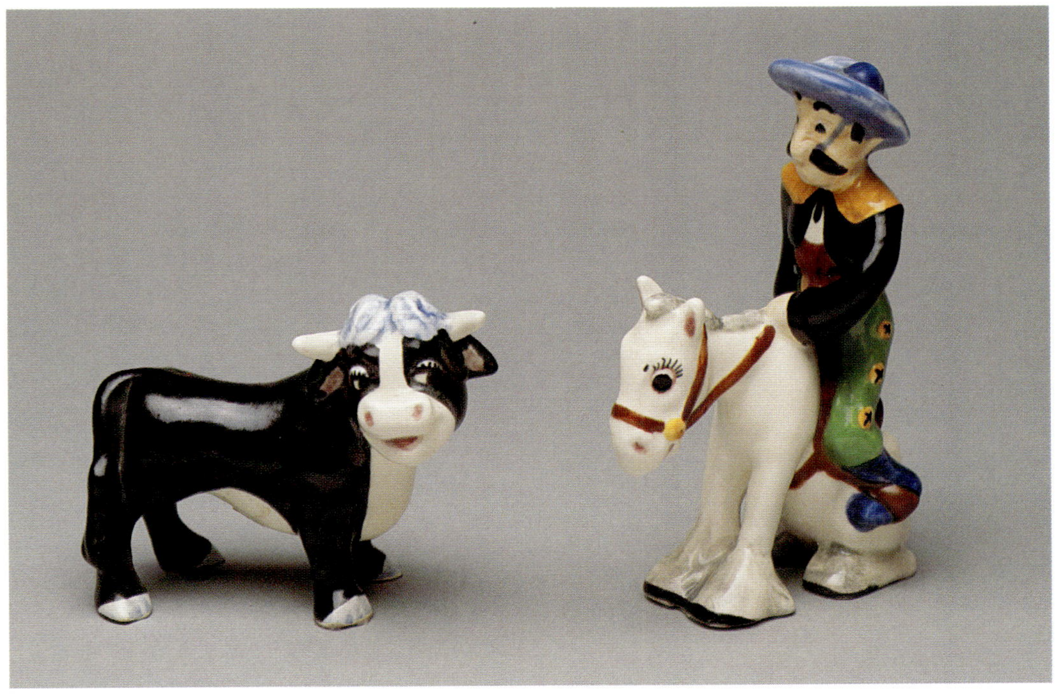

Ferdinand grown, in miniature 3 1/2" $300+ and miniature horse sitting down 6 1/4"

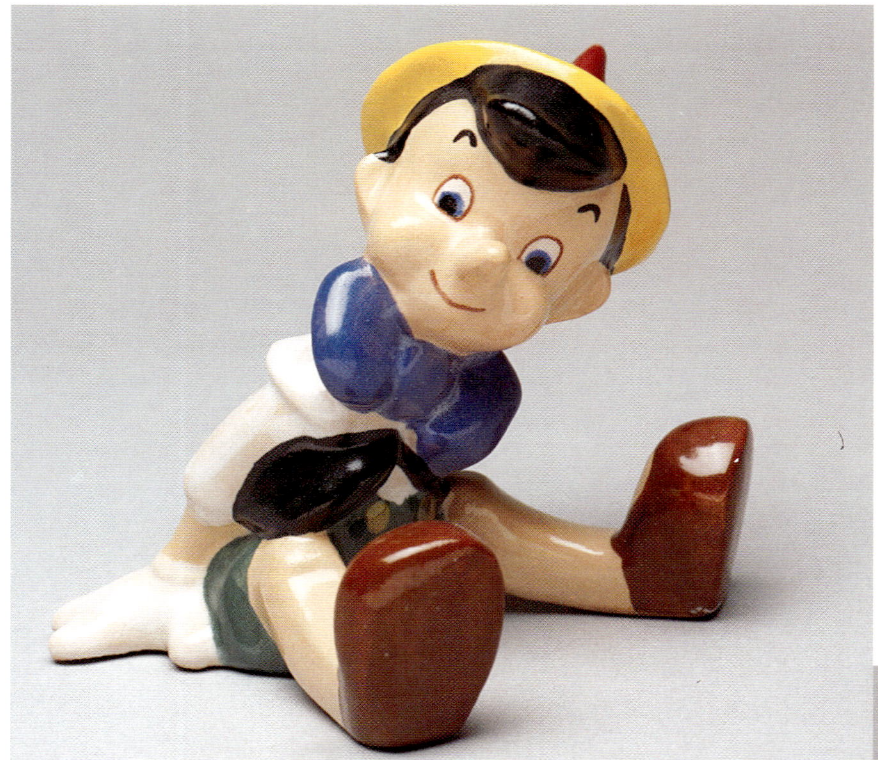

Pinocchio sitting without Jiminy 4" $600.

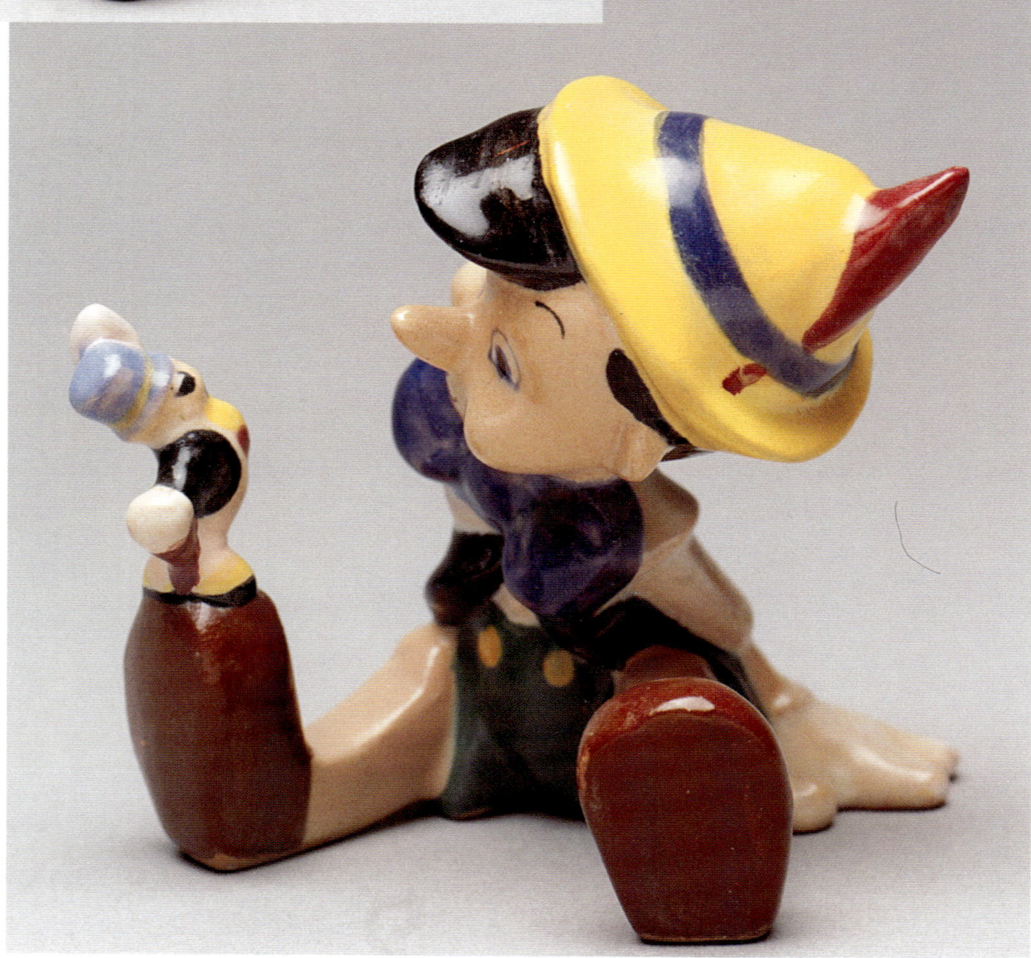

Pinocchio sitting with Jiminy Cricket on shoe 4" $800+.

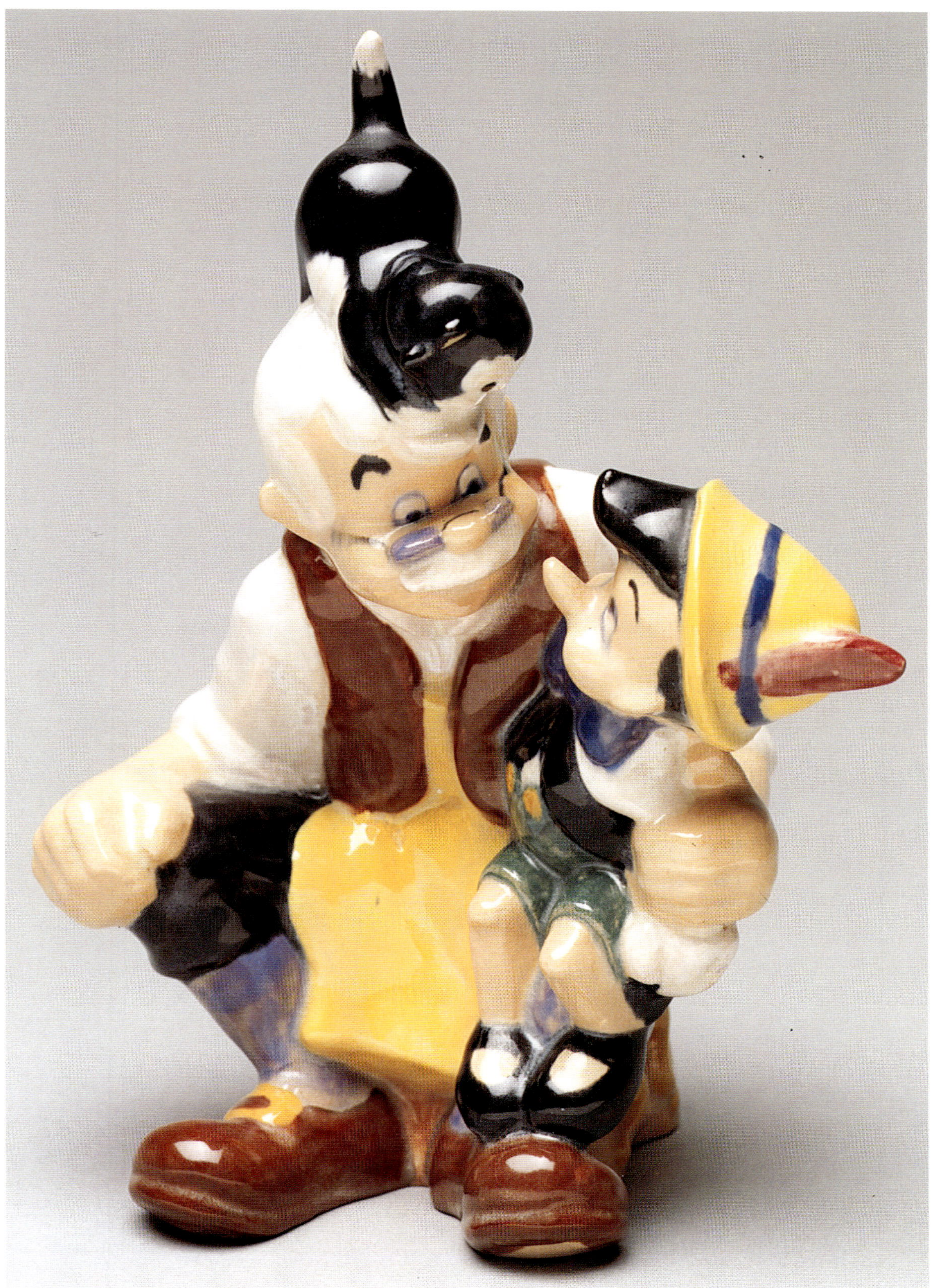

Pinocchio group 9 1/2" $2000+.

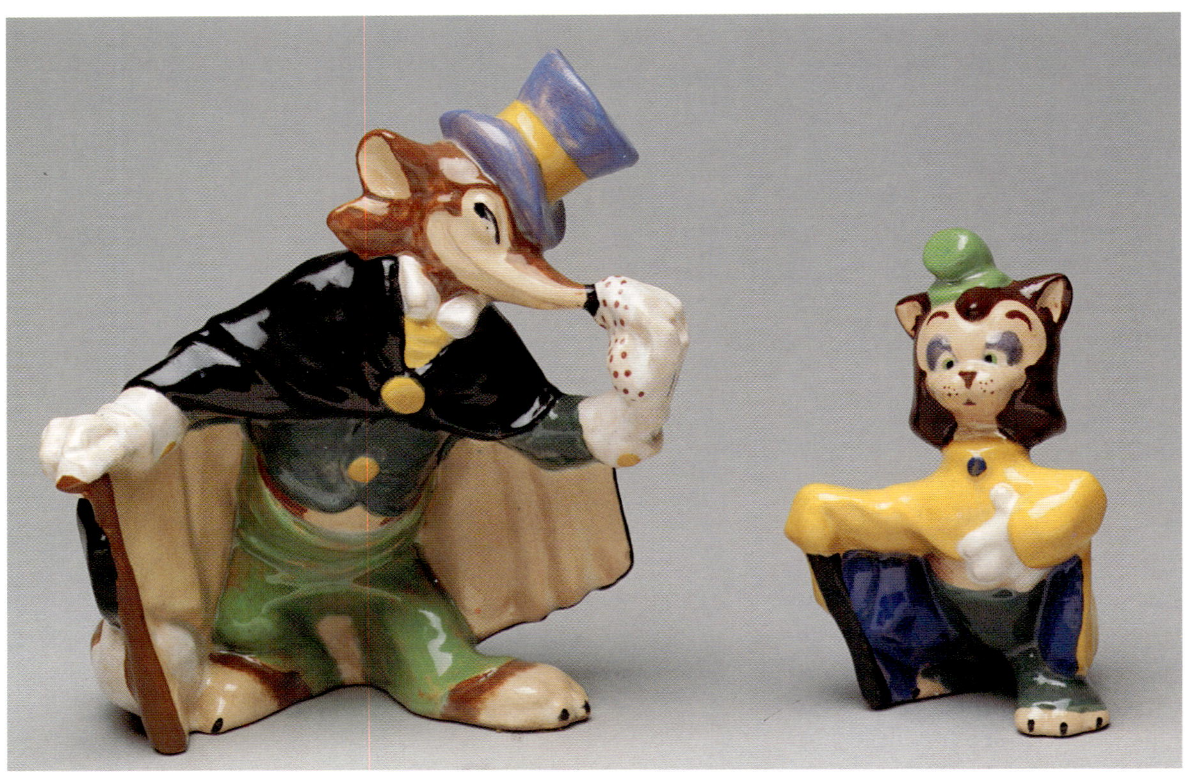

Honest John 6 1/2" $1000+ and Gideon 4 3/4 $800+.

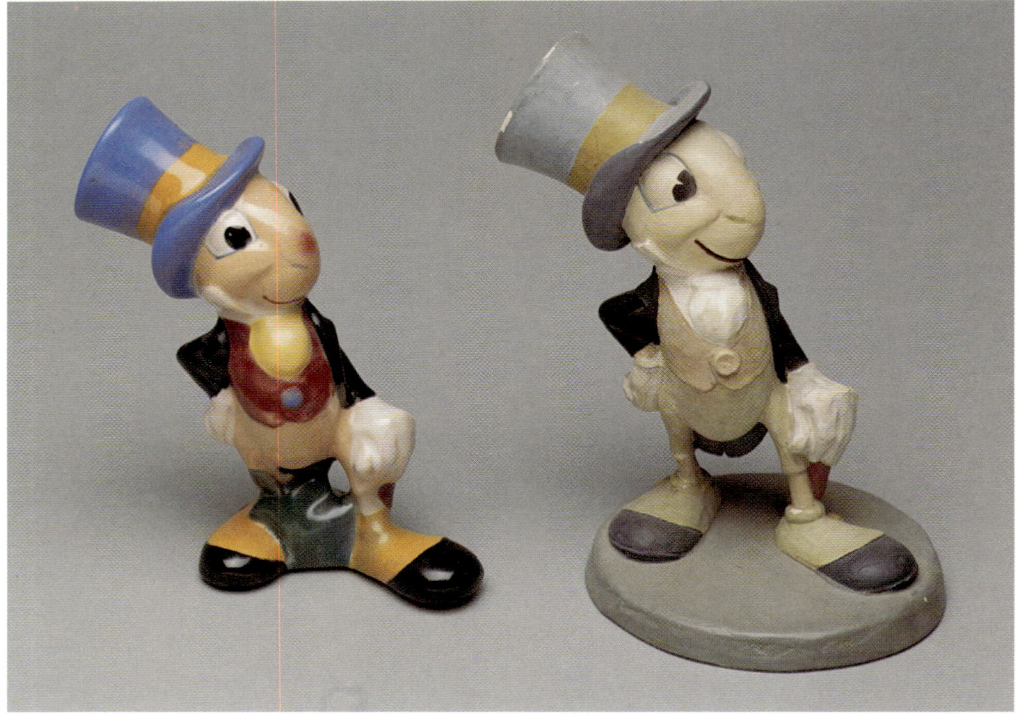

Large Jiminy Cricket 5 1/2" $1000+. Animators model used in the production of molds for Brayton.

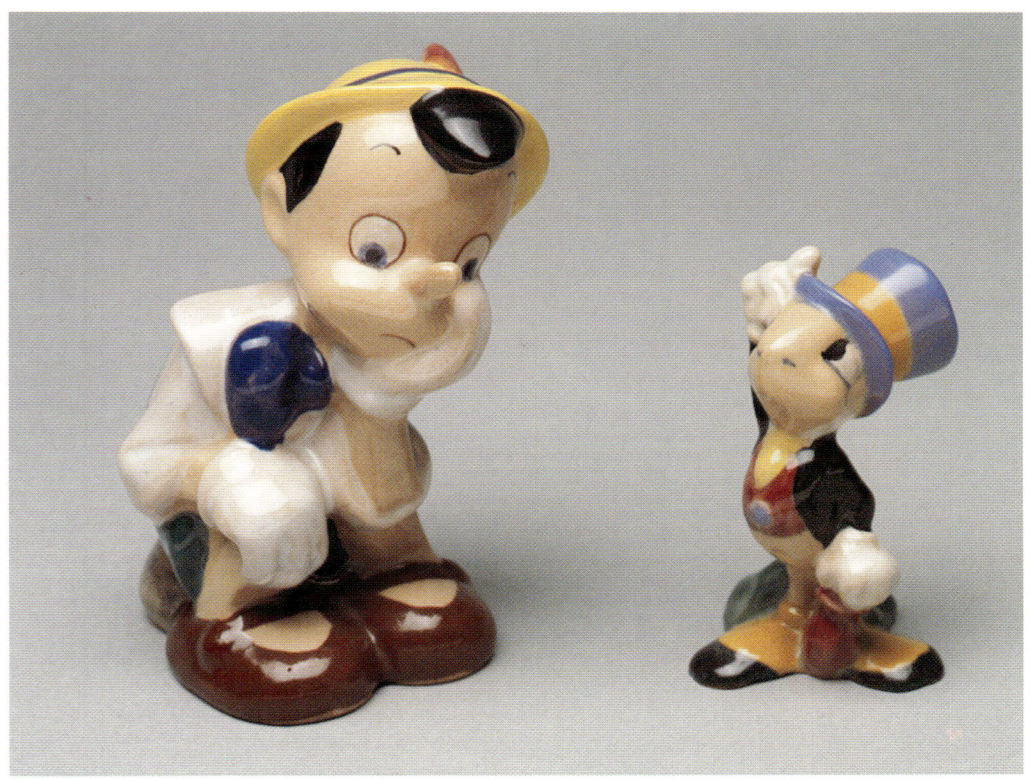

Pinocchio sitting on rock 4 3/4" $400+, Jiminy with arm up 3 1/4" $600+.

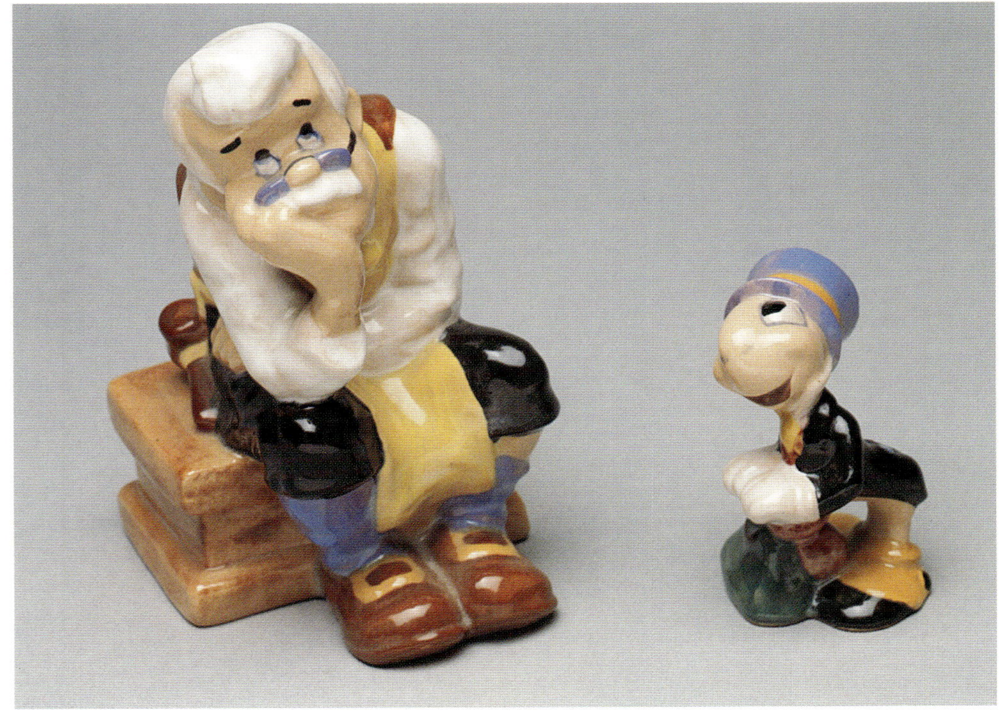

Geppetto sitting on box 5 3/4" $500+, Jiminy with carpet bag 3" $600.

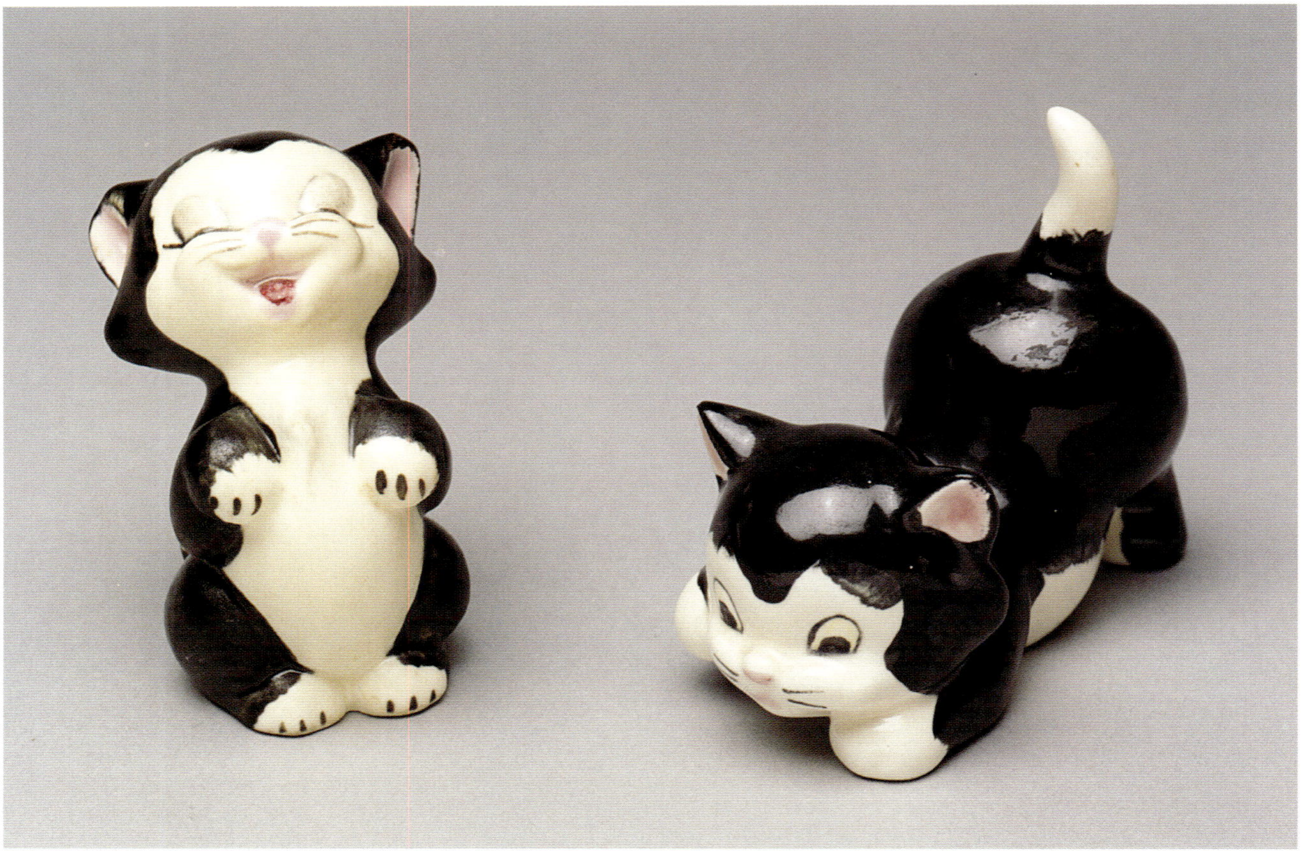

Figaro the kitten begging 3 3/4" and Figaro on the prowl 3 1/2" $150-250 each.

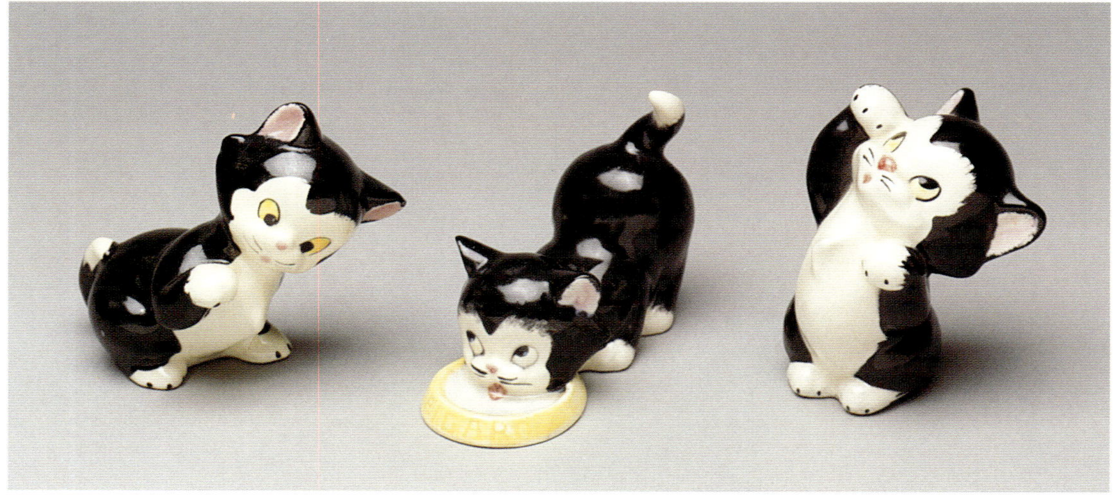

Figaro playing 4" $150-250, Figaro drinking from dish 3 1/2" $200-300, Figaro paw up 4" $150-250.

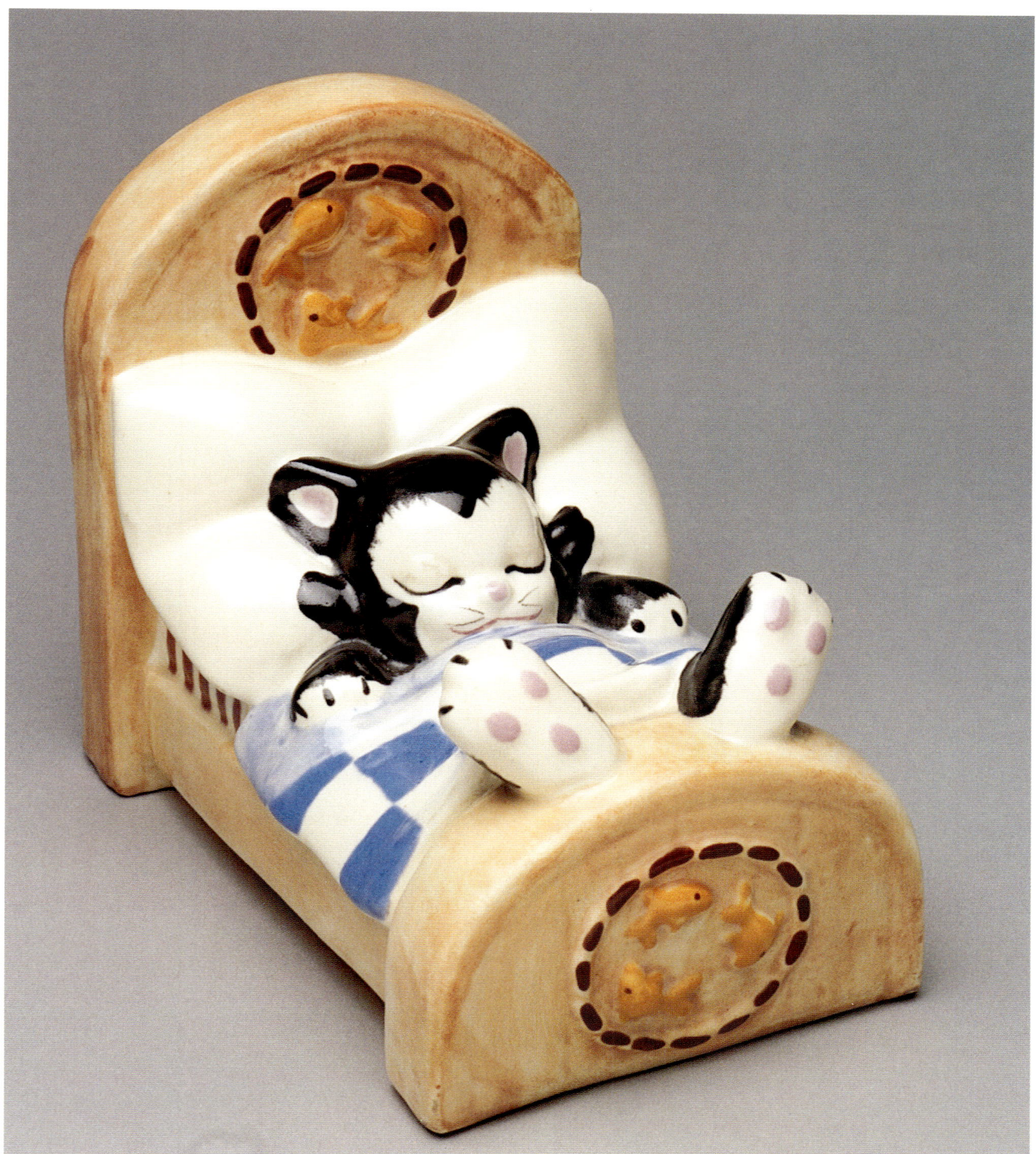

Figaro in bed 6" $1000+.

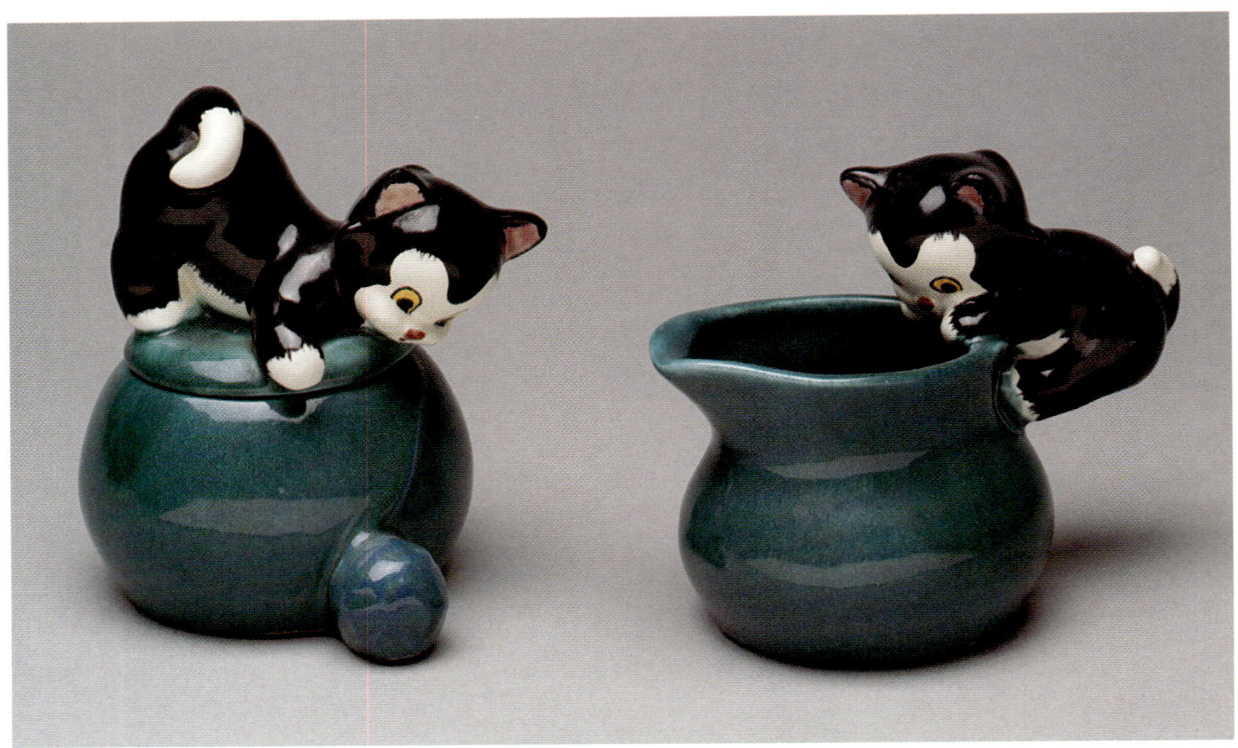

Figaro sugar bowl 5 3/4" $500+, Figaro creamer 5" $500+.

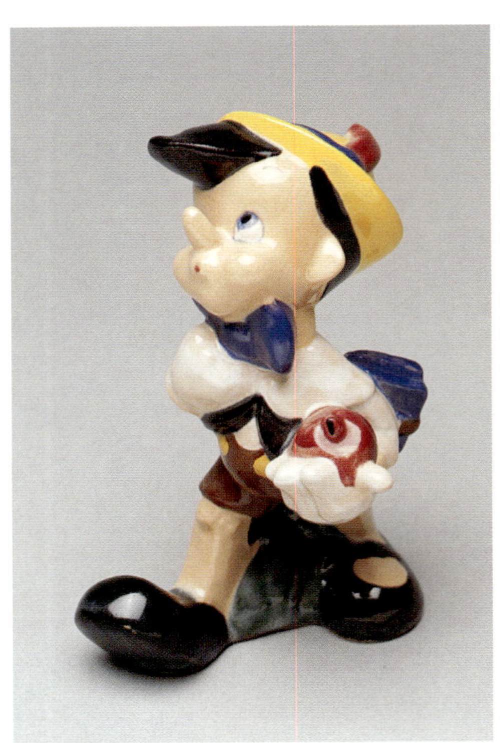

Pinocchio with apple 6" $500+.

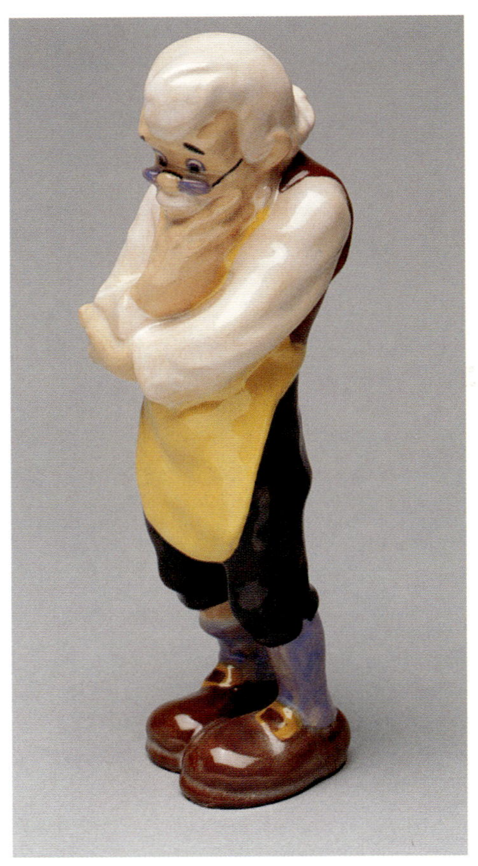

Geppetto standing 8 1/4" $800+

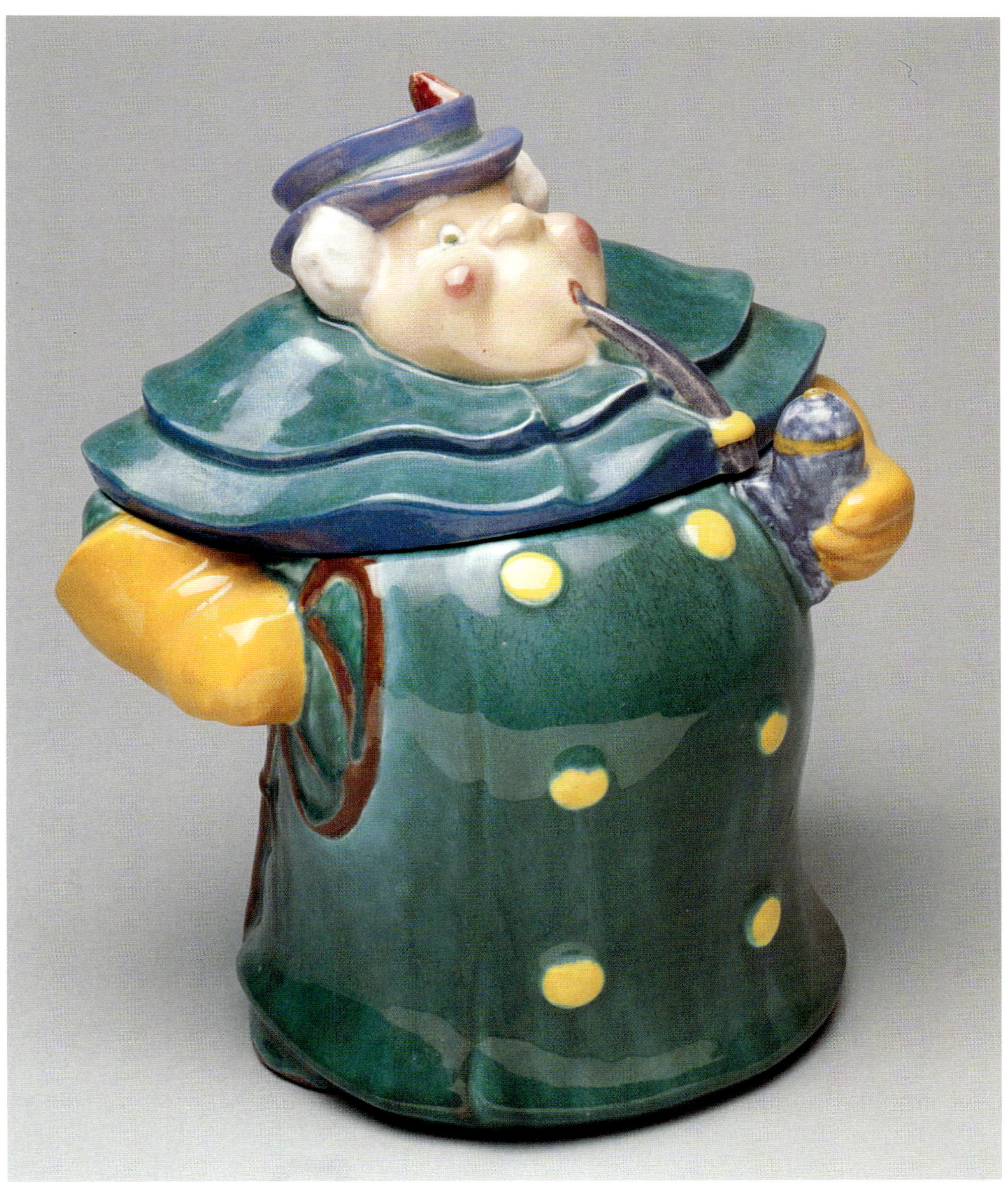

Coachman candy jar 9 1/2" $3000+.

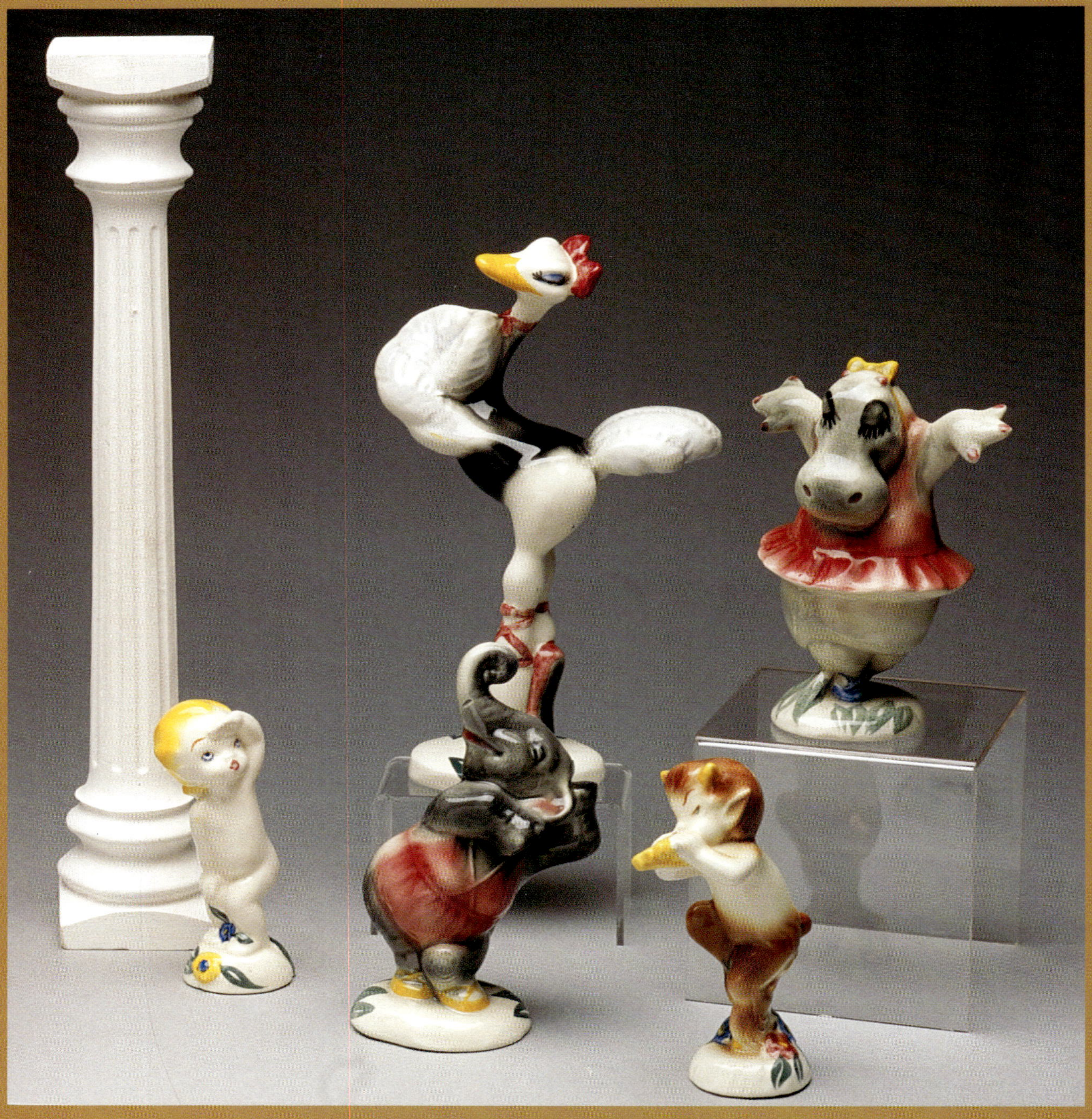

Vernon Kilns 1940-1942

Over its years of operation, Vernon Kilns had made a name for itself as a quality ceramics operation. Its use of high caliber materials in its development process, including clays, glazes, decoration and the hiring of unsurpassed California design talent in production, is what quite possibly led the Disney organization to the concern for the creation of fine ceramic reproductions from their new and state-of-the-art film, *Fantasia*.

Vernon began modestly in 1912, then being named Poxon Pottery after its founder George Poxon. Situated at 2300 East 52nd Street in the then rural farming community of Vernon, located just outside of downtown Los Angeles, the small Poxon plant produced vibrantly glazed bowls, vases, advertising and numerous decal-embellished china dishes throughout its first years.

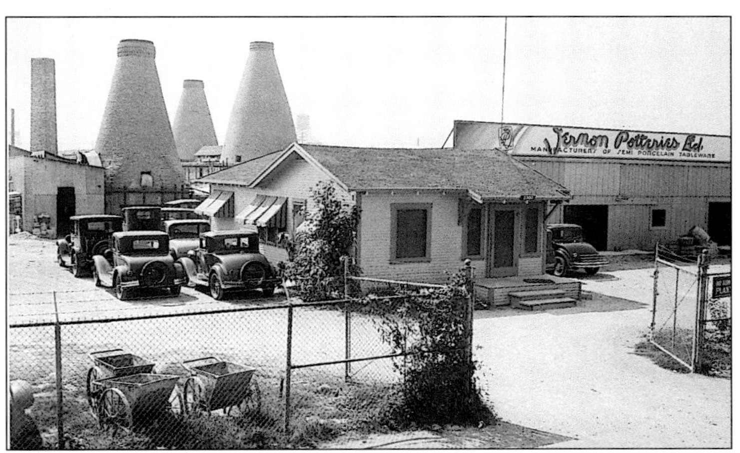

Exterior view of Vernon Kilns plant in 1933.

Mr. Faye Bennison, a retailer by trade, purchased the Poxon plant in 1931 and changed its name to the city in which it was located. Mr. Bennison believed in hard work and the production of an outstanding quality product. This belief helped Vernon Kilns through its infant years, a devastating earthquake and the nation's hard-hitting Depression. At this time and throughout its history, Vernon was at the forefront in ceramic dinnerware design for California and the West's rapidly growing middle income and its popular patio culture.

The company's product became a housewife's best friend for a stylish get-together with names like Ultra California, Organdie, and Coronado. By creating beautiful place settings in rich pastel colors and discriminating design as well as detailed hand decoration, Vernon achieved a distinction that would set the company apart from its competitors for its entire life.

The midpart of the Depression decade brought changes to the company with the introduction of the artwear department. On the advice of his gifted artist daughter, many talented designers were brought in by Bennison to develop decorative as well as functional ceramics during what many collectors today call the firm's golden years, 1935-1942.

Artists such as Harry Bird and Gale Turnbull contributed their own personal decorative style of glazed birds and vibrant handpainted designs to the company's product mix. In 1937 the creative and award-winning sister duo of May and Vieve Hamilton designed numerous art deco style objects d' art. Hamilton's work, featuring busts and bowls, were made available for the home as well as attractive corresponding Rhythmic and Rippled dinnerware.

Bennison's own artist daughter, Jane Bennison, a graduate from the University of Southern California, contributed unique and even fanciful bowls, vases and candlesticks to the line. Even though the artwear department itself was discontinued about 1938, Mr. Bennison continued the hiring of famous artists to design artwork for his profitable ceramic dinnerware lines including the famed "Moby Dick" and "Salamina" book illustrator Rockwell Kent and the Hawaiian poet, Don Blanding.

Walt Disney's innovative film *Fantasia* had its world premiere at the Broadway Theater in New York City on November 13, 1940. Exactly one month earlier on October 10, 1940, a contract was signed by Vernon Kilns with Walt Disney Studios to produce ceramic figurines and decorative bowls and vases of some of the characters that appear in the film *Fantasia* as well as the studio's then upcoming releases *Dumbo* and *The Reluctant Dragon*. Select dinnerware patterns inspired by *Fantasia* were also to be designed.

Fantasia was considered the grand experiment in animation for its creative adaptation to classical music. The two hour film was actually eight animated artistic interpretations set to popular classical music. Tchaikovsky's "Nutcracker Suite" was interpreted with mystical fairies, the changing of the seasons and dancing thistles, flowers and mushrooms.

The "Pastoral Symphony" brought Ludwig van Beethoven's Springtime melody to a mythical Greek age with Satyrs, Centaurs, and Centaurettes joyfully cavorting with Bacchus and gods Zeus and Vulcan. Other movie segments included Bach's "Toccata and Fugue in D Minor", Stravinsky's "The Rite of Spring", Ponchielli's "Dance of the Hours", Mussorgsky's "Night on Bald Mountain", Schubert's "Ave Maria" and the movie's centerpiece Dukas "The Sorcerer's Apprentice".

Although the film received some criticism mainly for score edits and pictorial ideas, its subject matter was strongly ahead of its time and therefore the presentation drew few into the theaters and failed at its initial box-office release. Today the music-visual laden film is considered a masterpiece and is being added-to and enhanced as originally intended by Walt Disney. The musical score was initially conducted by Leopold Stokowski and the Philadelphia Orchestra. Deems Taylor was the film's narrator.

The Vernon company quickly began production of the fine ceramics. As with the Brayton Laguna Pinocchio pieces, the molds for the ceramics were made from the actual hand- sculpted maquettes or three dimensional models that were used as visual references by the animators in the creation of the film's characters. For production purposes, some of the original models had to be altered and plaster case molds smoothed out to ease in the production efficiency of the ceramics.

As with any mass production of ceramics, all the pieces were handpoured in plaster molds and allowed to set to a certain thickness. All mold lines and imperfections were cleaned with a dull knife. No clay detail work was performed as all pieces were pulled from a single mold. The figures were then dried, kilned, carefully hand decorated with vibrant paints, brushes and airbrushes. Decorators were instructed to carefully follow a finished sample guide, recreating the delicate brush strokes that appear on the pieces.

Advertisement in House and Garden magazine for Vernon's Fantasia ceramics, May 1941.

Most of the figures and some of the decorated bowls and vases display intricate layering of the paint where the brush is used to grade the paint's intensity from light to very dark. Many collectors notice that there was a definite change in decoration over time. Most of the firm's early pieces such as the Satyr are completely brush decorated while other examples display a large amount of air-brush detailing. Some of the larger figures took roughly one half hour to handpaint while the airbrush technique was less time consuming. After being dipped in a high gloss silica glaze, the figures went through their second and final kilning. It has been stated that Vernon employed the finest quality clays, paint, decoration and silica glazes in its product. The firm was proud that its glazes would never craze or crack as was a constant with other potteries of the day. Over fifty years after their production, few pieces show signs of craze.

Thirty-six individual ceramics were produced from the film including the mythical Satyrs, Sprites, Unicorns, Centaurettes, Pegasus, and a Centaur from "The Pastoral Symphony". Elephants, Hippos, and Ostriches were derived from the "Dance of the Hours" sequence. The Hop-Low shakers danced in "The Nutcracker Suite". The

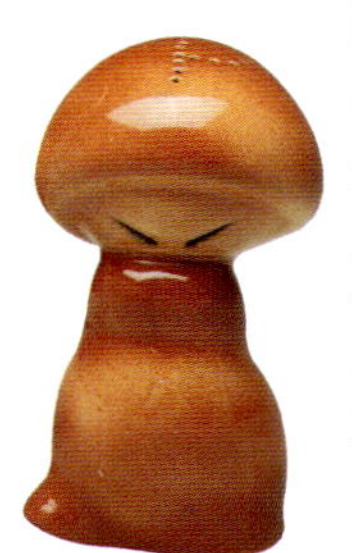

highly glazed figures were professionally produced in quality ceramic, decoration and clean mold lines and today are considered museum quality. The Walt Disney Archives has validated the listed known ceramics and feels that Vernon possibly never made a Sorcerer's Apprentice Mickey Mouse. However Mickey's portrait did find its way onto a Vernon plate in 1943. He can be found in his Burbank home on the Farmers Market map of Southern California. As with all the ceramic companies listed, few (if any) records were kept on what was made and how many were produced.

A ceramic Bacchus from Fantasia was produced in the 1960's by Vohann of Capistrano Beach, California. This God of Wine can be found as an ashtray or a bank and glazed in solid colors. A series of eight bas-relief Fantasia theme display bowls and flower vases were produced in solid and pastel colors of white, green (pistachio), blue, a pink or pearl salmon and two-tone. They can be found in rare hand decorated versions as well. All (but this is not done consistently) of the vases are numbered under glaze or in the base from 120 to 127. The Diana or Goddess vase #126 and the Pegasus vase #127 are considered rare. These pieces were sold to complement Vernon's various dinnerware lines and the individual figures. However, the vases and bowls create unique table decorations and centerpieces completely on their own.

The Fantasia dinnerware was produced on Vernon's stock shapes Ultra and Monticeto. Ultra was created by chief Vernon artist Gale Turnbull in the late 1930's and used as the design base for most of the fine artist designs. The eight designs sold were actually two designs with color variants in the pattern as well as options on hand decoration or not. Autumn Ballet, Fairyland, and Fantasia were an all-over transfer print found in brown, blue and maroon, all hand decorated. Milkweed Dance was available in plain blue or maroon line with no hand decoration.

The Flower Ballet, Enchantment, and Nutcracker lines were boarders on plates and other flatware and a complete all over design on hollowware such as teapots and sugars and creamers. Dewdrop Fairies was the exact same pattern in blueline minus the hand decoration. The pattern designs themselves were printing image transfers placed on the bisque ware, derived from an early form of direct printing.

As with other dinnerware and souvenir plates produced by the company about the same time, the completed artwork was etched into a reusable copper plate with the grooves being filled with colored ink. A thin tissue type paper was cut to the design and ceramics size specifications such as the rim of a 12" plate or outside of an individual sugar bowl and then laid or rolled over the copper image picking up the thick ink from the groove design. The tissue was hung wet side out on metal dowels before use. The decorators had to apply the tissues to the bisque rather quickly, to prevent the ink from running or drying out completely.

The pourous bisque would absorb the ink and once dried, decorated, glazed and fired, the design would be a permanent another begins. No decals were utilized.

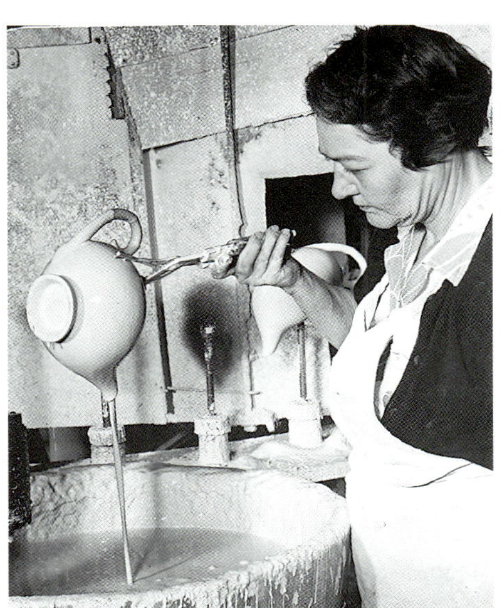

50's photo of ceramist demonstrating glazing process.

The Vernon ceramics were sold at better department stores and gift shops throughout the country including Macy's and Bloomingdale's in New York City, Foley's in Texas and Bullock's in Los Angeles.

Vernon Kilns also produced figures from the 1941 motion picture *Dumbo*, a tale about a baby pachyderm with aerodynamic ears. Two Dumbo the elephant poses, Timothy Mouse and the delayed delivery Stork and sassy Crow were also created. Baby Weems, the story of an infant with a very high I.Q. was produced from the movie *The Reluctant Dragon*, a 1941 live action/ animated tour of how cartoons are created at the Walt Disney Studio starring actor/ comedian Robert Benchley.

Most of Vernon's Disney ceramics are ink stamped with a copyright mark, date 1940 or 41, and the figure, vase or bowl number. Most of the figures have an impressed number in the inside unglazed body cavity, however some do not bear a mark for various reasons. Several of the bowls and vases have been found not marked. Because of the ceramic's high production cost, they were discon-tinued after only eighteen month of manufacture. All production rights, molds and inventory were turned over to American Pottery, see next chapter.

Vernon Kilns continued its varied and successful dinnerware lines and its hundreds of popular souvenir plates depicting historic people and places across the country. In 1947 a devastating fire destroyed most of the facility. The company opted to rebuild, replacing the beehive kilns with modern and more efficient tunnel kilns for increased production.

The 1950's brought the cowboy invasion and the popular big screen Westerns as Vernon introduced its cowboy inspired Winchester '73. In 1958 Vernon Kiln produced their last set of dinnerware and the company closed its doors due to added competition from foreign manufactures. Today Vernon Kilns and its many artistic pottery achievements are con sidered to be one of the "big five" in California pottery circles.

Baby Weems 6"
$250-375

Vases and Bowls

DISNEY
COPYRIGHT 1940
VERNON KILNS
U. S. A.

Figurines

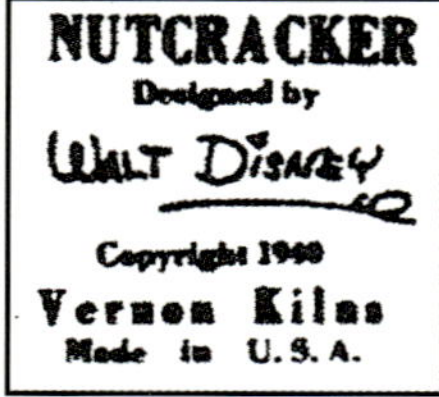

Dinnerware

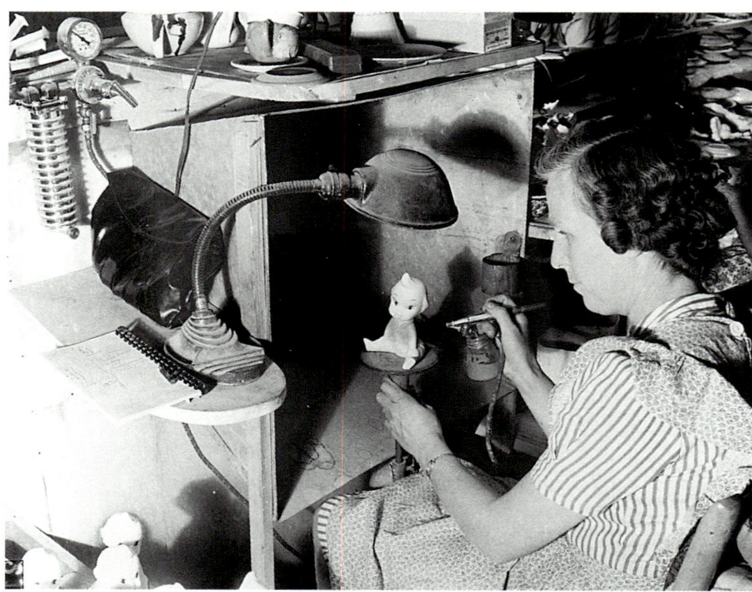

Vernon decorator gives Baby Weems a fresh coat of paint.

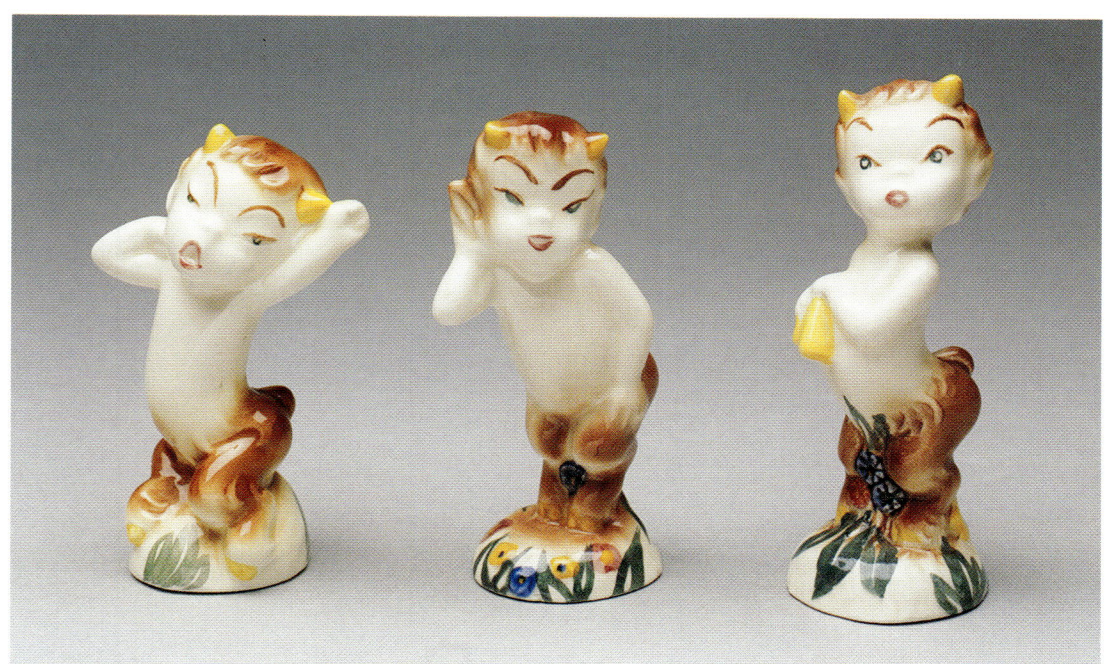

Satyrs #1, 2 and 3, 4 1/2" each, $200-300 each.

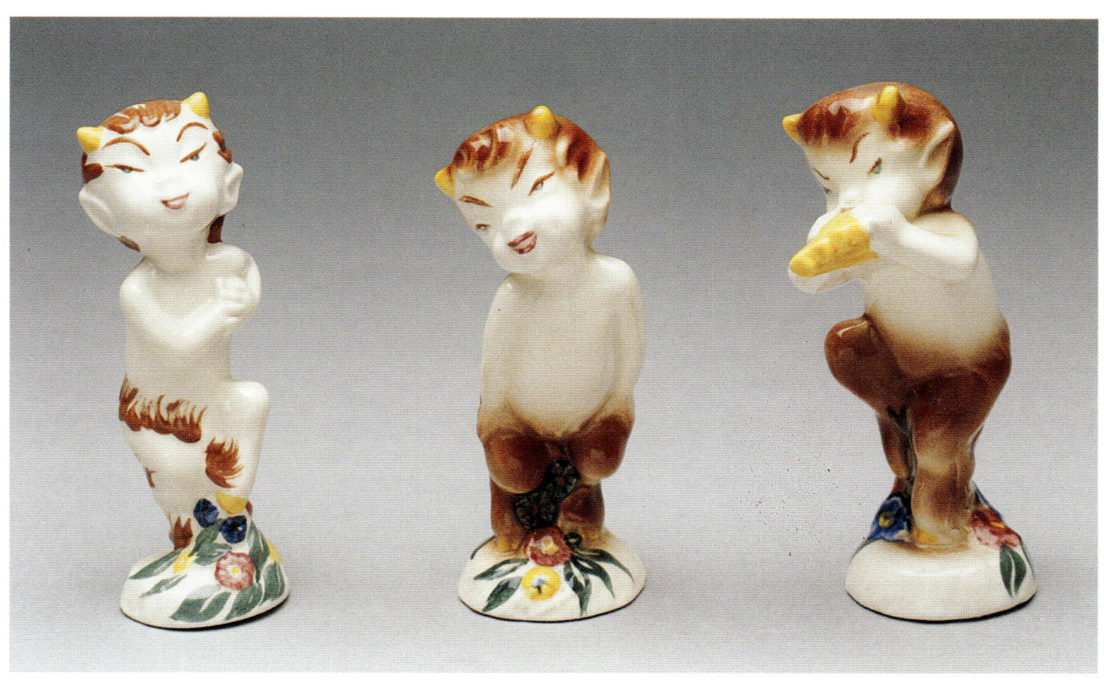

Satyrs #4, 5 and 6, 4 1/2" each, $200-300 each.

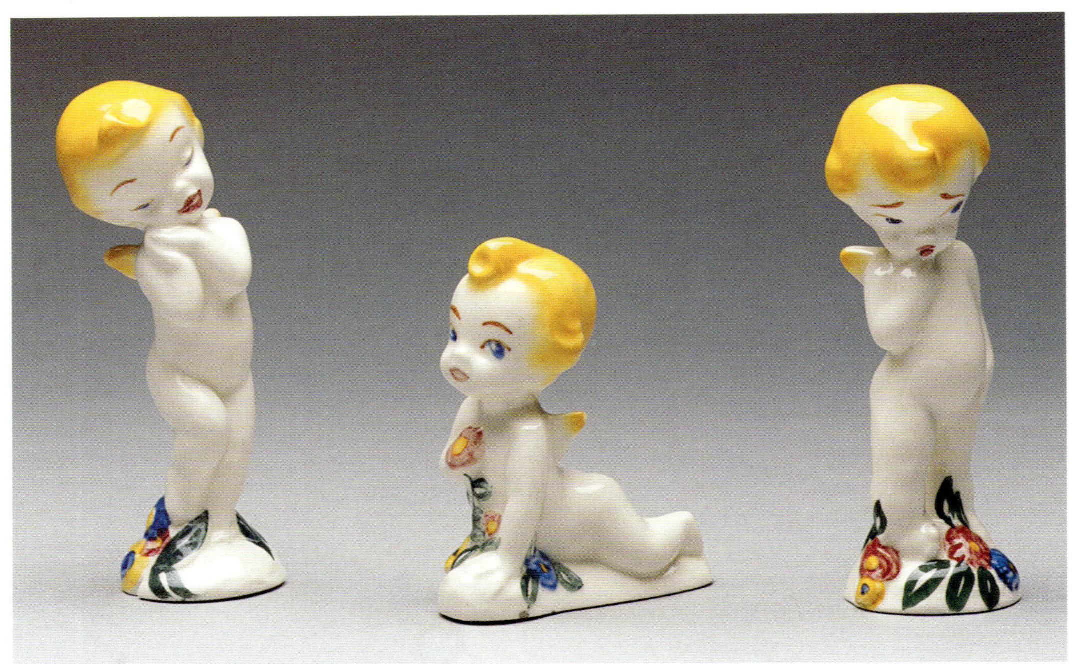

Sprites #7, 4 1/2", #8, 3" and #9, 4 1/2" $250-350 each.

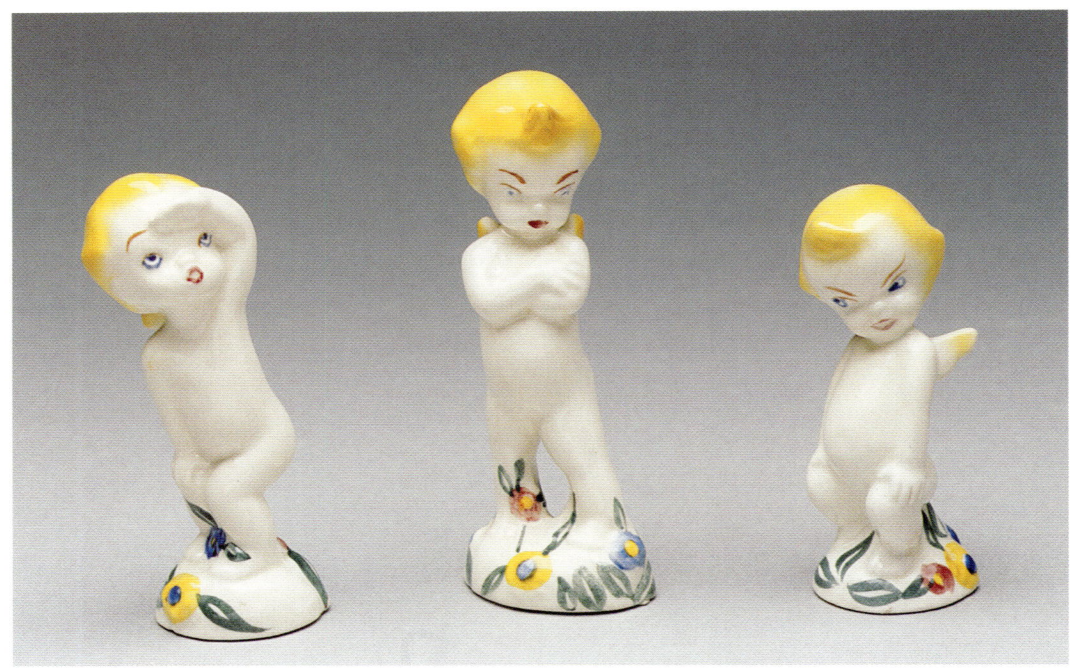

Sprites #10, 4 1/2", #11, 5" and #12, 4" $250-350 each.

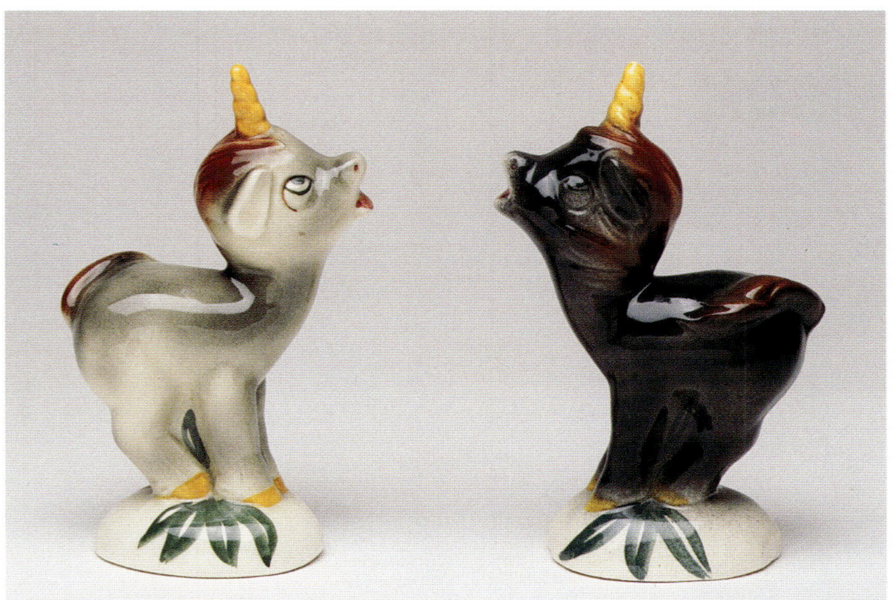

Unicorn #13 in gray and in black 5"each $350-450 each

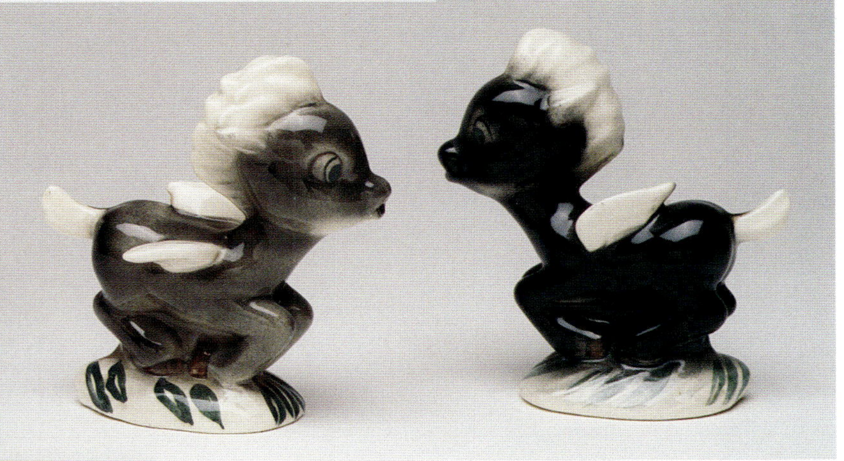

Baby black and gray pegasus #19, 4 1/2" each $350-450 each.

Sitting Unicorn #14, 5" $400-600. Example displayed was a decorator's sample

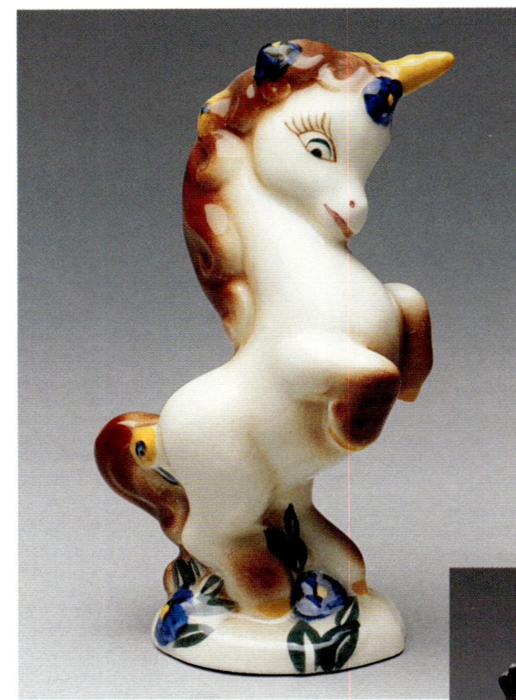

Rearing Unicorn #15, 6" $500-700.

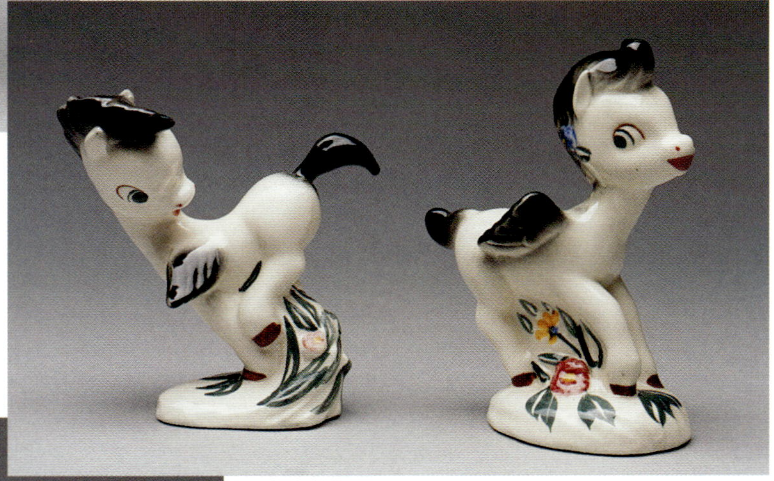

Pegasus head turned #20, 5" $700-900 and Pegasus #21, 5 1/2" $400-500.

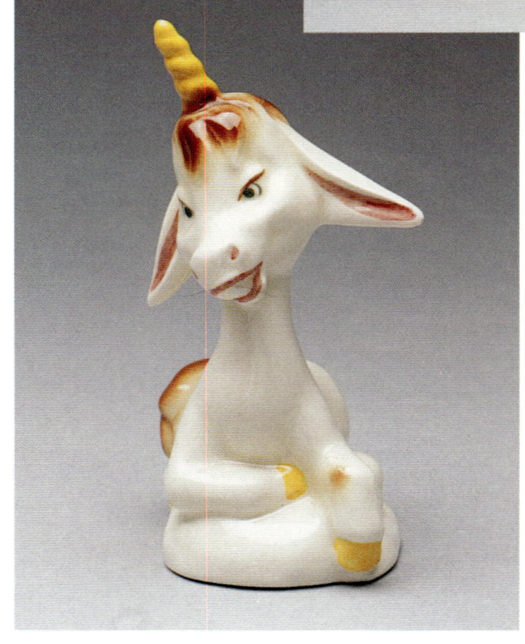

Donkey Unicorn #16, 5 1/2" $750-900. Bacchus' pal is quite hard to find

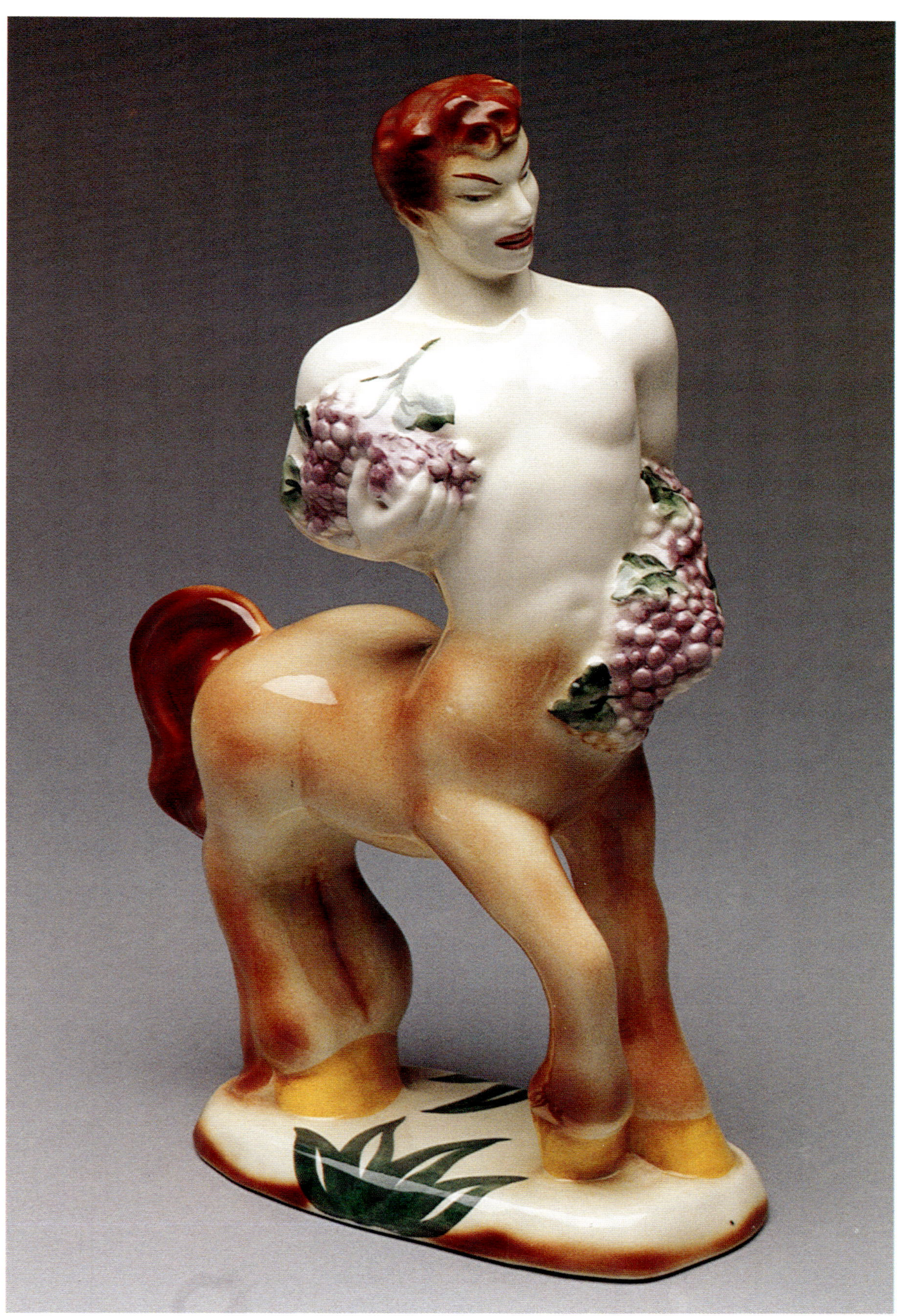

Centaur #31, 10" $1500-1800.

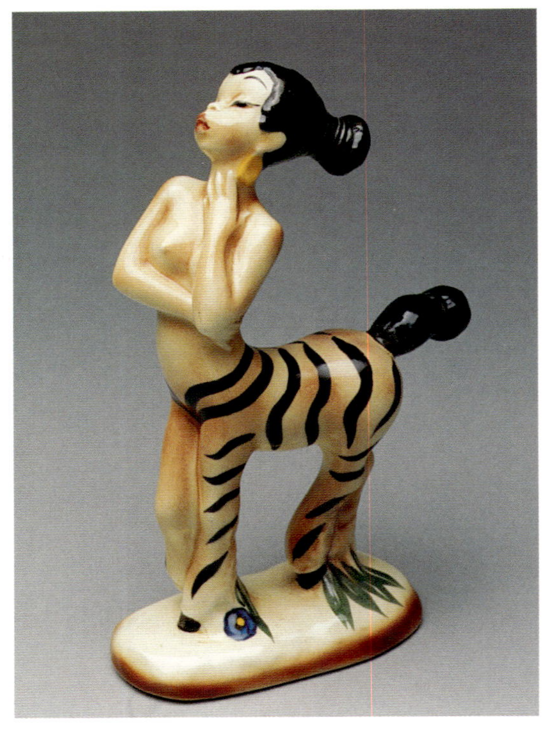

Nubian Centuarette #24, 7 1/2" $1000-1250.

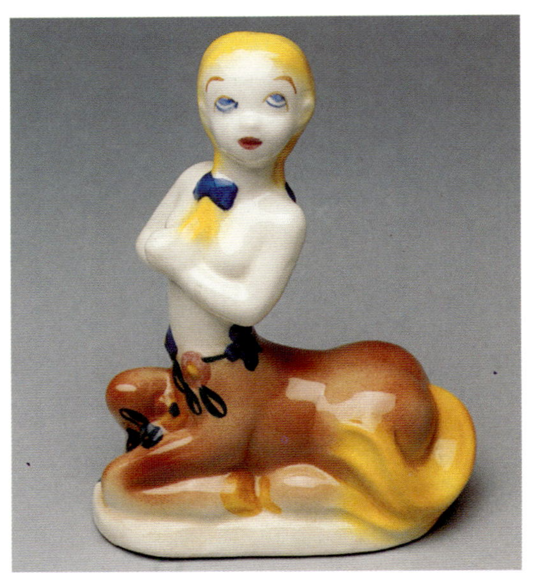

Reclining Centaurette #17, 5 1/2" $800-900.

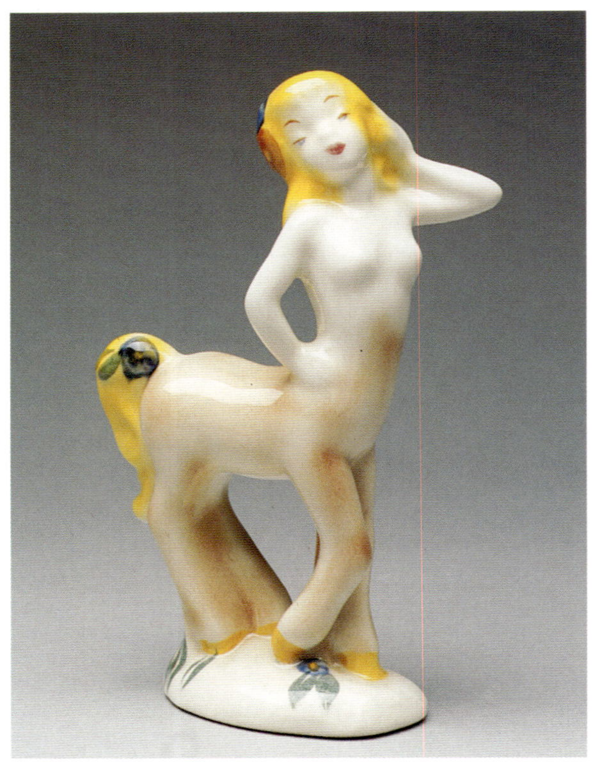

Centaurette #22, 8 1/2" $1400-1700.

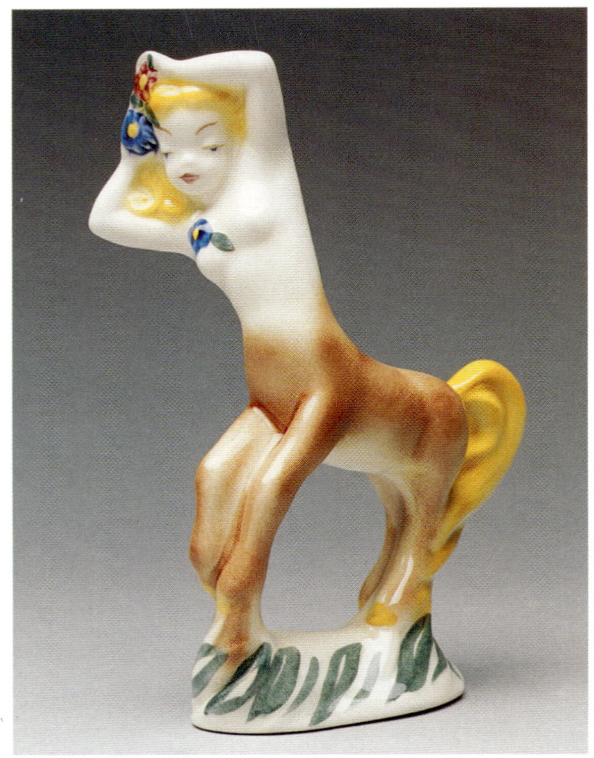

Centaurette #18, 7 1/2" $900-1200

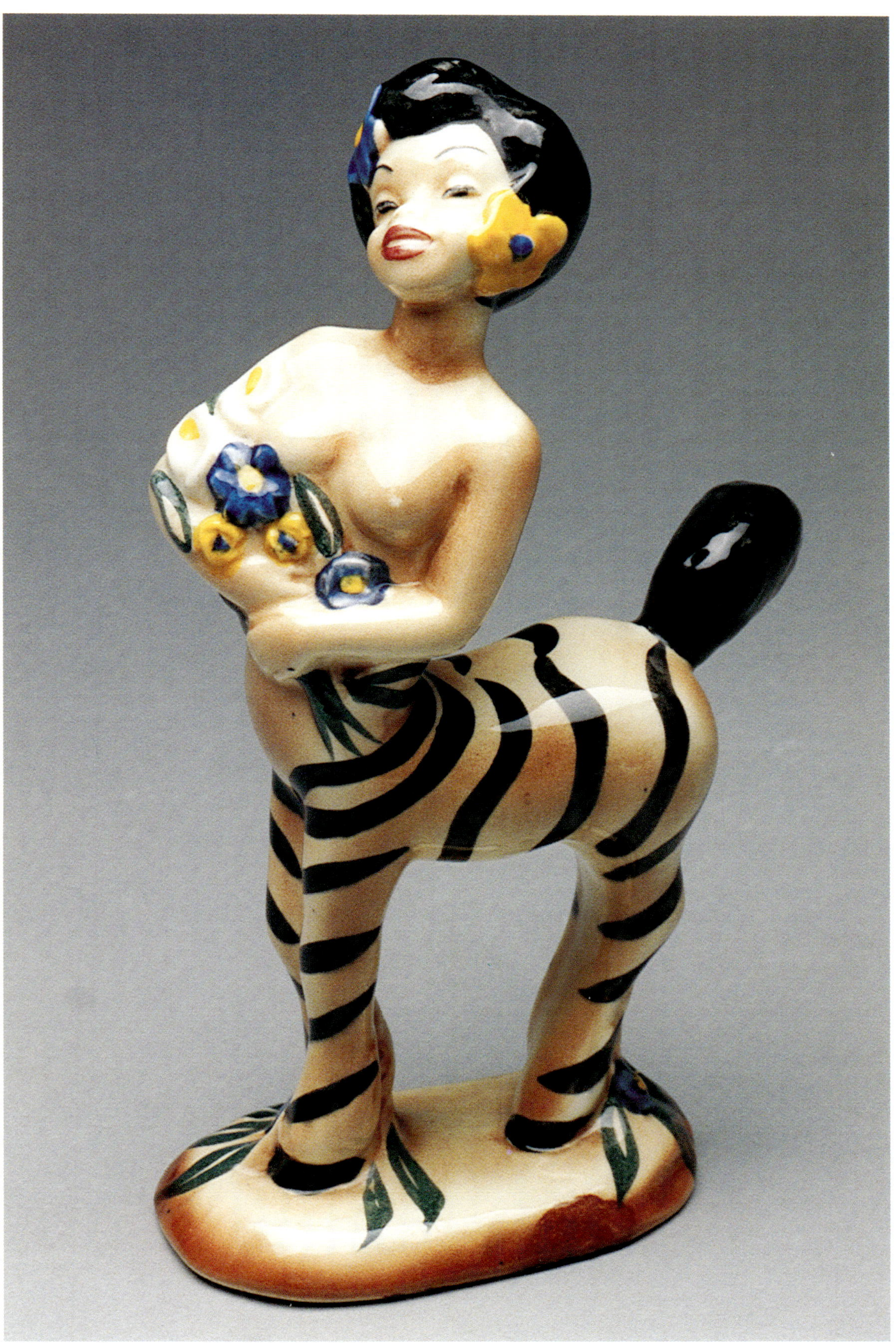

Nubian Centaurette #23, 8" $1400-1700

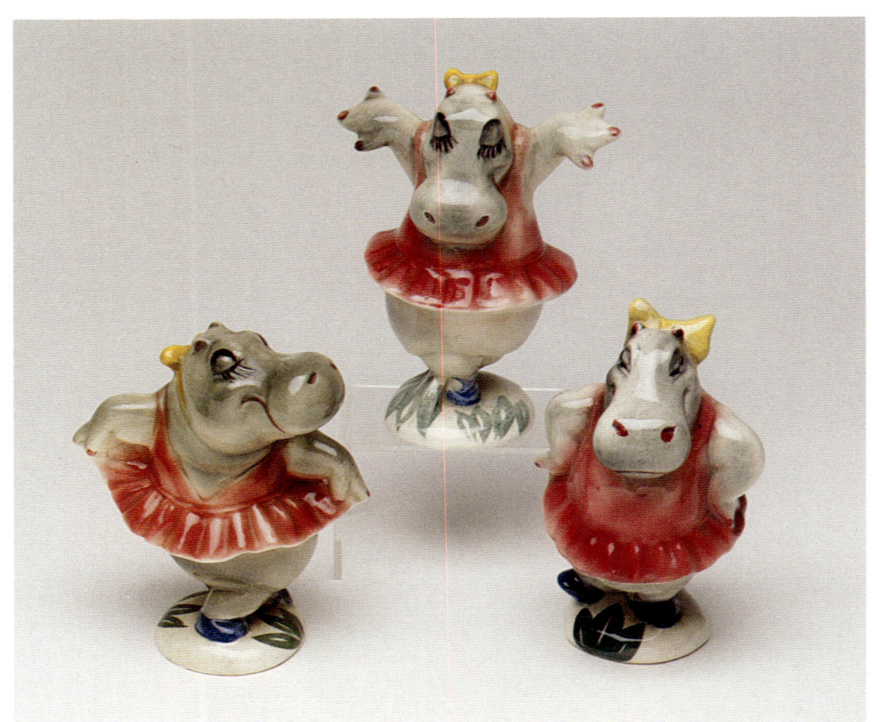

Hippo's #33, 5"$500-700,
#32 51/2" $400-500,
#34 5" $500-700.

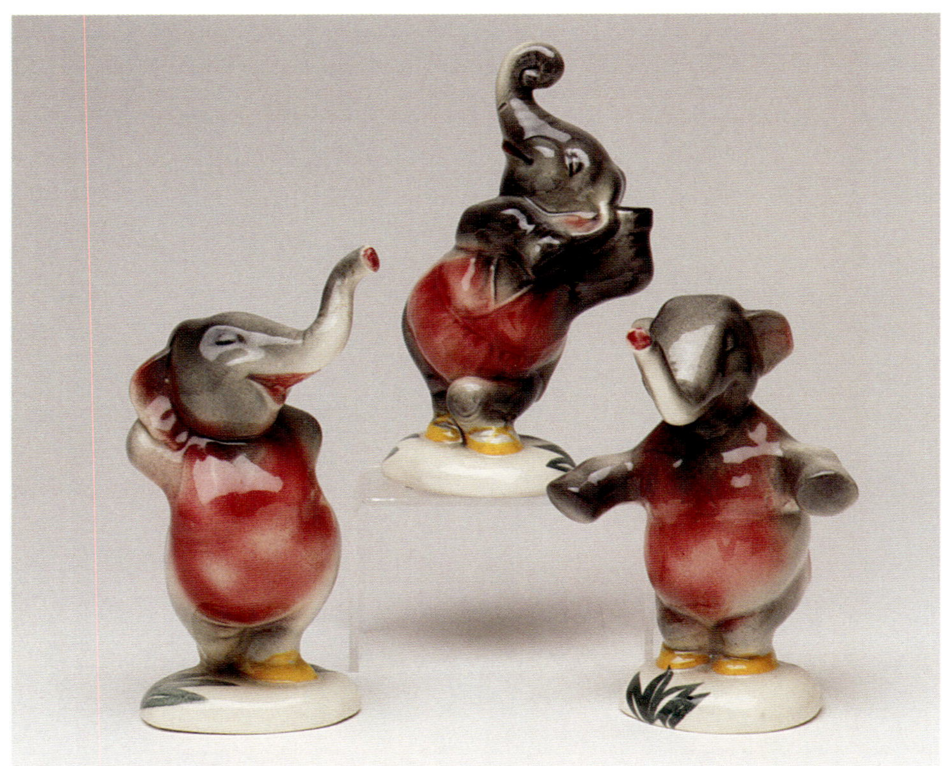

Elephants #25 5" $600-700,
#27 5 1/2" $600-800,
#26 6" $650-800.

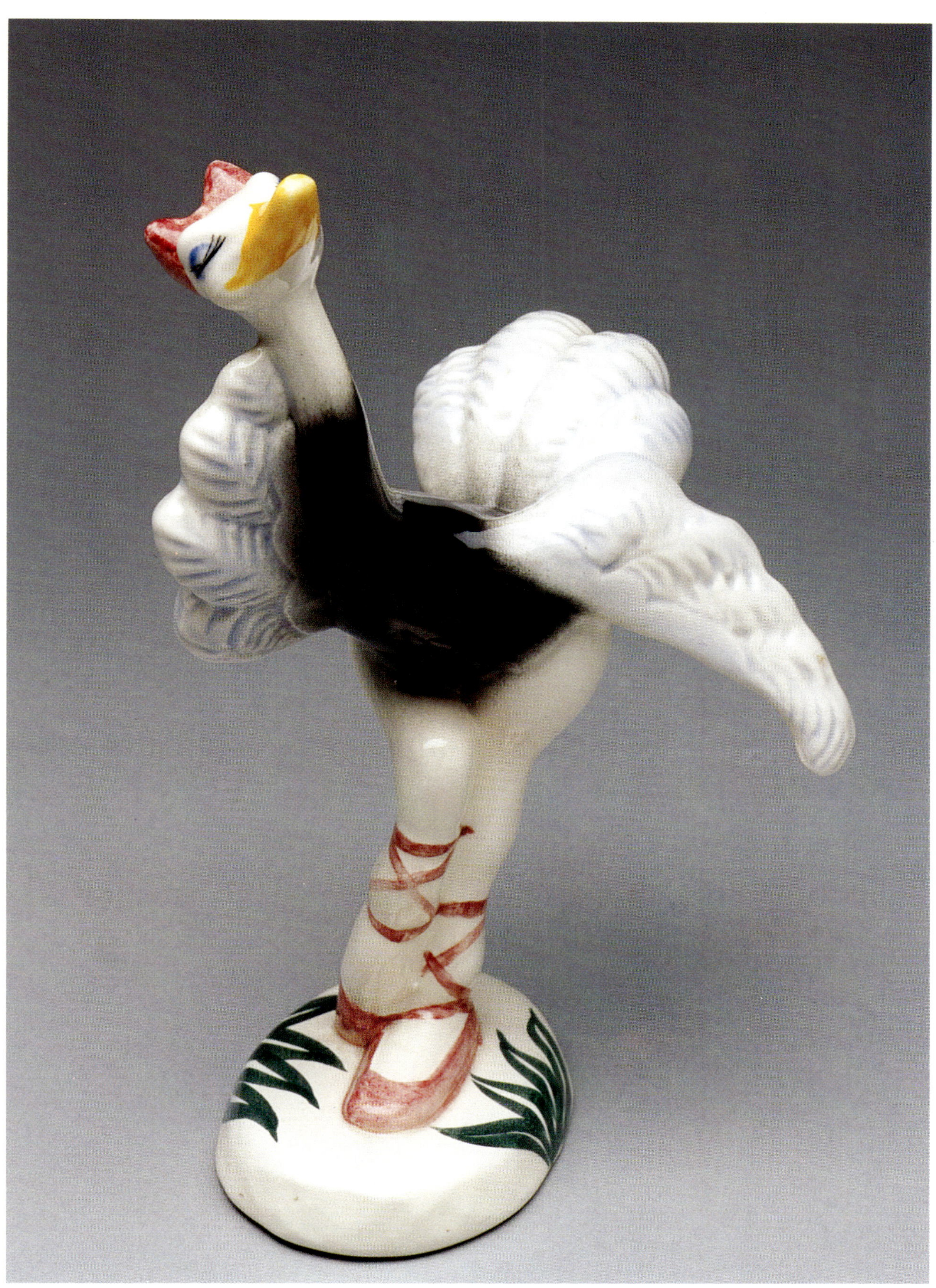

Ostrich #28 9" $1200-1800.

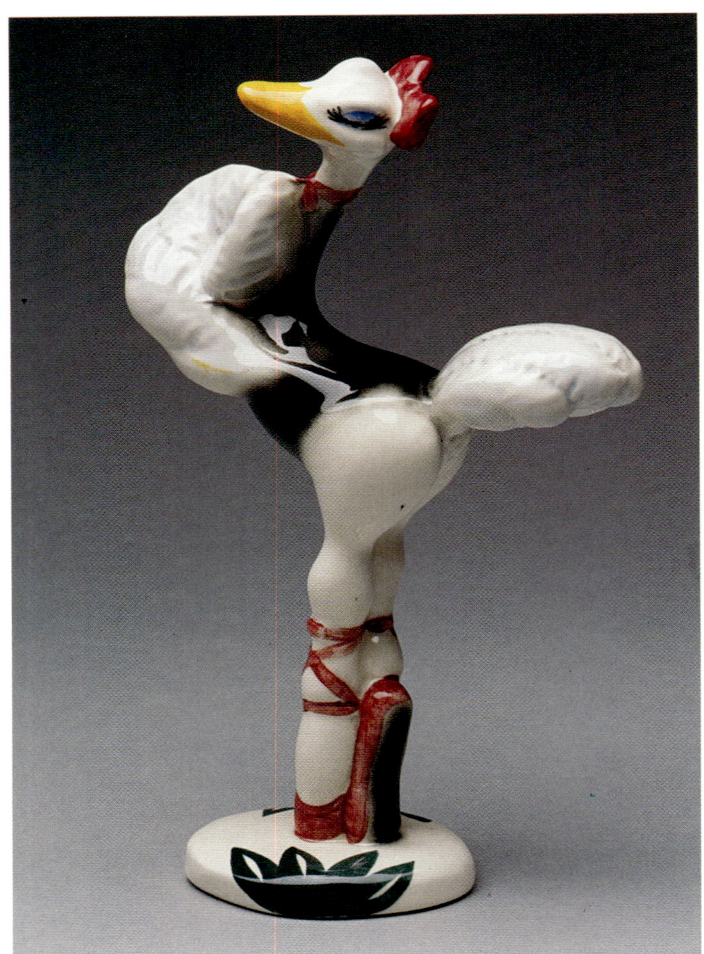

Ostrich #30 8 1/2" $1200-1800.

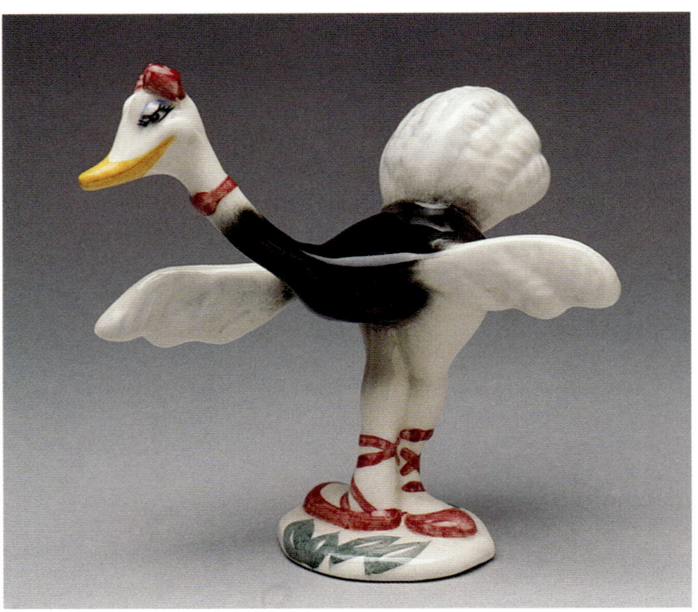

Ostrich #29 6" $1200-1800.

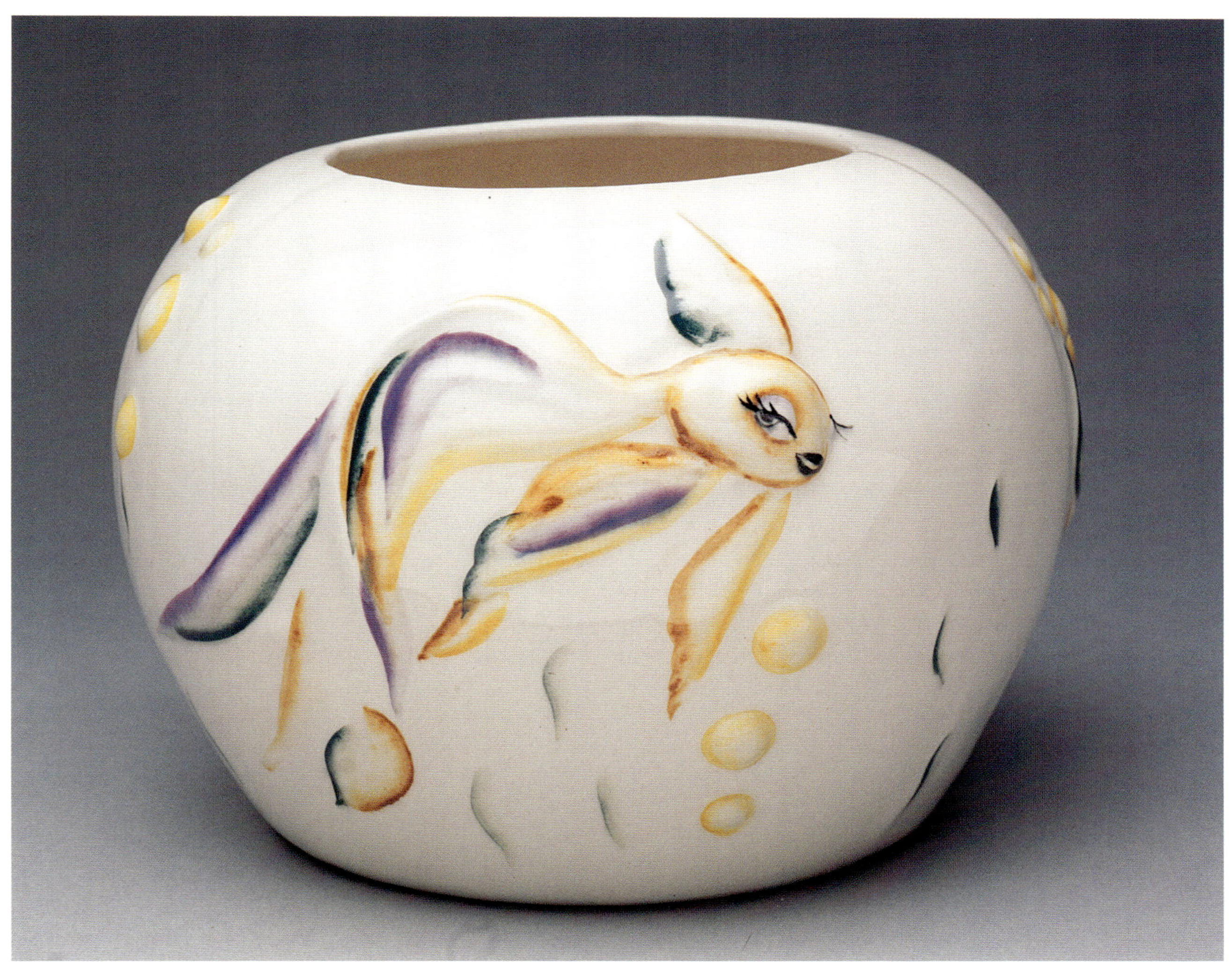

Goldfish bowl #121 6" $700-900 decorated.

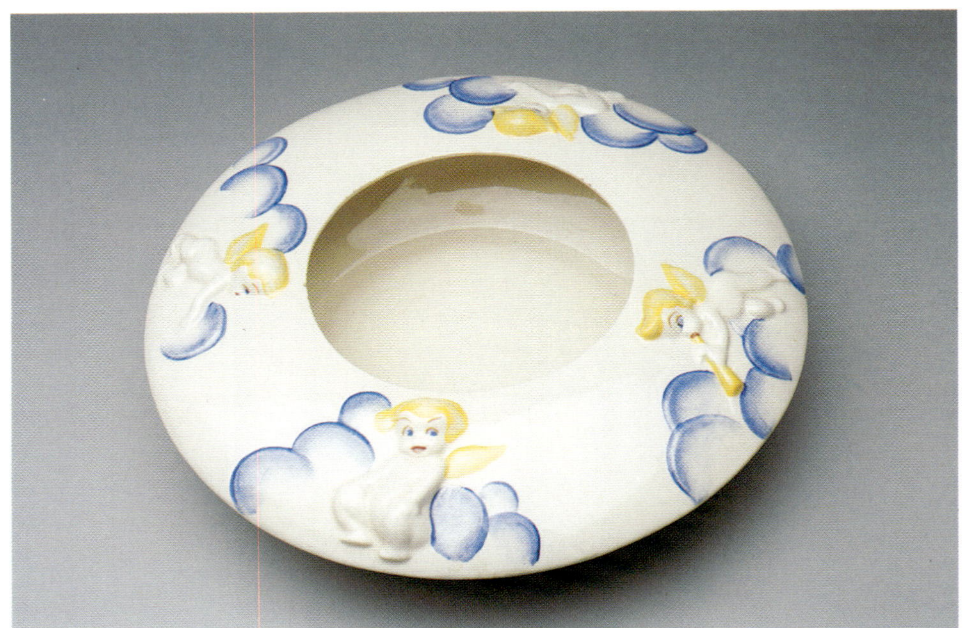

*Sprite bowl #125 3"*high *6 1/2"*diameter*$600-800* decorated.

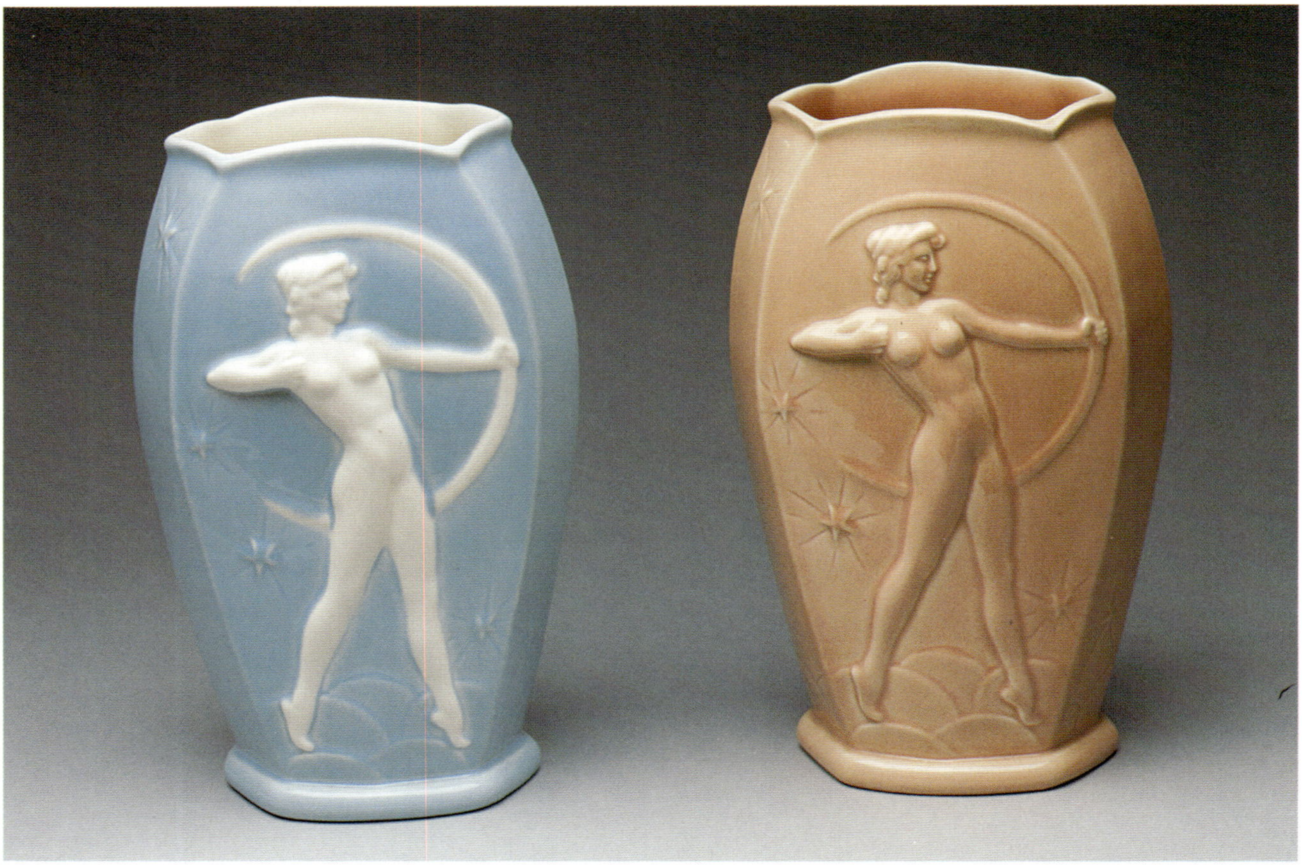

Goddess vase #126 10"$1000-1500 cameo decorated, $800-1200 solid color

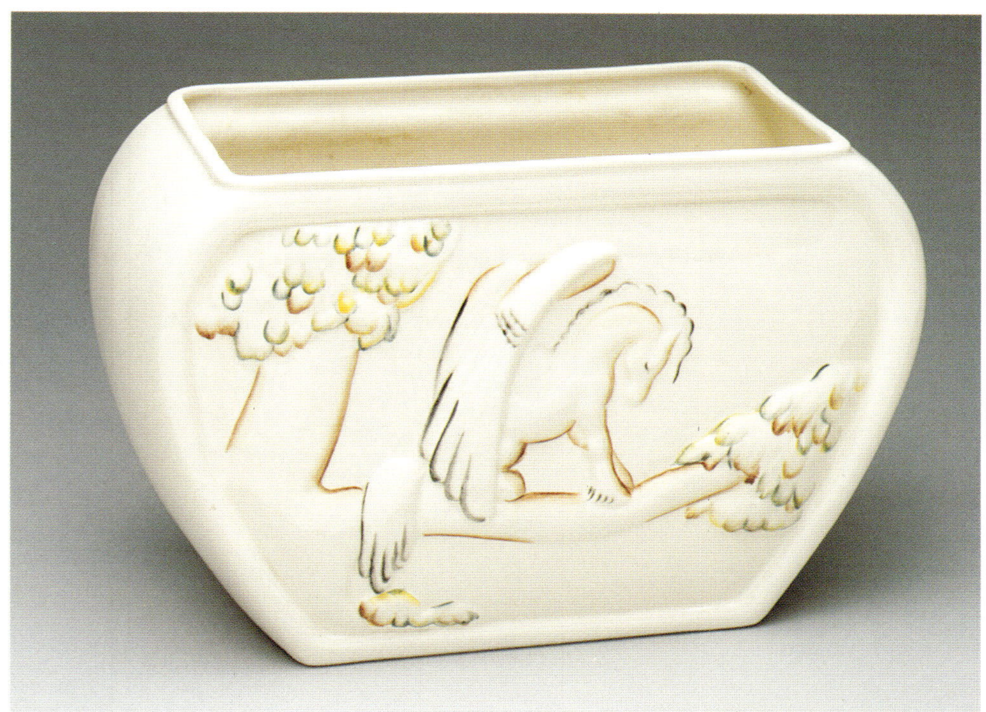

Pegasus vase #127 8" high *12" diameter 5"* deep *$1000-1500 decorated.*

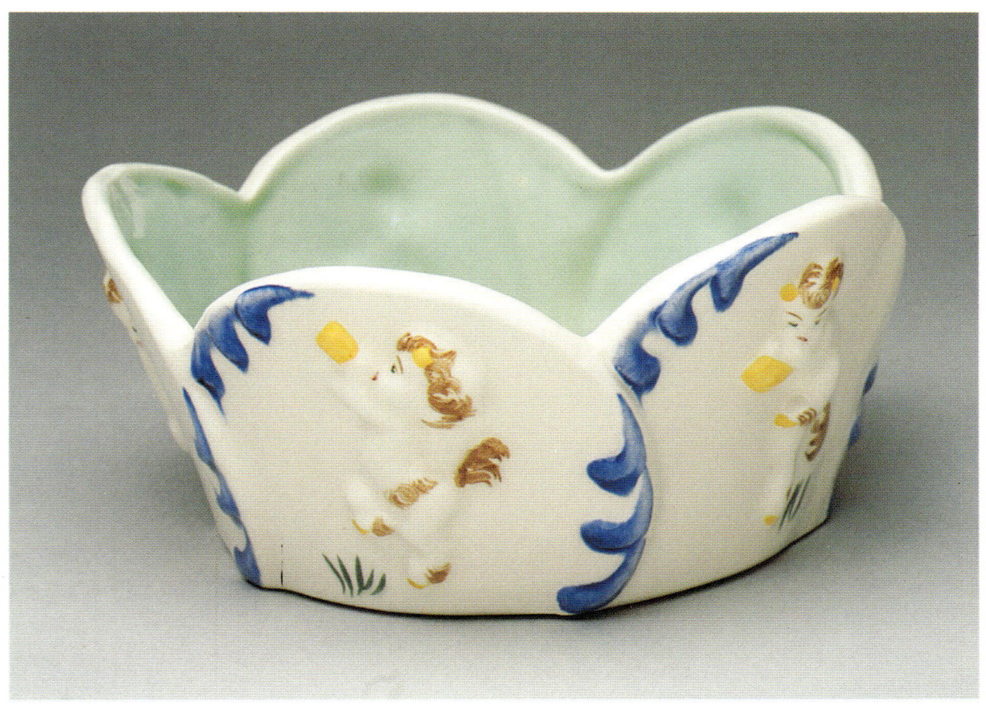

Satyr bowl #124 3" high 6 1/2" diameter $450-600 decorated.

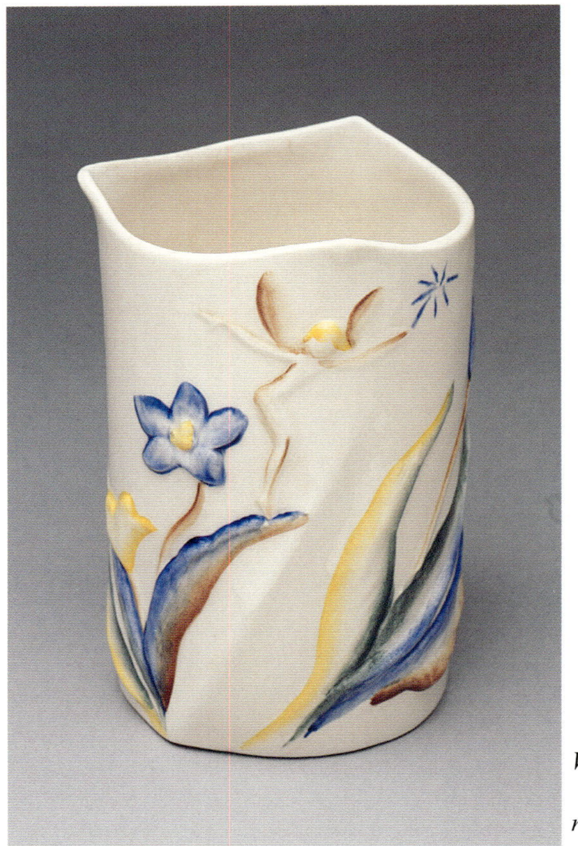

Winged Nymph vase #123
7" high *4"* diameter *$600-800 decorated.*

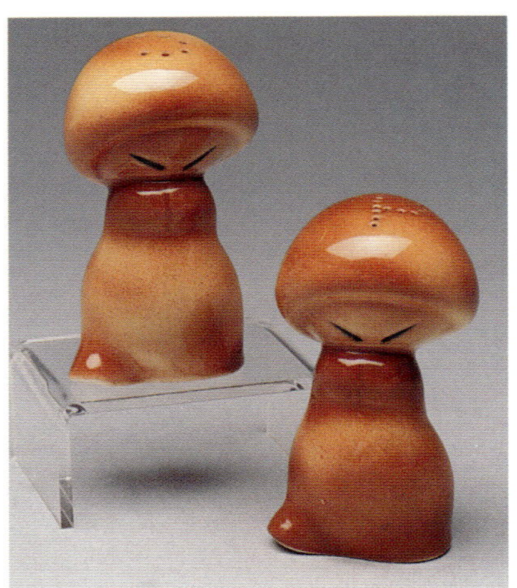

Hop-lo Mushroom salt and peppers 3 1/2" $90-125 pair

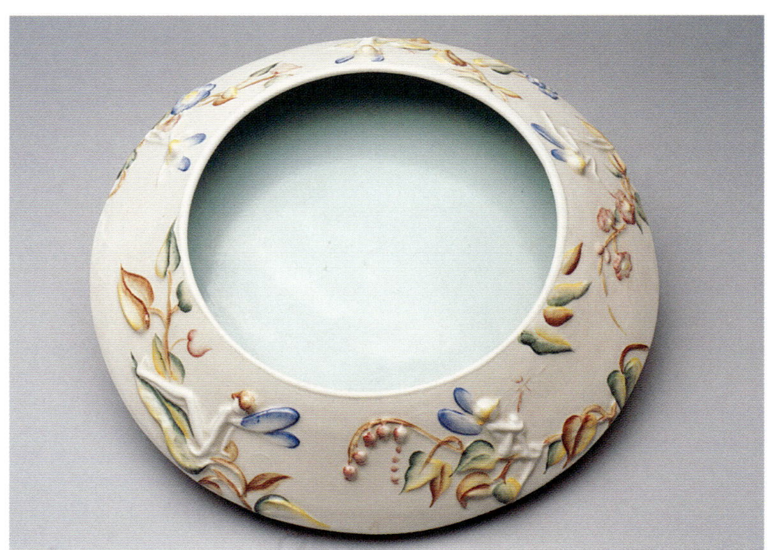

Winged Nymph bowl #120
2 1/2" high 12' base *$600-800 decorated.*

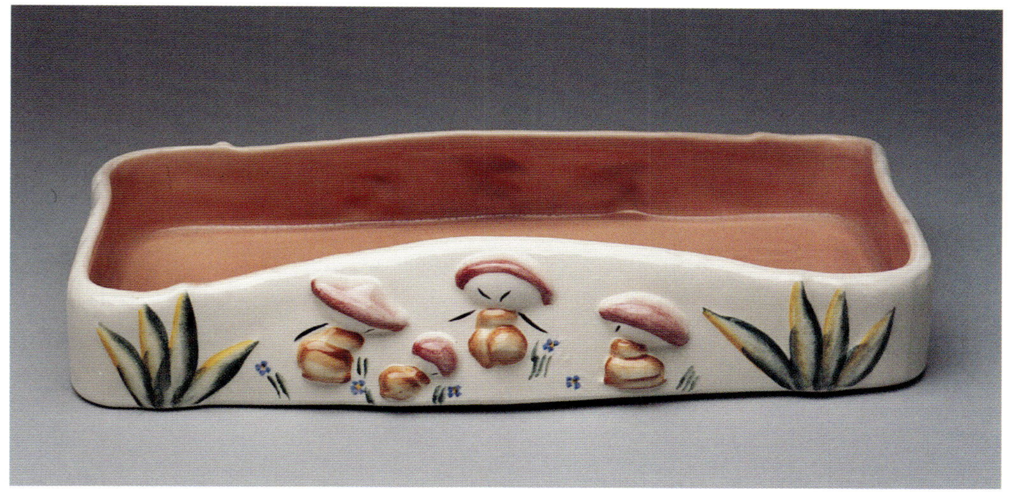

Mushroom bowl #120 2" high 12"x7" base $300-450 decorated.

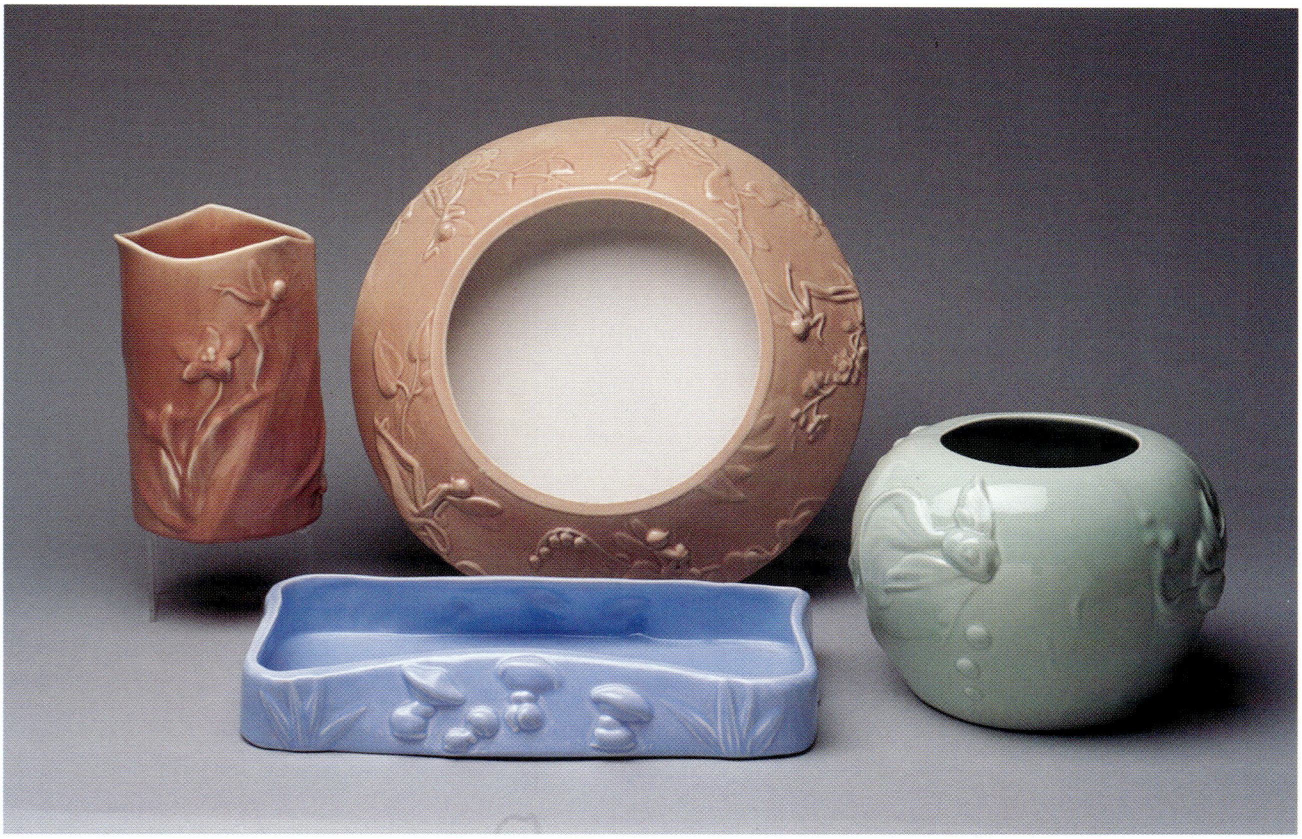

Fantasia bowls and vases in solid and two-tone glazing. $200-700 each.
Values approximately 50% less for solid colored vases.

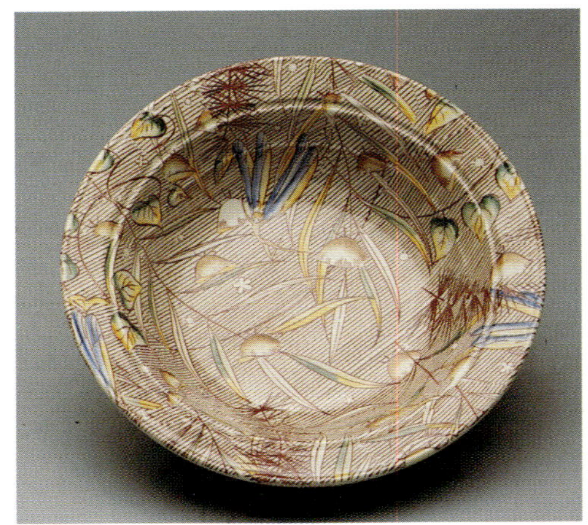

Autumn Ballet 9" bowl $200+.

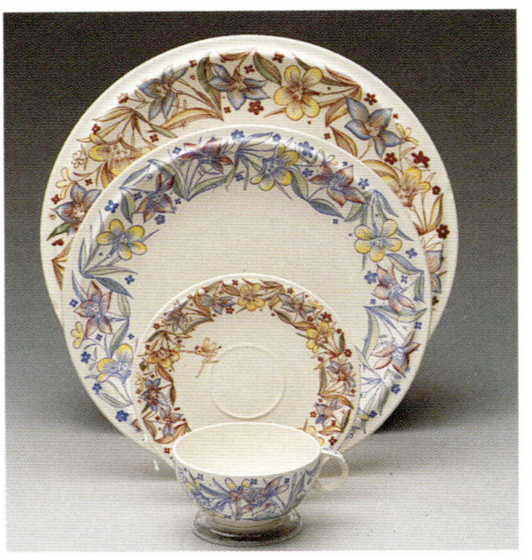

Flower Ballet and Enchantment dinner plates and teacup $75+ each.

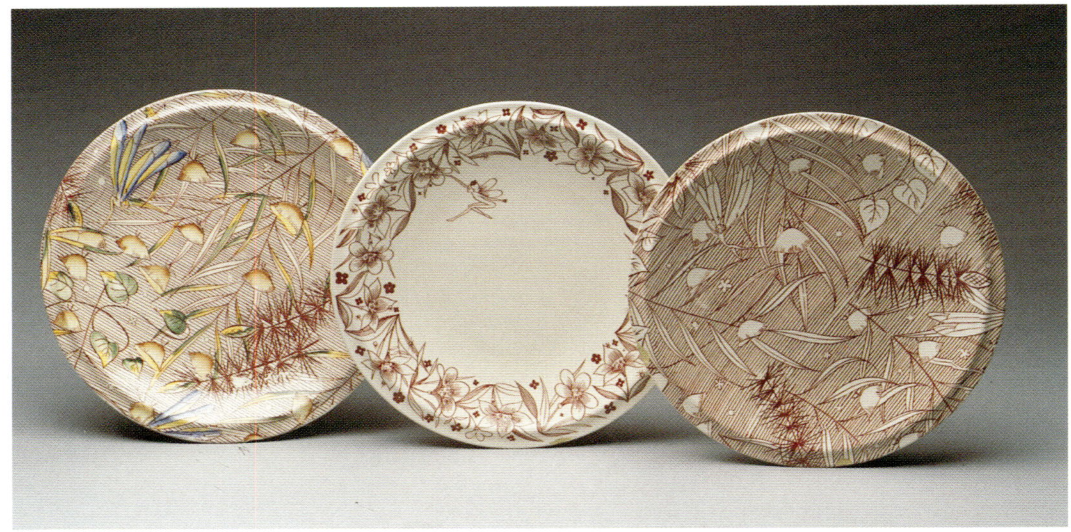

Autumn Ballet, Milkweed Dance and Dewdrop Fairies 9 1/2" dinner plates $100+ea

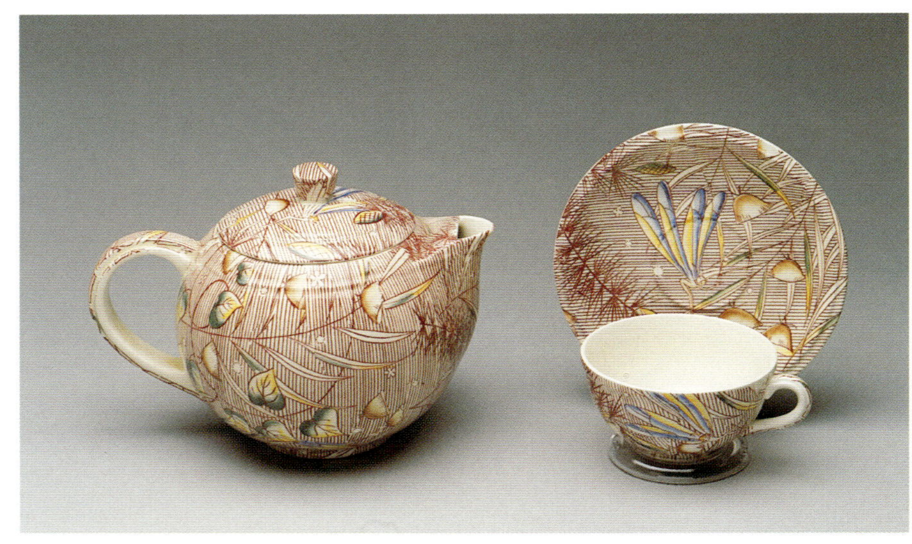

Autumn Ballet 6-cup Teapot on Montecito shape 500+, matching cup & saucer 100+.

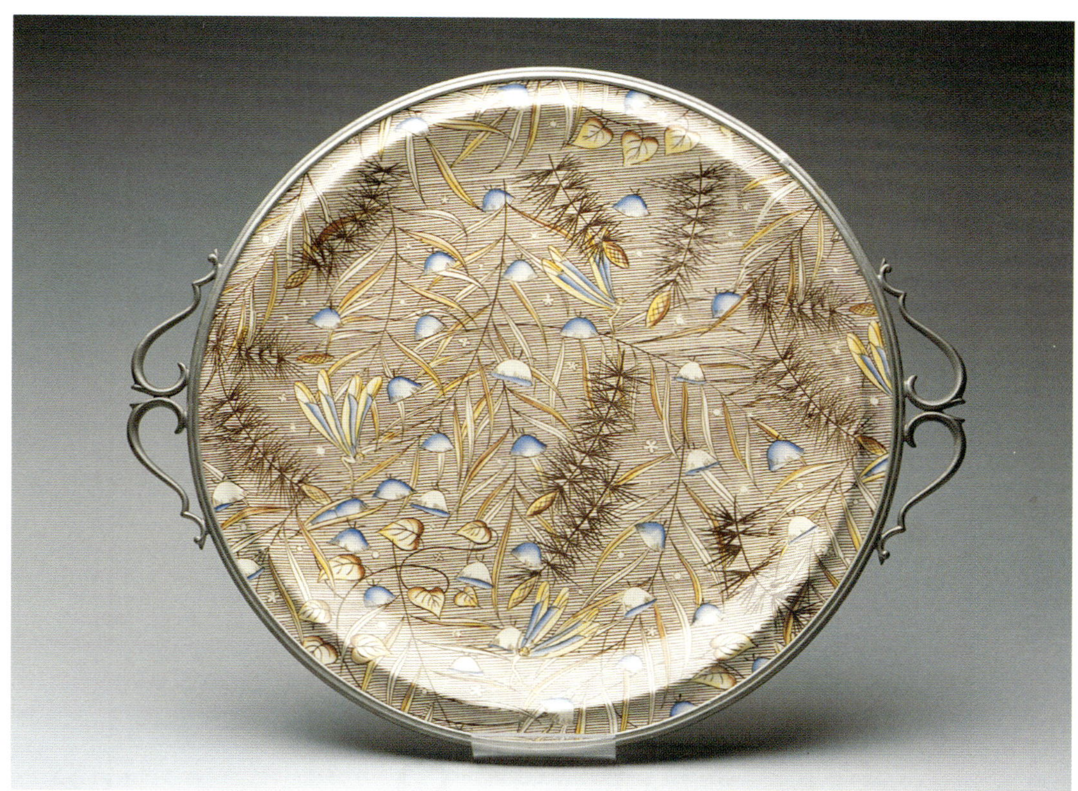

Fantasia 17" chop plate encased in pewter $800+.

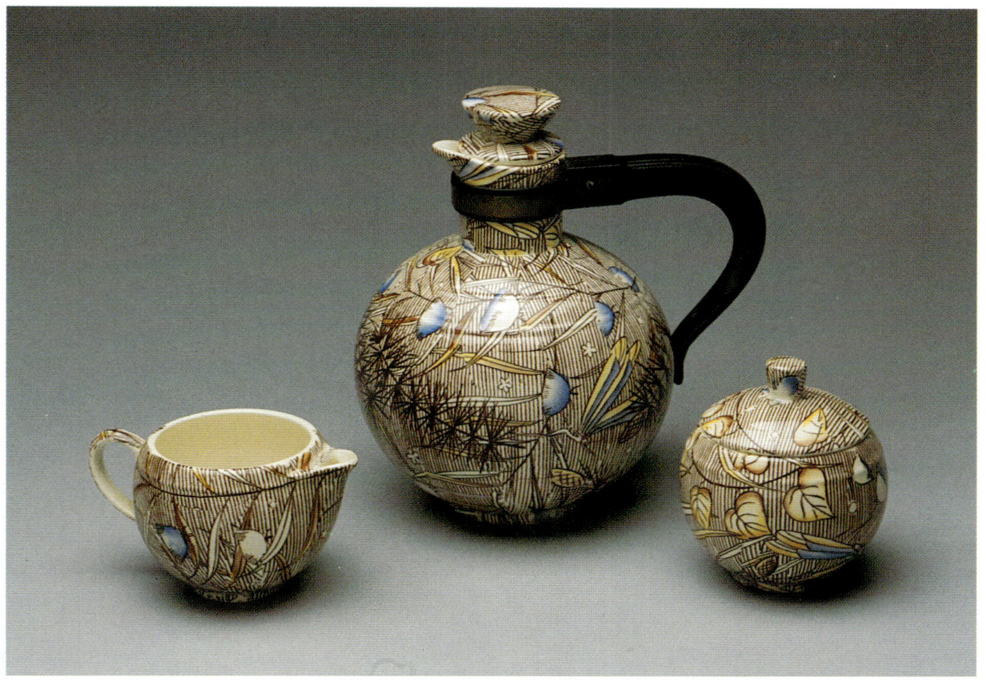

Fantasia coffee carafe with stopper on Montecito shape $500+, matching sugar bowl and creamer 300+ set.

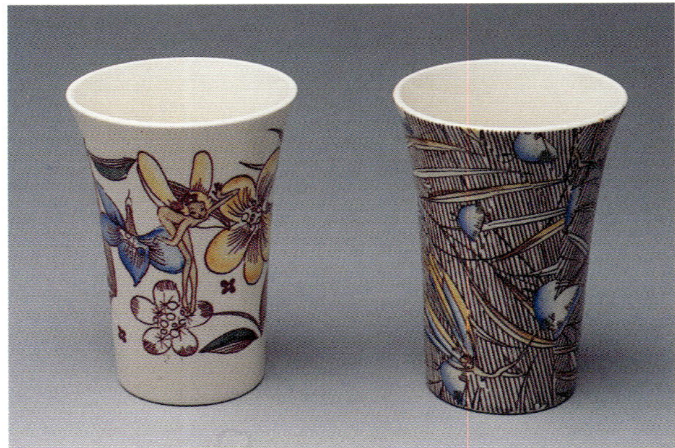

Flower ballet and Fantasia 6" tumblers $100+ each.

1 pint pitcher with cover on Ultra shape $300+, 6-cup Teapot $500+ and eggcup $100+ all in Nutcracker pattern

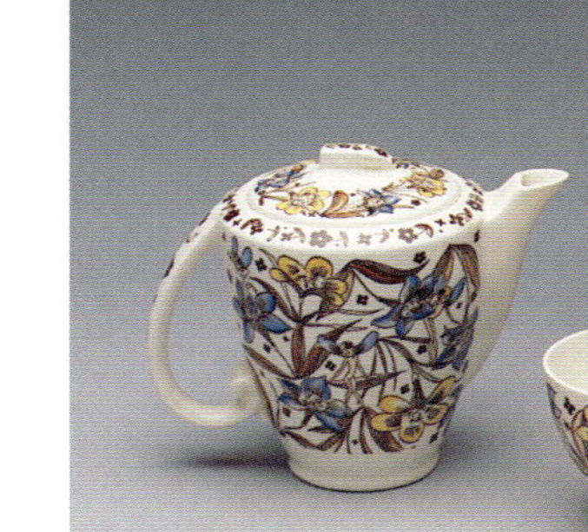

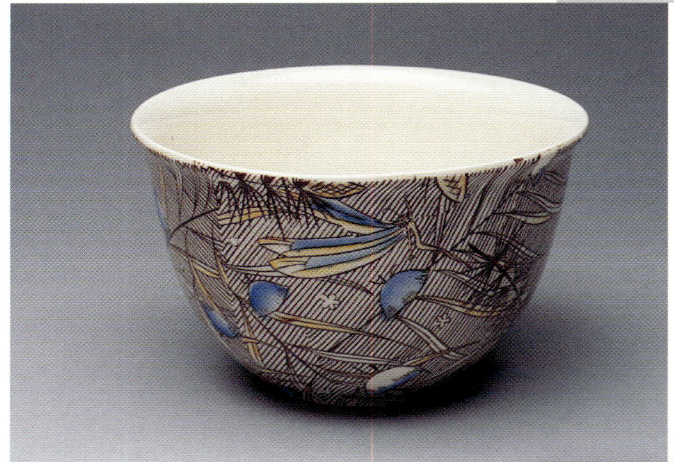

Fantasia mixing bowl $300+.

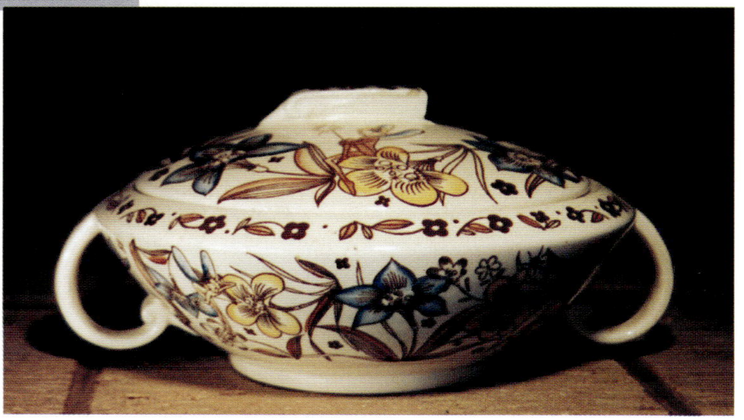

Casserole $500+

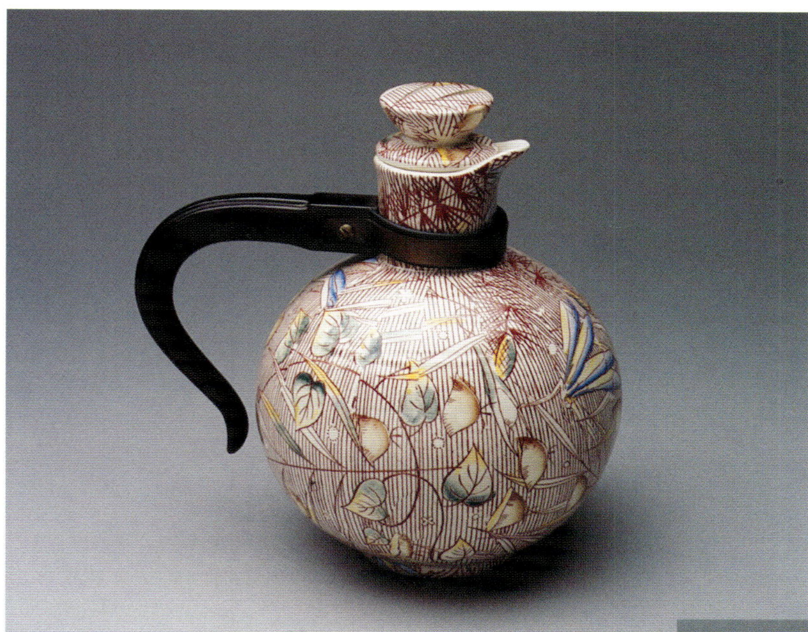

Autumn Ballet coffee carafe with stopper $500+

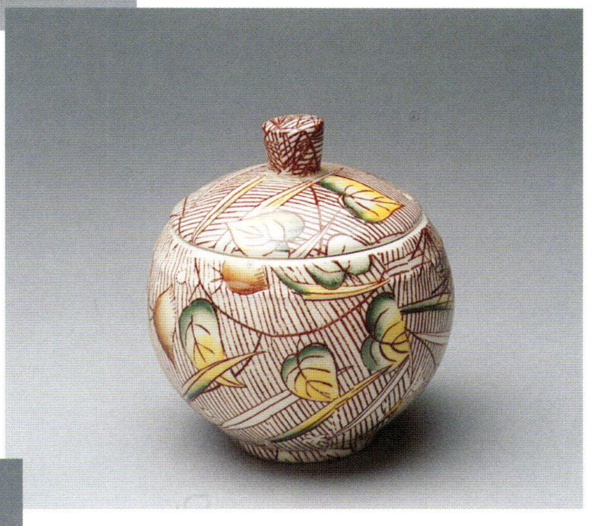

Autumn Ballet sugar bowl on Montecito shape 100+

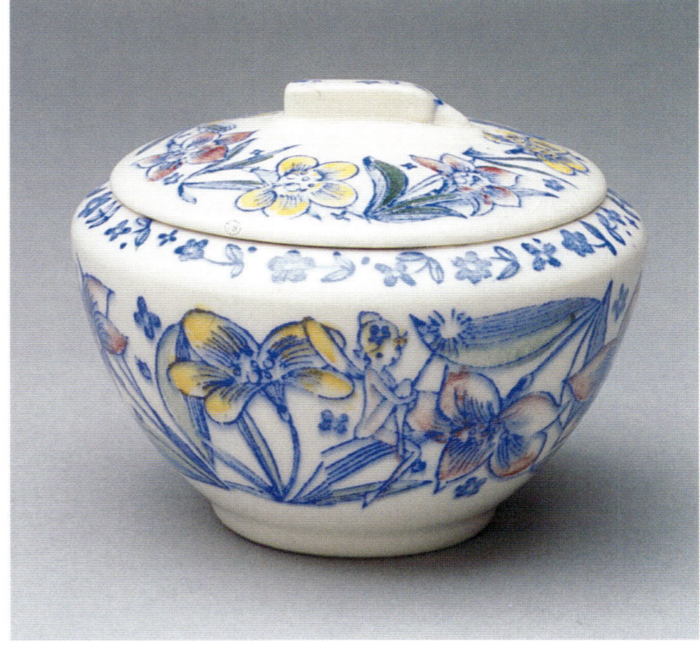

Enchantment individual sugar bowl $75+

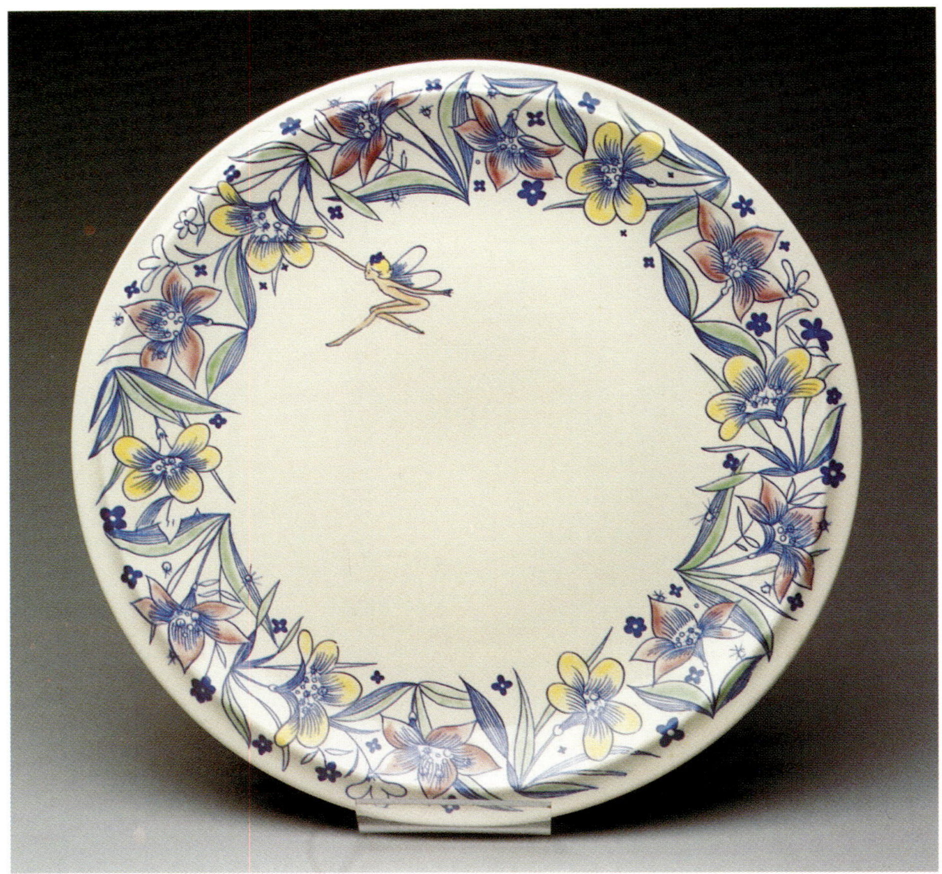

Enchantment *14" chop plate $400+.*

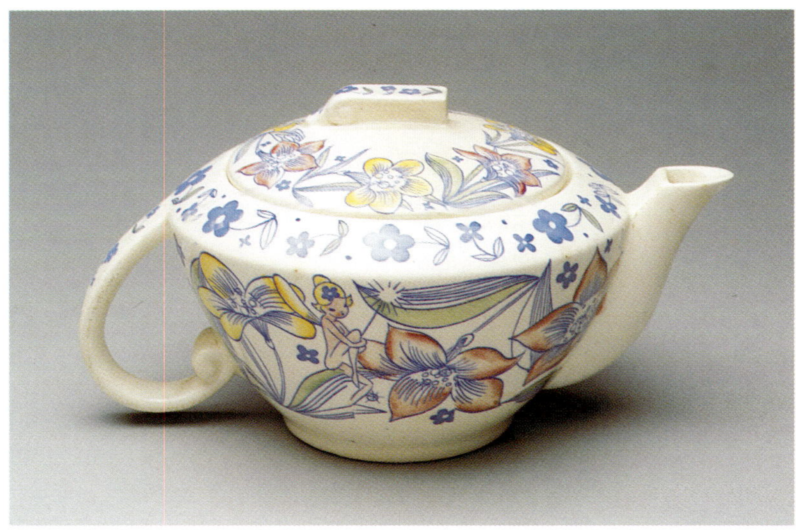

Enchantment *6-cup teapot on* Ultra *shape $500+.*

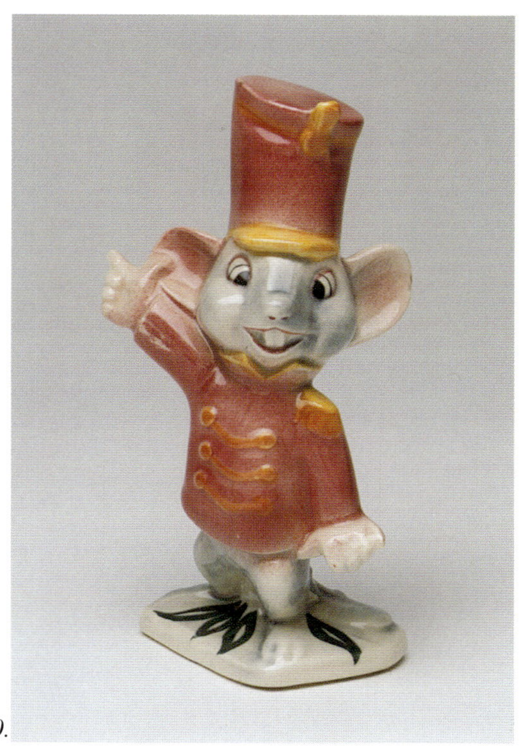

Timothy Mouse #38 6" $400-600.

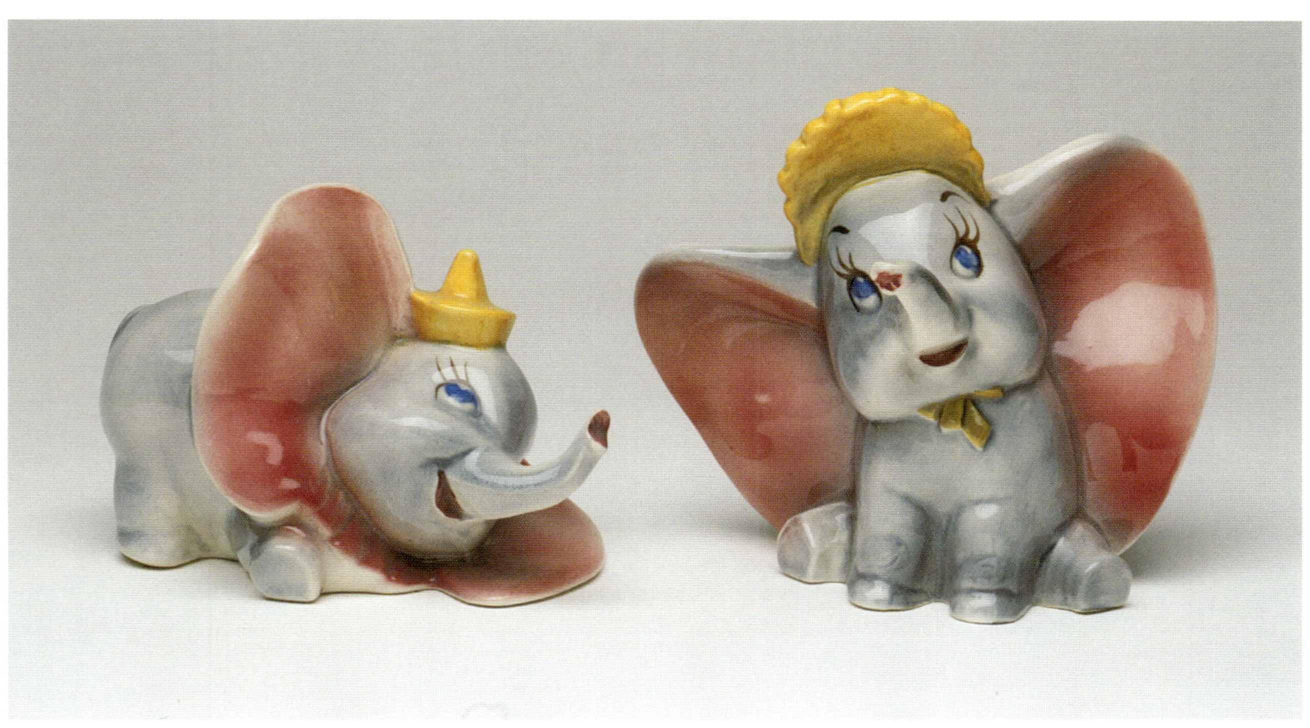

Dumbo on ear #40 4", and sitting #41 5" $200-300 each.

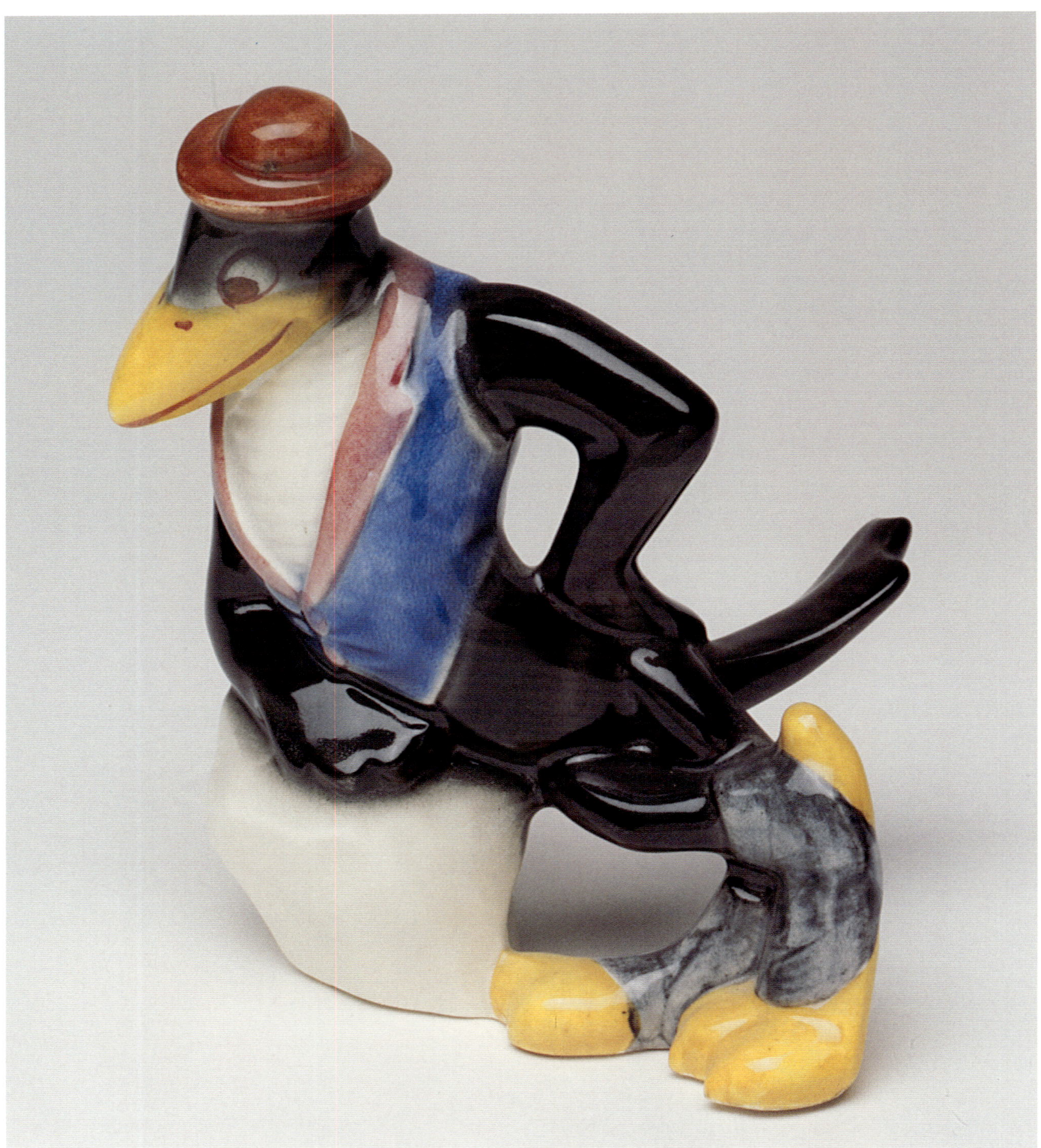

Crow #39 5 3/4 $2000+.

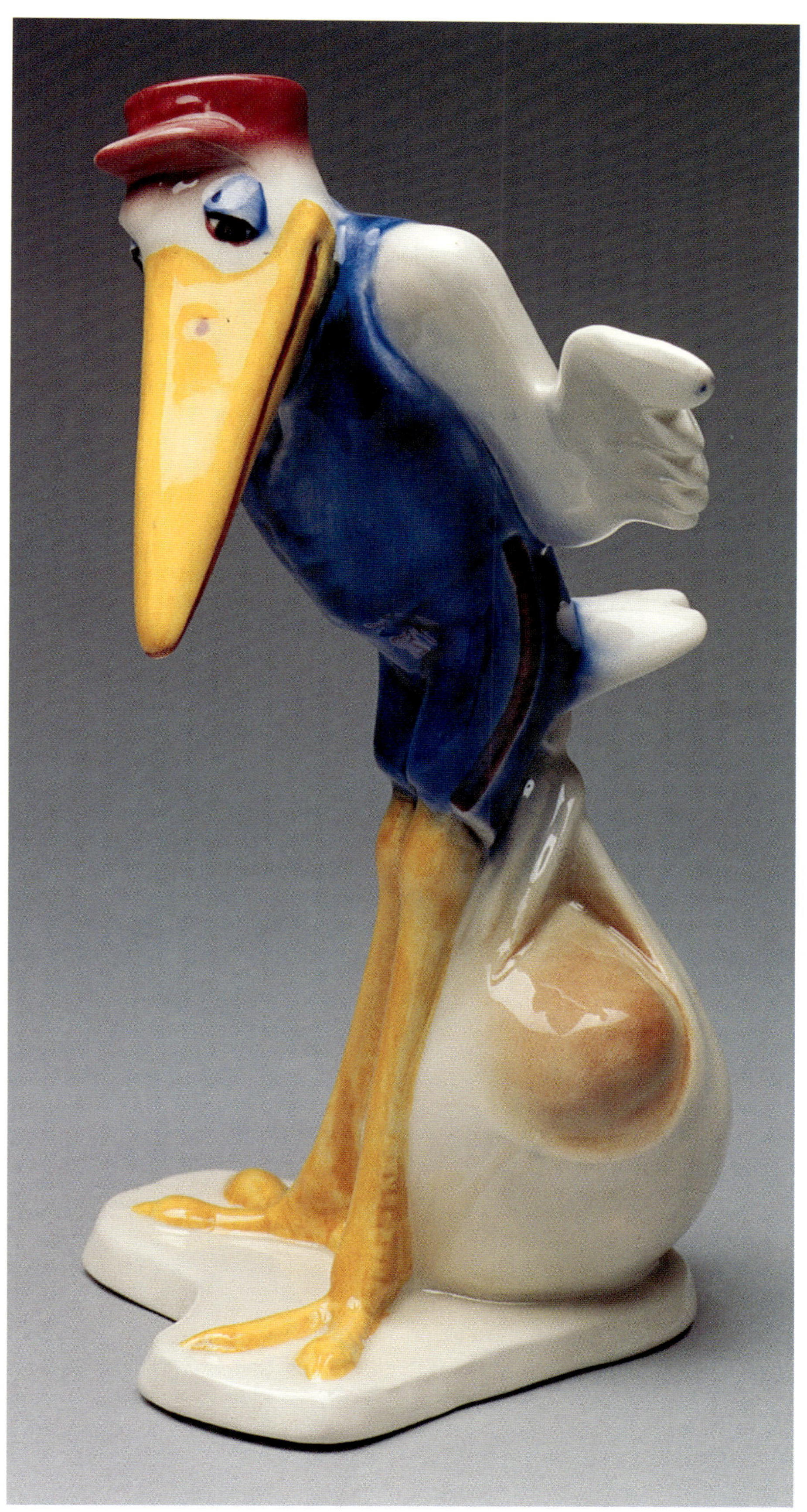

Mr. Stork #42 8 3/4" $2000+.

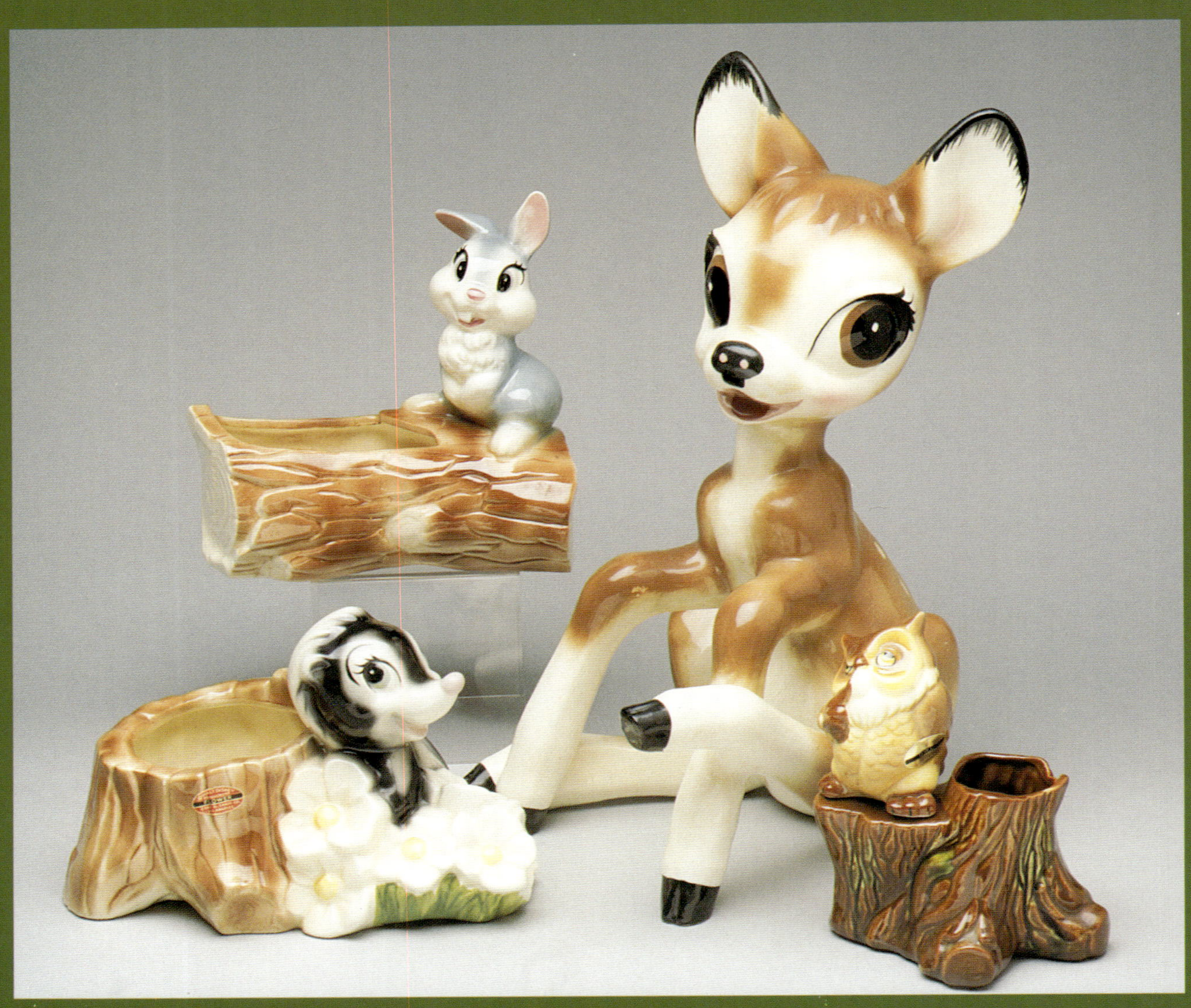

American Pottery/Evan K. Shaw 1943-1955

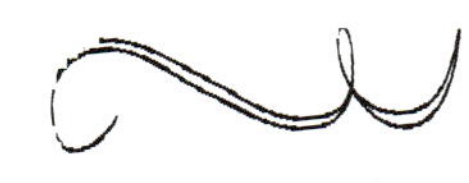

The Evan K. Shaw licensing saga and the production of its Disney ceramics involved a known total of three companies, production shops or licensing firms. American Pottery was a large ceramics outfit in Los Angeles, with its office address listed at 527 W. 7th Street. The company was initiated in the late1930's by one time Vernon Kiln employee Evan K. Shaw. American Pottery initially produced small and somewhat crudely made ceramic figures, bowls and vases as well as some beautiful bird and animal figures.

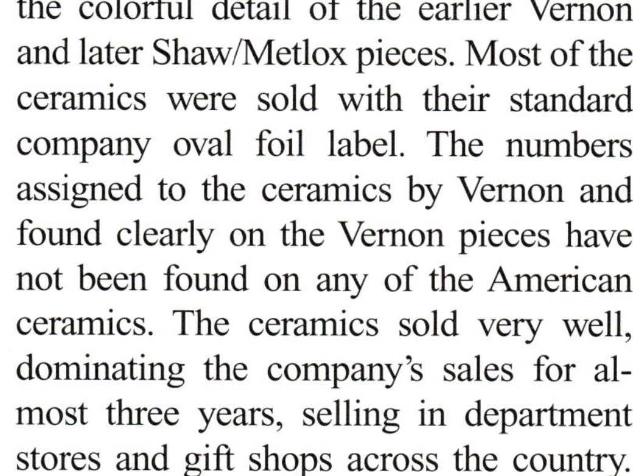

Evan K. Shaw

On July 22, 1942, Vernon Kiln for financial reasons discontinued its Disney line and assigned their current contract to Evan K. Shaw's fledgling American Pottery Company. This action gave the company a much needed shot in the arm by providing the firm a potentially profitable product along with all of Vernon's mold cases, its existing warehouse stock and the rights to continue to produce and finish the Fantasia and Dumbo designs for the number of months remaining on Vernon's existing contract.

Shaw's American Pottery signed its first contract with Disney on February 4, 1943. This contract and concurrent overlapping renewals would last through December 1955. The American Pottery contract would last through 1950, Shaw having earlier extended the contract in his own name from 1946 to 1955. After Vernon's existing stock had been depleted, American continued to produce some of the Fantasia designs including a sprite #10, Pegasus #20, mushroom shakers Hop Low #35,36, Hippo #34, and Elephant #25. Two Dumbo poses #40, 41 as well as a Timothy Mouse #38 were also continued in production.

A few new designs were introduced to the line including Mickey with a bouquet, Minnie with a broom, a Donald Duck, Pluto and a number of large Bambi and related figures. A few of these pieces have been found with an ink stamped mark "American Pottery copyright 1942 or 43". Several collectors have noticed in these first pieces most of the ceramics mold lines were cleaned hastily, the inside cavity was glazed and the pieces abruptly decorated with airbrushes and a lack of the colorful detail of the earlier Vernon and later Shaw/Metlox pieces. Most of the ceramics were sold with their standard company oval foil label. The numbers assigned to the ceramics by Vernon and found clearly on the Vernon pieces have not been found on any of the American ceramics. The ceramics sold very well, dominating the company's sales for almost three years, selling in department stores and gift shops across the country. In 1946, a devastating fire swept through the American Pottery facility, completely destroying the factory and everything in it.

With the onset of the second World War, many domestic manufacturers were forced into the production of war related materials. Fortunately this era was a profitable time for Shaw's production in that foreign trade had reduced gift merchandise imports to a mere trickle. American Pottery produced a tremendous amount of inventory for stores and gift-shops across the county while the war raged on. The firm also produced figurines from other cartoon creators including the Warner Bros. animation stable of Bugs Bunny, Elmer Fudd, Daffy Duck and Walter Lantz's Woody Woodpecker and Wally Walrus. With help from money

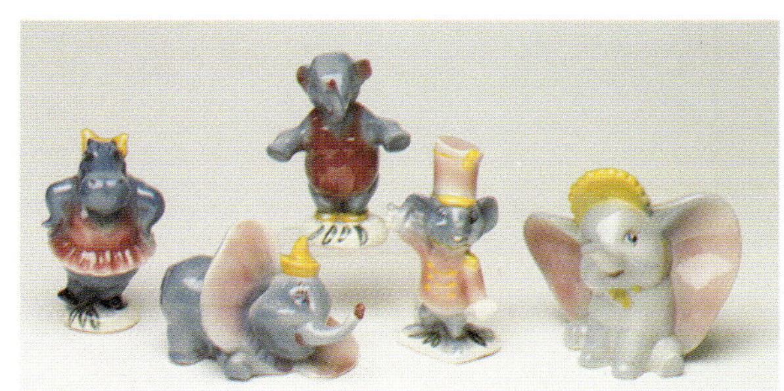

Group of American Pottery figurines from Vernon molds. Values approximately 50% less than Vernon figures.

collected from insurance payments for the destroyed American Pottery factory, Shaw purchased the Metlox facility in Manhattan Beach from Willis Prouty on November 8, 1946. For several months, Shaw did not have a studio in which to produce any ceramics. It has been suggested that Shaw feared if he had not renewed his contract with Disney while he was waiting to rebuild, Kay Kamen and Disney might have shopped around for another ceramics manufacturer, thus cutting off the lucrative ceramics bonanza and pizzazz of the Disney name and product. Also before Shaw purchased Metlox in 1946, several of the Disney figures were produced in a nameless facility in Mexico. These ceramics were supposedly licensed through Shaw as some examples display Shaw paper labels and are photographed in Shaw-American publicity stills. The made-in-Mexico pieces are half the size of the American made ceramics and are heavily glazed. Many collectors notice that these creations do not contain the amount of care and detail that even the American pieces have. For this reason it is believed another license was granted to Shaw by Disney from 1945 to 1950. Metlox's long production output began in 1927 when T.C. Prouty and his son Willis formed a company producing sturdy ceramic and metal signs for California and the west's growing cities and their numerous business establishments. The Metlox name was a combined abbreviation for the company's main material used for bonding ceramic tiles to metal-metal oxide. Two of the company's most prominent signs were the neon-embellished Pantages Theater marquee in Hollywood and Manhattan Beach's own pier.

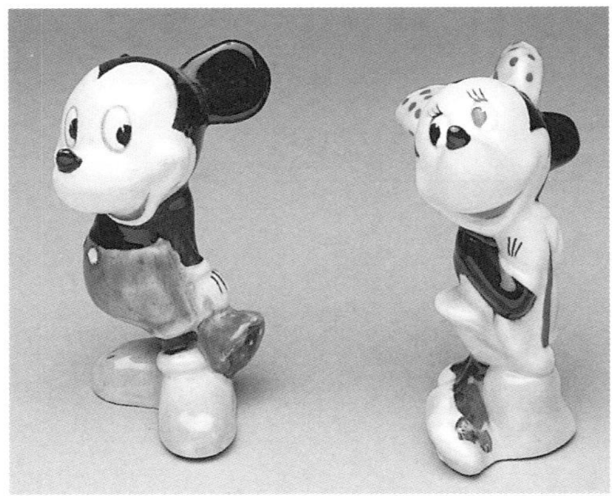

Mexican Mickey 4 1/2" & Minnie 4 1/2"

With the onset of a devastating depression and death of founder T.C. Prouty in 1931, son Willis veered the company's direction from that of costly and complex advertising signs to profitable dinnerware lines. Throughout the 1930's and 40's, the company produced an abundant amount of hand-decorated, colorful place settings. California Pottery and Poppytrail were popular lines along with Mission Bell settings created and sold exclusively at Sears department stores across the country. The war years brought changes to the firm with the production of aircraft parts for B-25 bombers and in the postwar victory, the output of children's metal toys. With Shaw's purchase of Metlox a new era for the company began by producing beautifully detailed and vividly decorated ceramics from Disney's many animated films. Today much of the product produced at Metlox is considered by many collectors to be some of the best representations of the classic characters. When Shaw purchased the old Metlox plant, the facility was completely rundown and saddled in huge debt due to minuscule profits achieved during the war. Within two short years the company's original 165 employees had peaked to over 400 working in a refurbished environment with thousands invested in modern production equipment.

With the new dinnerware lines and profitable Disney creations, the firm was in its renaissance. Snow White and the Seven Dwarfs, Pinocchio, new versions of Dumbo, Bambi, The Three Caballeros, Brer Rabbit from *Song of the South,* Little Toot from *Melody Time* and the whole staple of other Disney characters rounded out the collection.

Many artists contributed to the line including Brad Keeler, who had worked as a designer of birds and animals earlier for American Pottery. Keeler would leave Shaw to head his own company creating his famous bird figures and lobster dinnerware. Frank Irwin and Shirley Soderstrom were considered responsible for sculpting for the line. Artist Melvin Shaw in story development for Disney's *Bambi* and other films was responsible

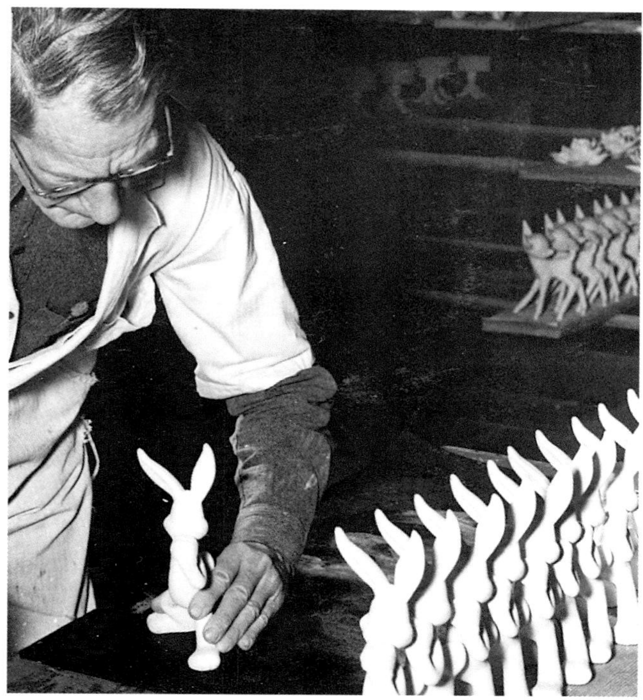

for designing some of Metlox dinnerware shapes and decoration. Mel Shaw was no relation to Evan K. Shaw.

After a character was chosen for ceramic reproduction, the Disney Studios would provide the talented Metlox artists with animator model sheets to be used as a guide on how the character should look. Each new design was subject to approval by Shaw and the Disney Studio artists and licensing division before any production could begin. Mold maker Stanley Skee worked for Metlox on a freelance basis in the 1940's. His talented skills were needed only when new molds were to be made. He remembers the original Disney sculptures were created from freelance artists and were sculpted only for use by Metlox. "The sculptures I believe went directly to the Disney Studio, where they were approved before being mass produced at the factory," Stan recalls.

Around 1950, Shaw/Metlox released two beautiful ceramic sets and included them with select previously created Disney ceramics in a retail promotion entitled "Walt Disney's World of Enchantment in Ceramics." A colorful collector's book printed for this promotion mistakenly compares these modern cast production ceramics with one-of-a-kind art of hand-built Native American pottery. Cinderella featured ceramic creations of Cinderella in rags and dressed for the ball, each featuring a hollow indentation for flowers. A Prince Charming planter, mice Jaq and Gus, Mama Mouse, Baby Mouse, two Bibbidi Birds, and two poses of Cindy's dog Bruno completed this story book selection.

The Alice in Wonderland set featured the famous rabbit-chasing blonde along with the Mad Hatter, March Hare, Dormouse, White Rabbit, Tweedle Dee and his twin Tweedle Dum and the Walrus. Four very unique teapots were also made for inclusion in the set, but were mostly used in store displays with few actually being sold. Some of the decorators liked to experiment on these teapots by painting different designs for their own personal enjoyment.

These ceramics precisely capture the personality and look of the screen characters with their charming poses and vivid animation coloring. Even with all these pluses, some corners were cut to ease production. Cinderella's Bruno dog, both sitting and prone, are prior Pluto castings painted a darker color and displaying a somber expression.

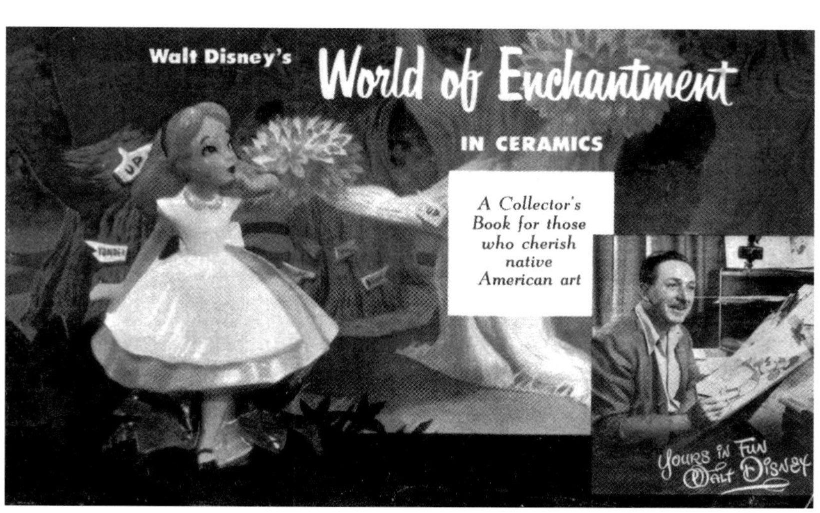

Cinderella's Baby Mouse is also cast as Alice's Dormouse, painted his respective colors.

Many of these bright ceramics were sold in the collectibles, gifts, children's or even the furniture department of America's premier department stores including the fine Bullock's chain in Southern California and Marshall Field's in Chicago. Shaw also introduced its only Disney dinnerware set for children featuring a plate, bowl, mug and pitcher decorated with a colorful Bambi design.

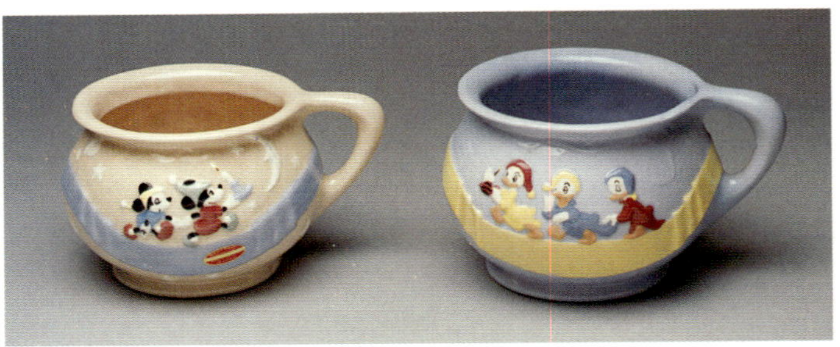

Given as gifts from Walt Disney to new parents. Pink for a girl and blue for a boy, the baby's name was cold-painted on the ribbon and flaked-off easily. $1800+ each

The set was unveiled in New York City at Macy's department store in 1950.

Probably some of the rarest examples of Disney ceramics were the pink and blue potties Metlox made for Walt Disney in the 1950's. In a gesture of congratulations to staff members and friends who had new babies, Walt Disney would present the parents with the ceramic potty filled with flowering baby sweet peas. Disney commissioned his artists to design various characters in their night clothes sleepily slumping off to bed.

The bas-relief pieces were fired, decorated and glazed at Metlox, while a studio staff artist would paint the name of the child on the pot's decorative ceramic ribbon. Because the name was painted over the glaze, the dry unprotected paint could easily be wiped away or chip off the glaze. Most examples found are without personalization.

The ceramic chamber pots were produced in previously said lots of 500 and in two slightly different mold versions but it is unclear how many lots were actually made. Hagen-Renaker would, in 1960 produce a similar potty for Walt Disney in a listed quantity of 100. In 1947 and 48, the Railley Lamp Corporation of Cleveland, Ohio was licensed to produce a series of lamps using the Shaw molds. The characters included Donald, Jose and Panchito as well as Mickey and Minnie Mouse. The rare children's lamps are decorated in darker hues and are generally found on the collector's market minus their beautifully printed paper lampshades and electrical hardware.

"Modern Ceramic Products" more commonly called M.C.P., produced Disney ceramics in Sydney, Australia. Some of them might be confused with the American/Shaw pieces. M.C.P. acquired the rights to produce ceramic Disney figurines through Walt Disney Merchandising as early as 1948 through 1960 and probably had no dealings with the Evan K. Shaw company, although most records were destroyed.

Most M.C.P.'s are smaller versions of the Shaw figures, though some, like their Alice in Wonderland set, were produced in a larger size. They were all sold with an identifying M.C.P. silver and blue foil paper label with Disney copyright and character name in red. Once these labels were removed, no identifying mark would remain.

The Sydney pieces are quite rare and valuable, and the authors do not want to dissuade interest in Modern Ceramic product figurines, but merely want to make collectors aware of these for proper identification.

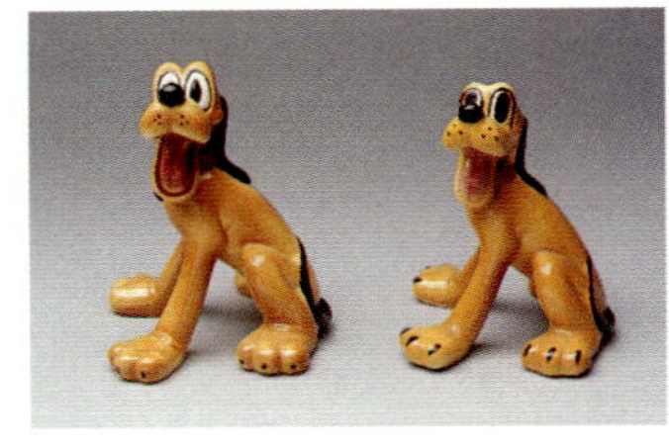

American's Pluto 5 °" as compared to Australian M.C.P Pluto 5"

By 1953 and to the end of Shaw's license, two years later, the ceramics in general had reduced in size with a full variety of miniature designs were introduced. A Peter Pan set of Peter, Nana, Tinker Bell, Wendy, Michael, and a Mermaid were sold separately, each in a clear plastic presentation box. Other characters were produced for the miniature series including Snow White and the Seven Dwarfs, the Three Little Pigs, Dumbo, Bambi, Lady and the Tramp, and Mickey, Donald and Pluto among others. Stormy a colt from a live action short *Stormy - The Thoroughbred with an Inferiority Complex*, 1954 was also produced in two miniature poses.

In comparing the earlier American to the later Shaw product, most of the first American pieces including Dumbo, Timothy Mouse and some of the Fantasia designs have the appearance of being hastily produced and quickly decorated with air brushes. The glaze also seems to be of an uneven quality and craze is considerably evident. As the pottery progressed and introduced more figures, the decoration and design appears to improve overall. In the production process some color decoration was painted overglaze to achieve its proper hue. For example bright red paint would turn a dark brown color if fired under glaze. Therefore bright reds on the earlier pieces would be applied to the figure after glazing and subject to wear and flaking. Swift painting is not the case with the Shaw-Metlox pieces. A combination of detailed airbrush, masking and full hand brush decorating appear on all of the Metlox and future pieces. American Pottery oval paper labels were used to identify most if not all the ceramics produced at American. The American labels under the Shaw contract were continued on some of the ceramics originated at American before the fire but continued in production at Metlox until the late 1940's. Evan K. Shaw labels were used in tandem from 1946-1955.

Because Evan K. Shaw had the longest license with the Disney company, questions arise on how long a particular ceramic figurine was produced. A character's popularity with the public had a great deal to do with a figure's production. Shaw produced a beautifully detailed Snow White set at American begining in 1945 and continued its production at Metlox until 1952. The Bambi figures, Donald, and Pinocchio were also very popular in retail stores.

Others that were not as popular and today are considered hard to find in the collector's market were items to be used such as planters and in the kitchen. The company produced the ceramics in an abundant amount. Although no records have been found on how many pieces were produced, it is assumed by most Shaw employees that each design listed in company catalogs and records was produced for at least a short time but in the thousands. Many pieces produced could be considered limited in number due to their large size,fragile state or unique purpose.

For example a large sitting Bambi is believed to be extremely rare because of its enormous size and complication in production as well as its high price.

Ceramic flower containers were generally sold in florist shops and hospital gifts shops. The ceramic gift/flower arrangement would be presented to a new mother, who would in turn decorate the nursery with the character ceramic. Few of the planters exist today due to toddler breakage and actual use of the piece as a planter.

The Disney line was very profitable to both Shaw and Metlox. Shaw paid Disney only 5% of the sales profit. After the Disney license expired, Metlox continued producing its popular dinner sets, including California Ivy shown in the kitchen set of the "I Love Lucy" television show and Red Rooster. In 1958 the company purchased the then closed Vernon pattern and some stock and continued to make decorative planters, figures and cookie jars for many years. Metlox Pottery today is considered one of the "big five" in California pottery circles. It was the last of the "old timers" to close its doors in June of 1989.

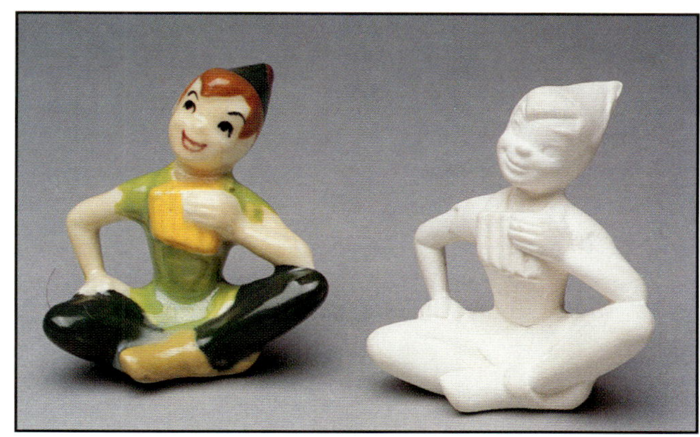

Peter Pan undecorated (right) and, ready for a child's room.

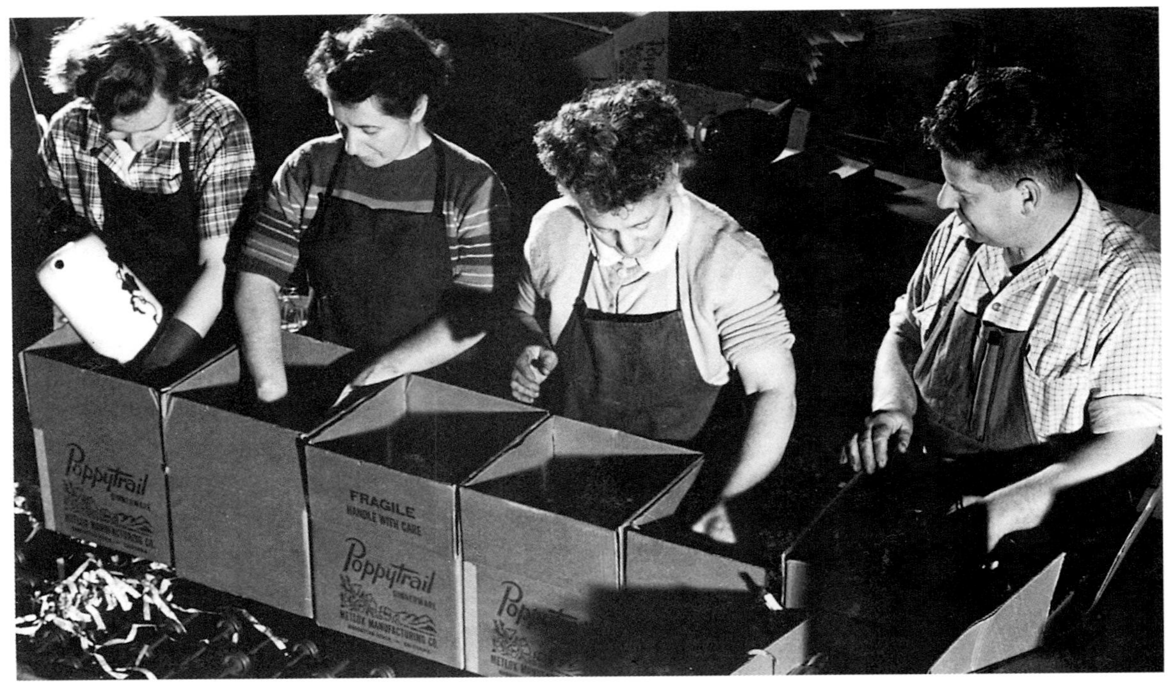

From the Metlox 1951 catalog, packers.

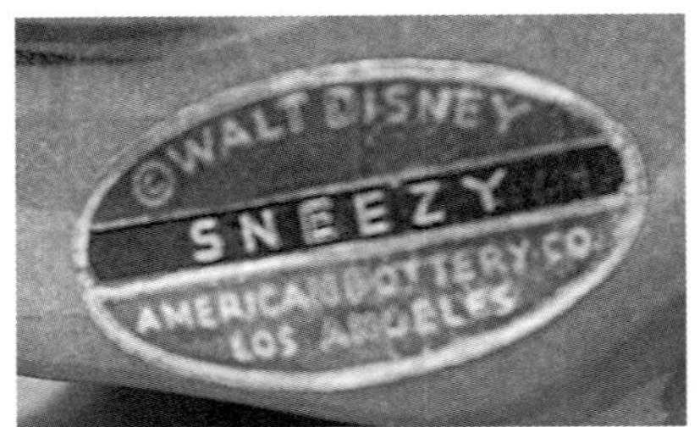

American foil label

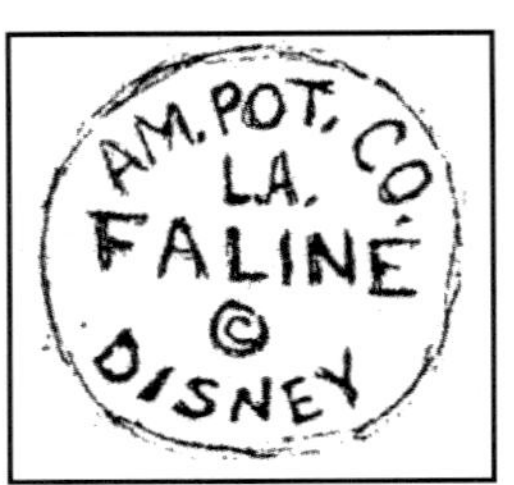

Circular stamp

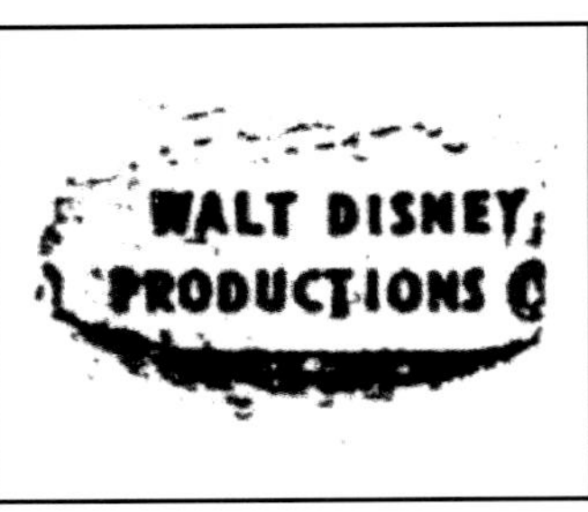

Miniatures label

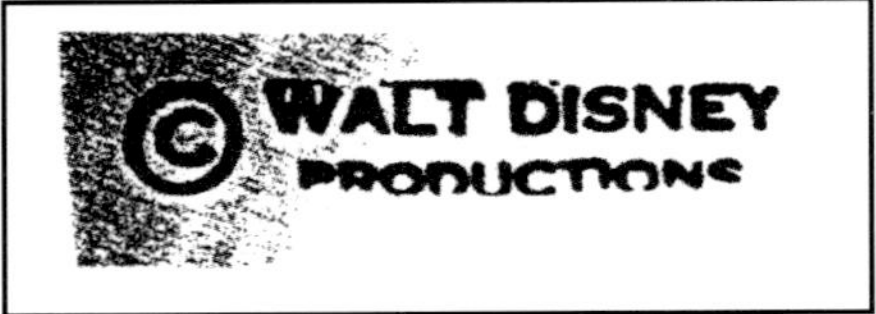

Bambi Dinnerware stamp

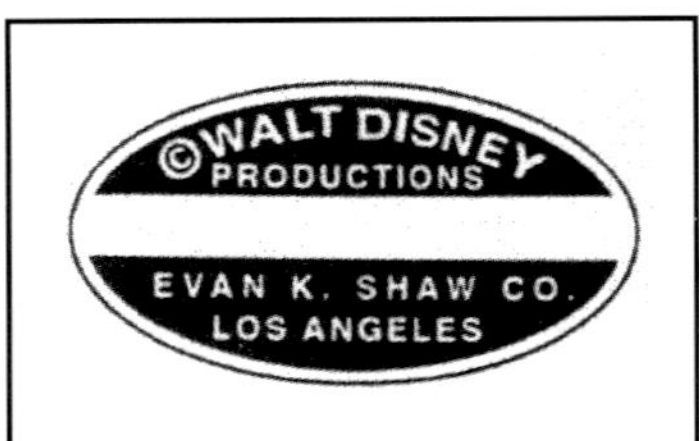

Shaw foil label

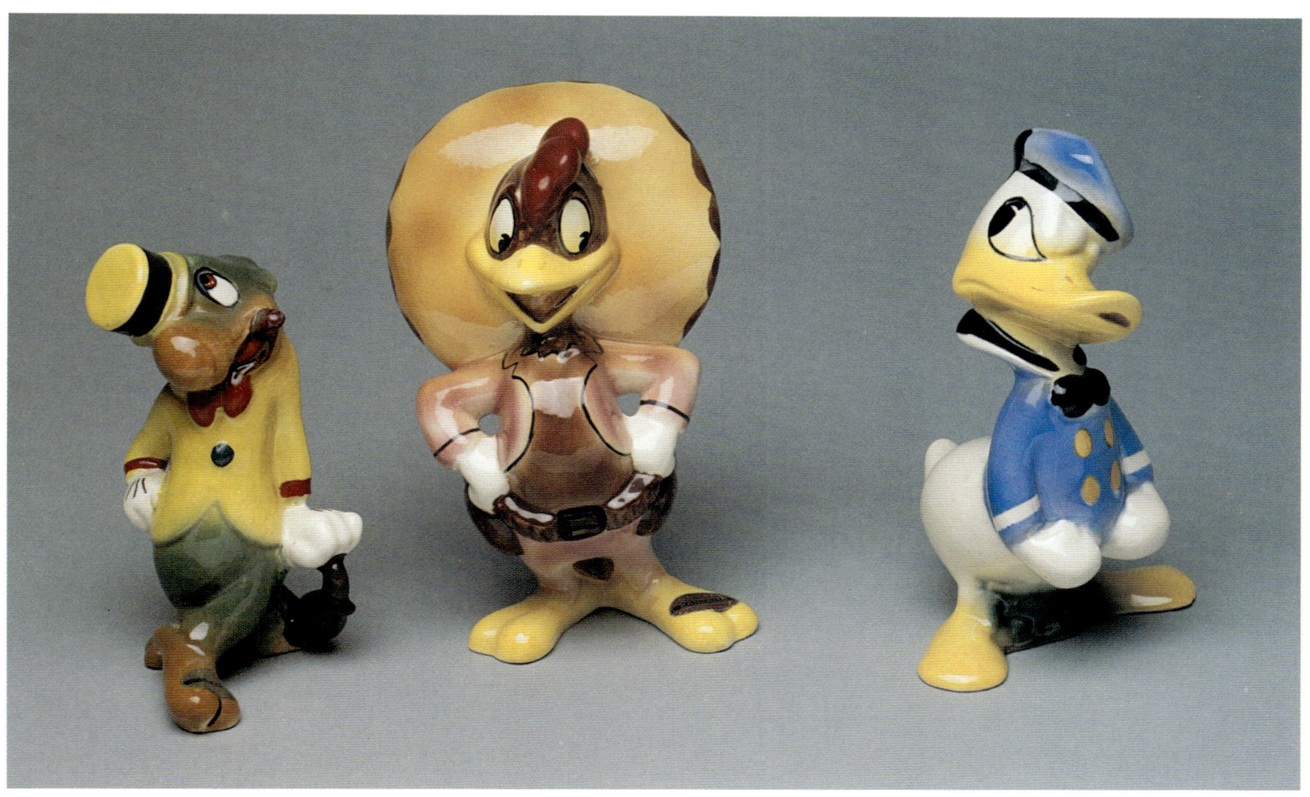

Jose Carioca 6 1/2" $125-175, Panchito 6 1/2" $185-250, Donald Duck 6 1/2" $250-300

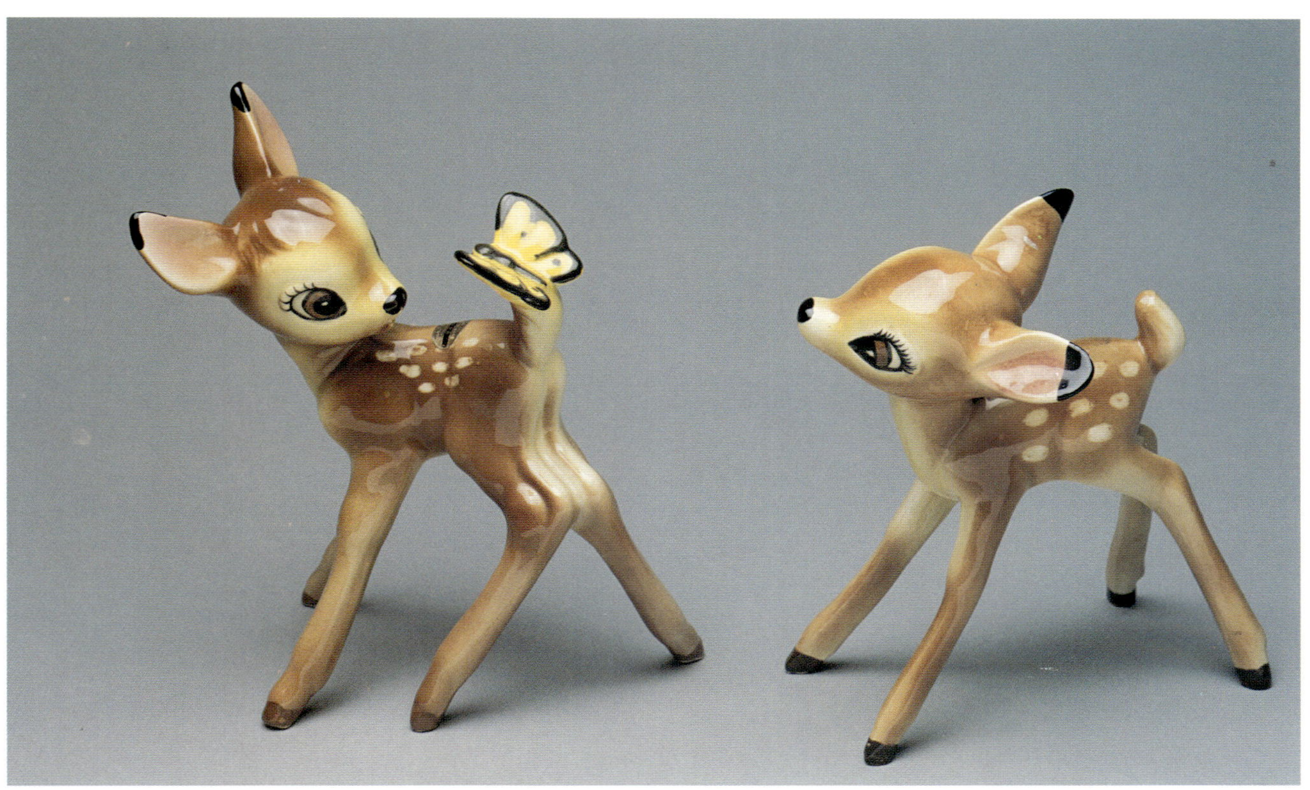

Shaw Bambi with yellow butterfly 8 1/2" $165-200, American Bambi 7 1/2" $125-175.

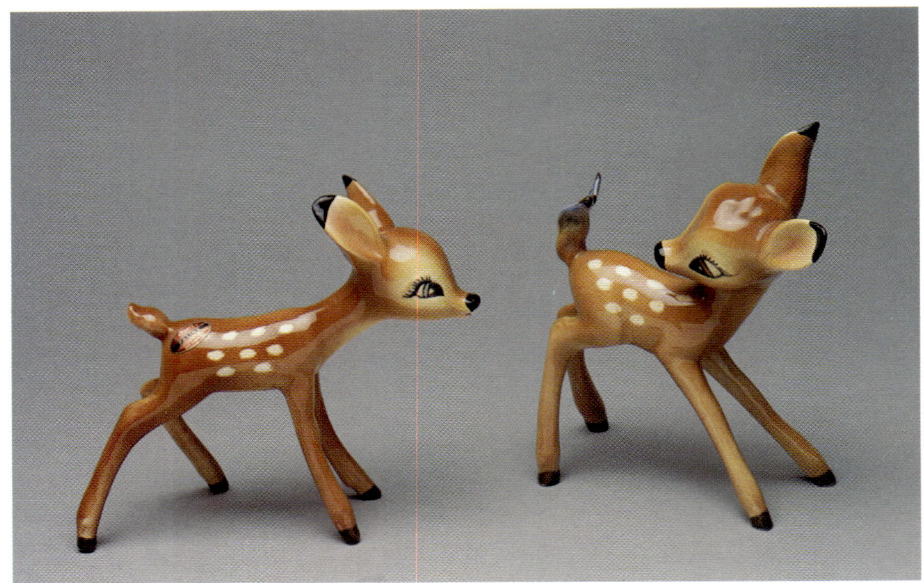

American Faline 7" $135-165, American Bambi with blue butterfly 8" $150-185.

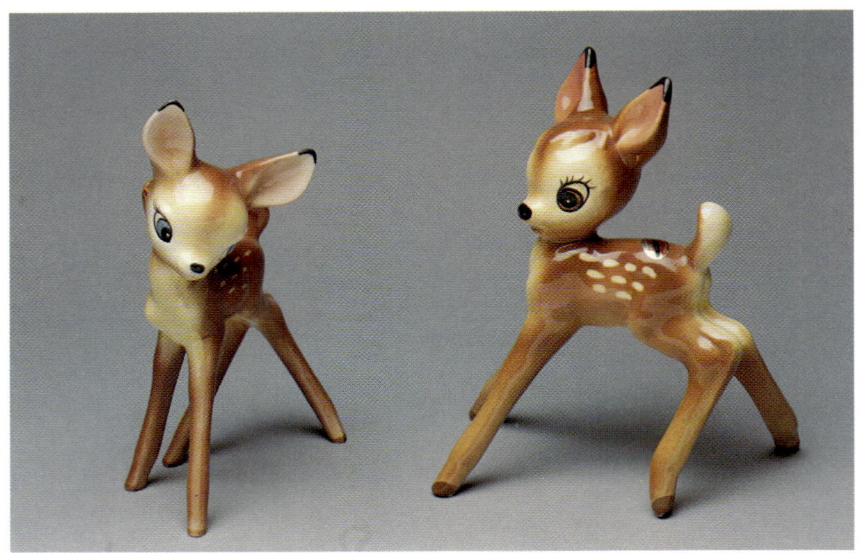

Shaw Faline 8 1/2" $150-195, Shaw surprised Bambi 8" $175-200.

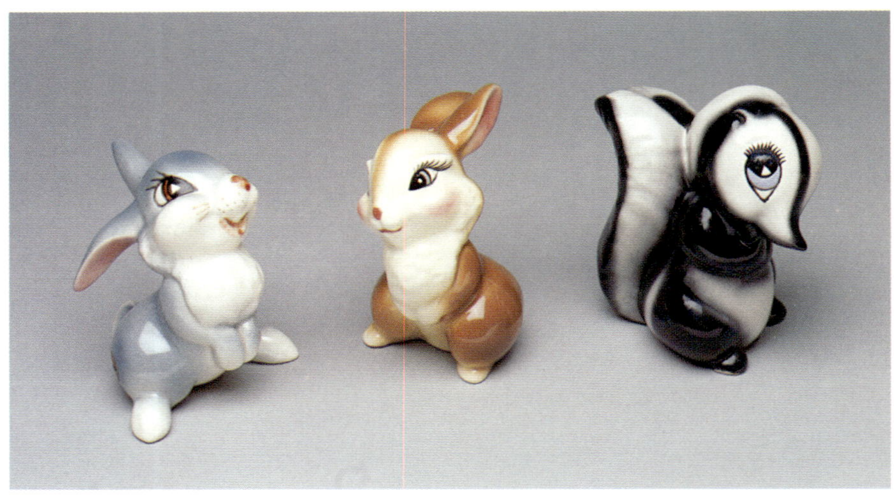

Thumper (gray) 4" $45-85, Girlfriend 4 1/4" $55-95, Flower 4 1/2" $45-75.

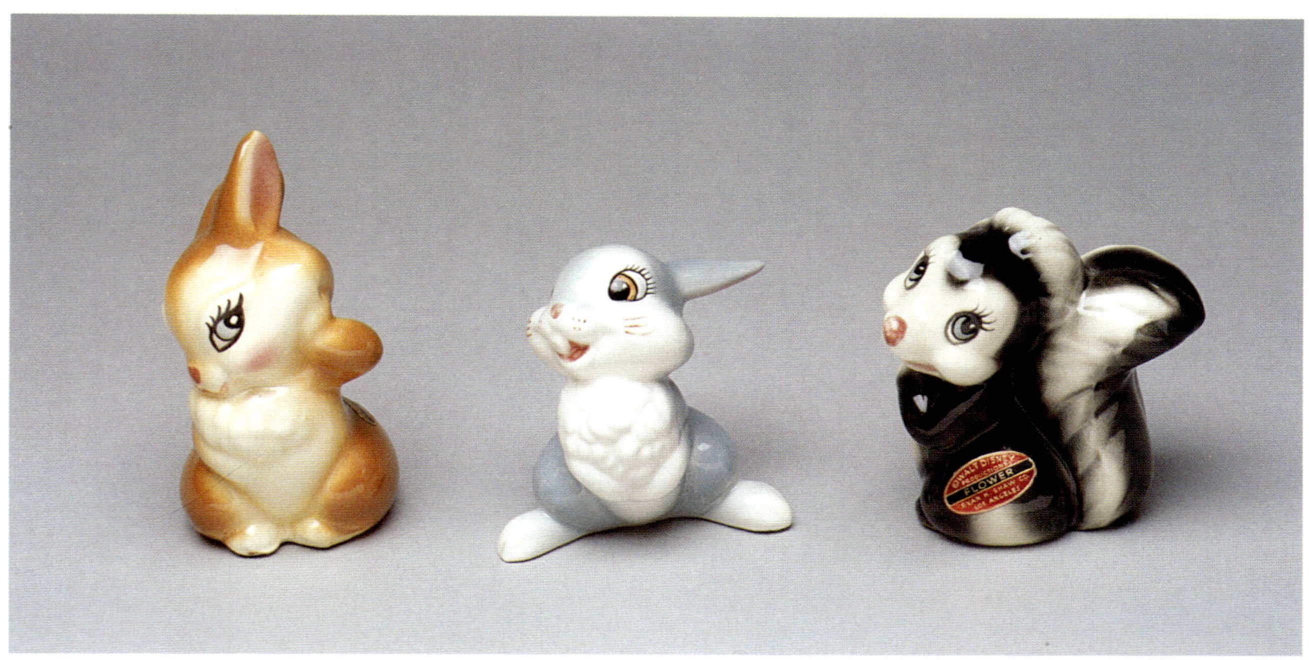

Small Girlfriend 4" $100-125, medium Thumper 3" $75-100, medium Flower 3 1/4" $85-100.

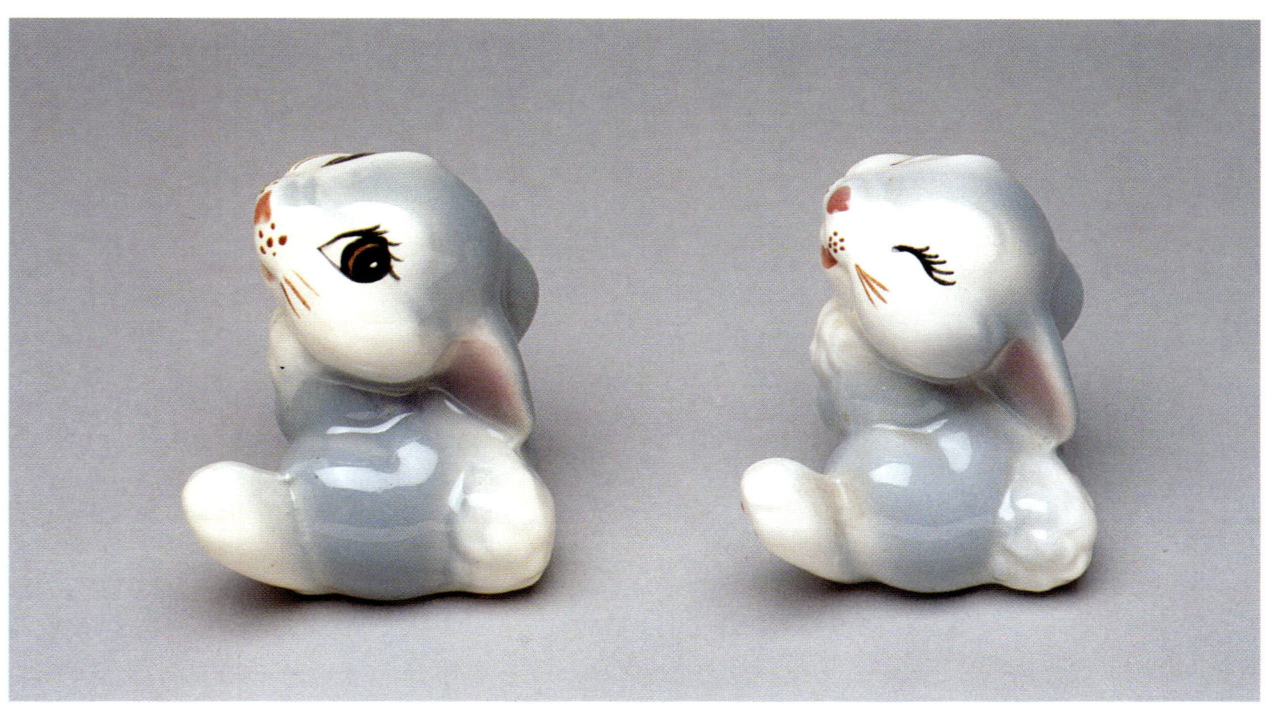

Thumper thumping, eyes open or closed 3" $100-125 each.

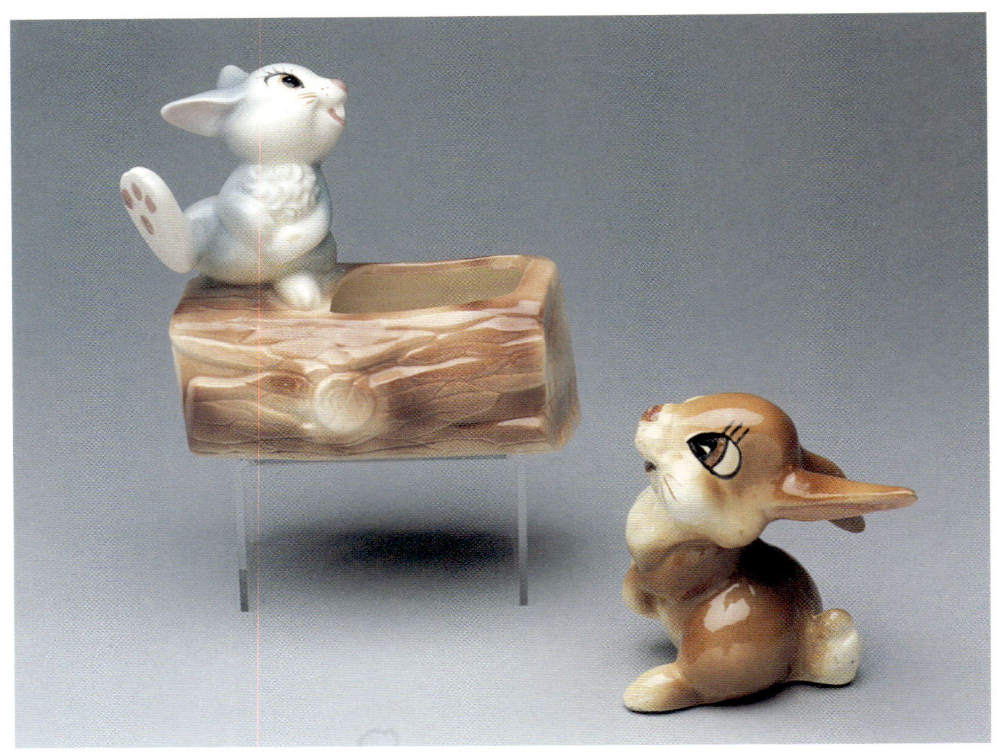

Small Thumper on log (planter) 5" $250-375, Thumper (brown) 4" $45-85.

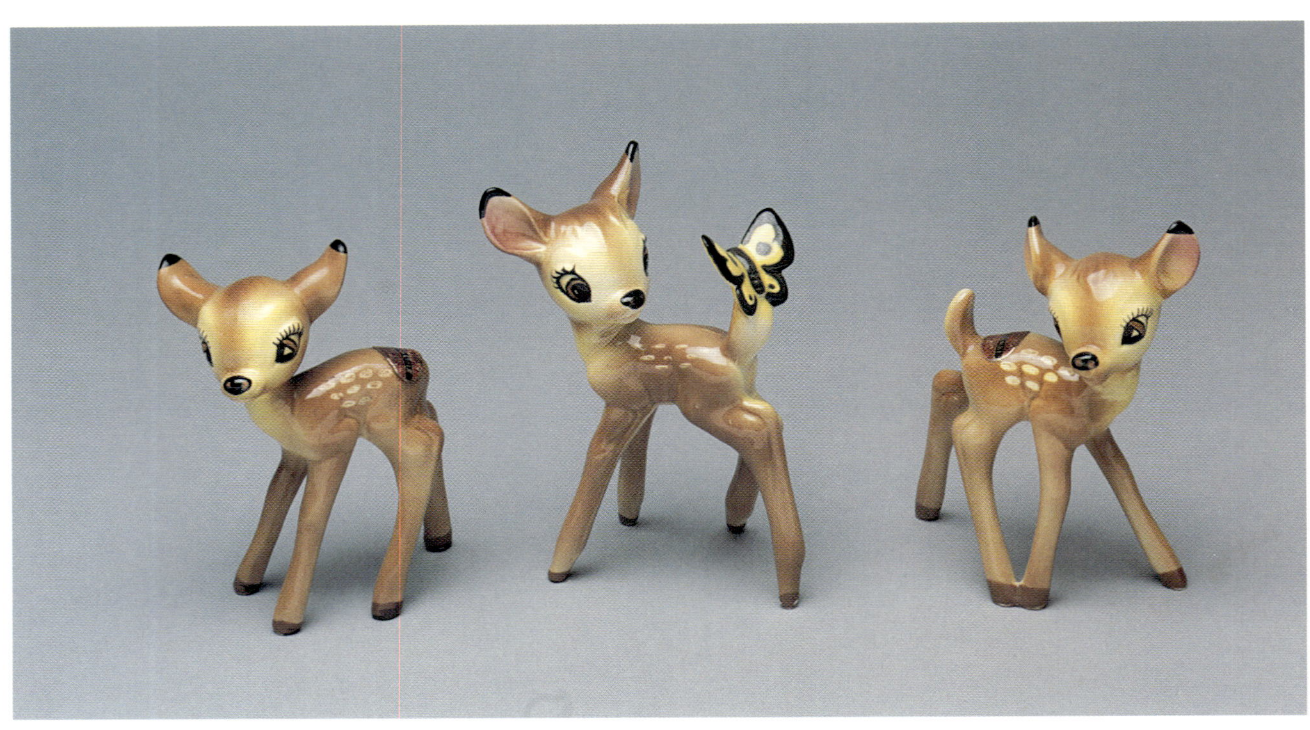

Small Faline 4 1/2" $95-125, small Bambi with butterfly 5" 150-175, small Bambi 4 1/2" $95-125.

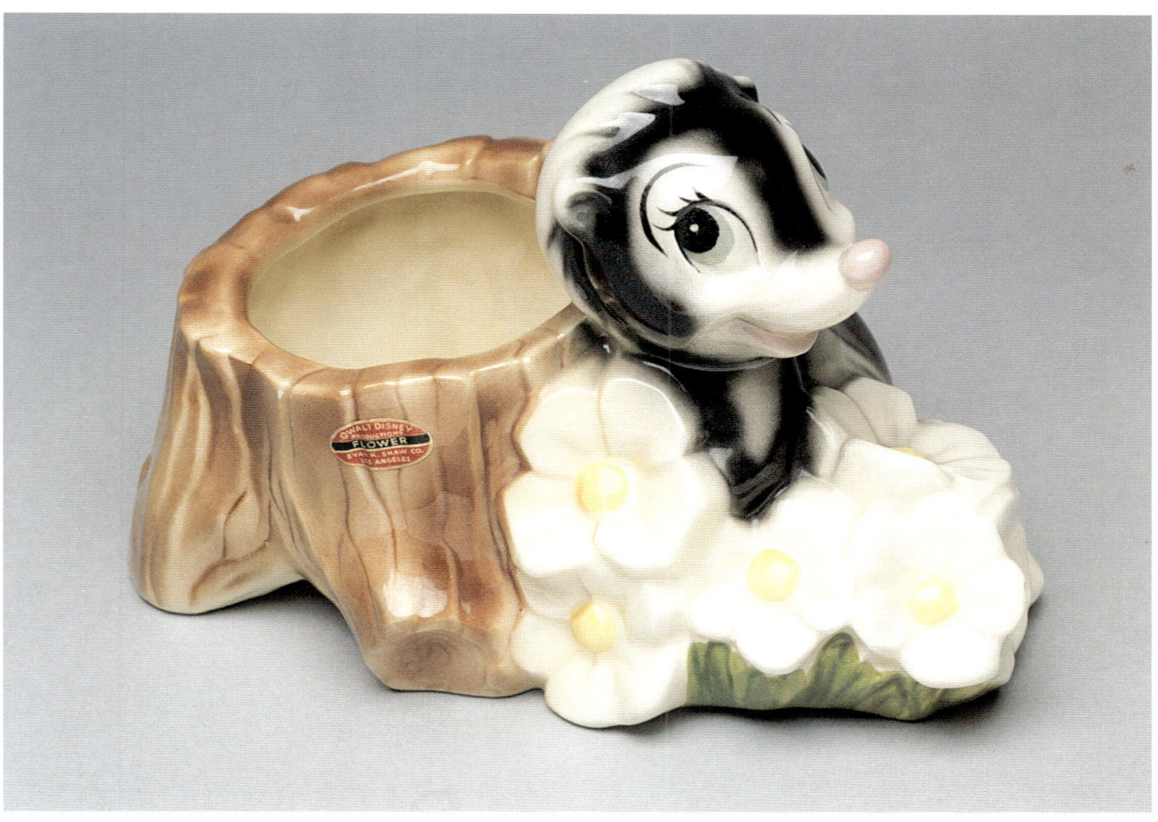

Large Flower planter 6" $500+.

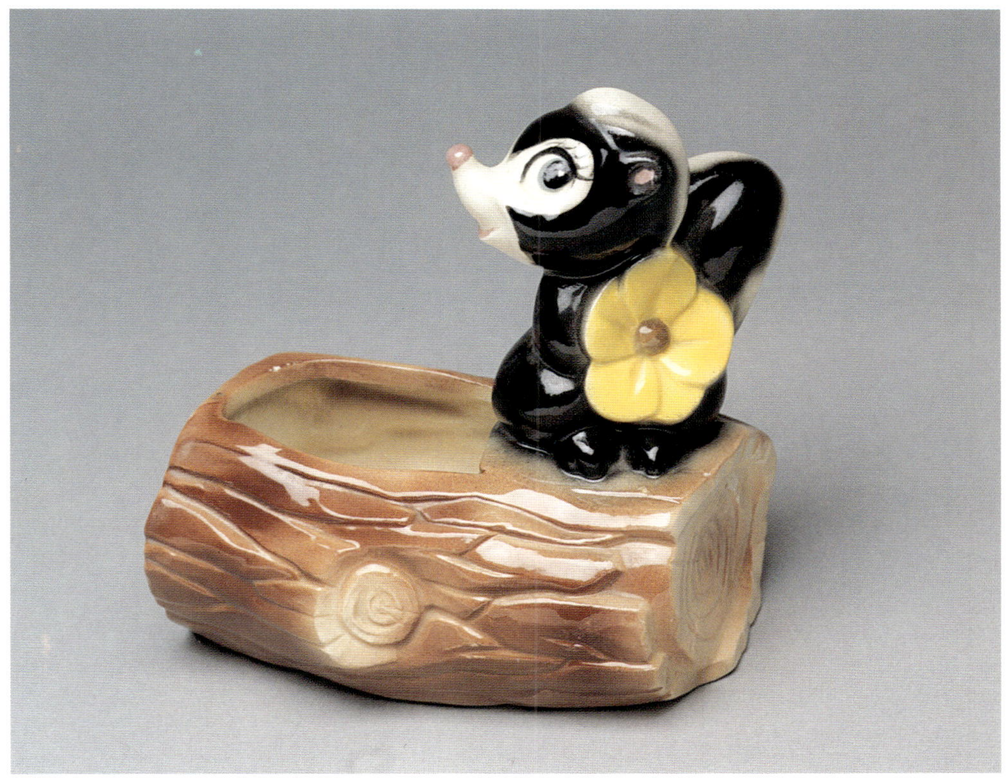

Flower on log (planter) 5" $250+.

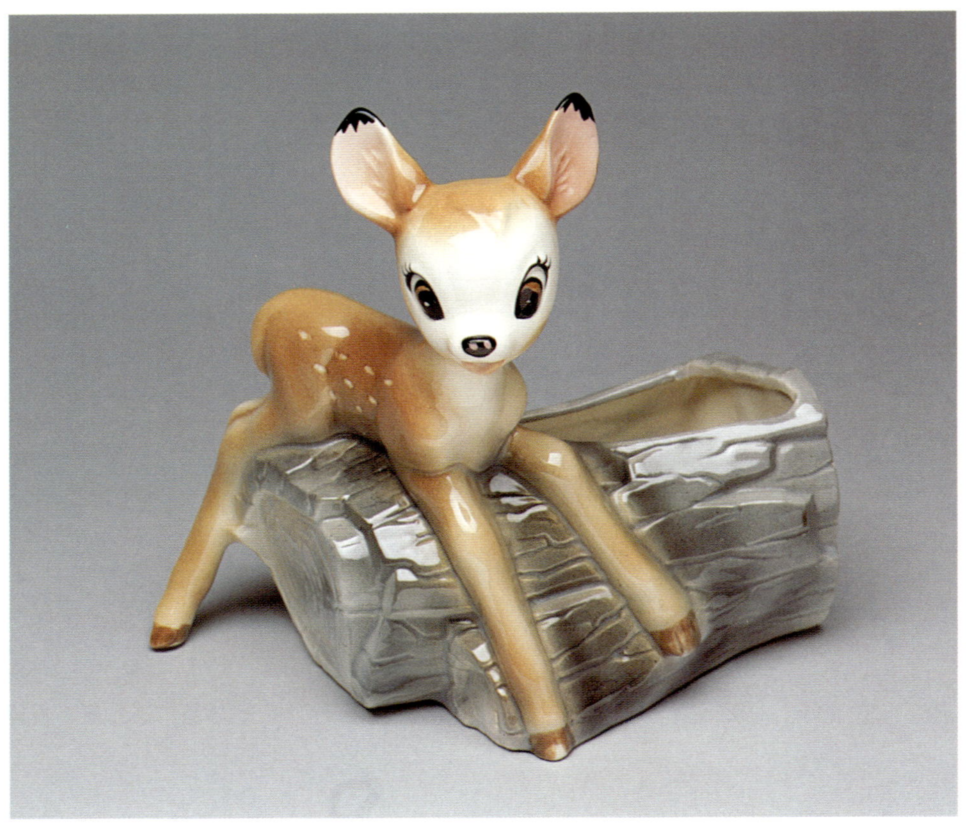

Large Bambi planter on log 8 1/2" $350+

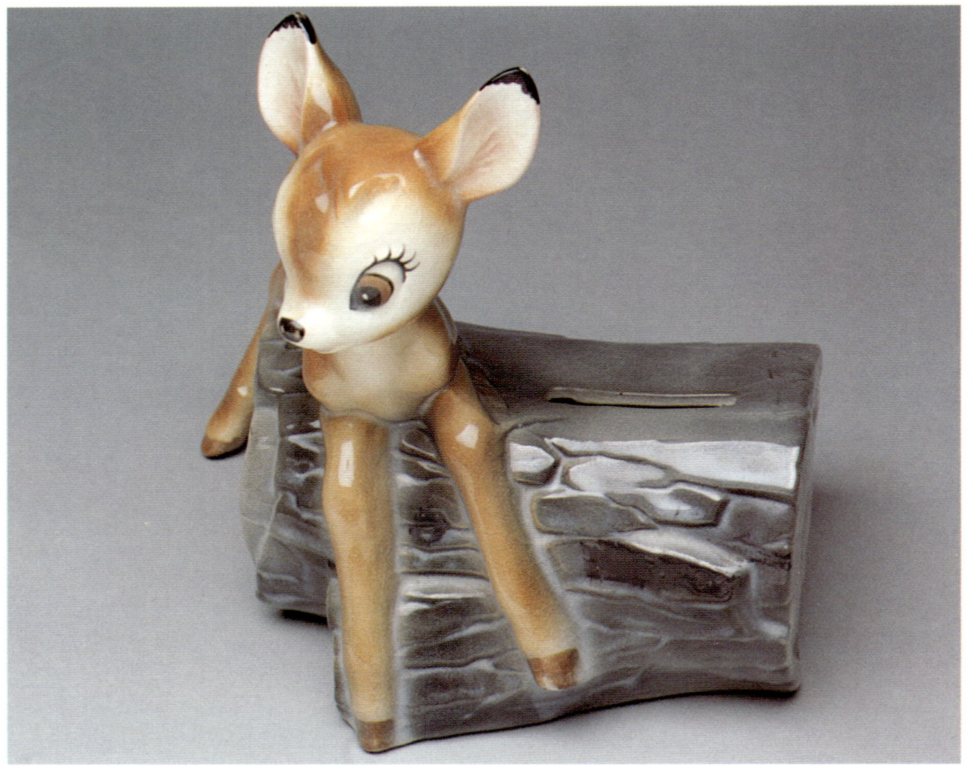

Large Bambi on log in form of a bank $NPA

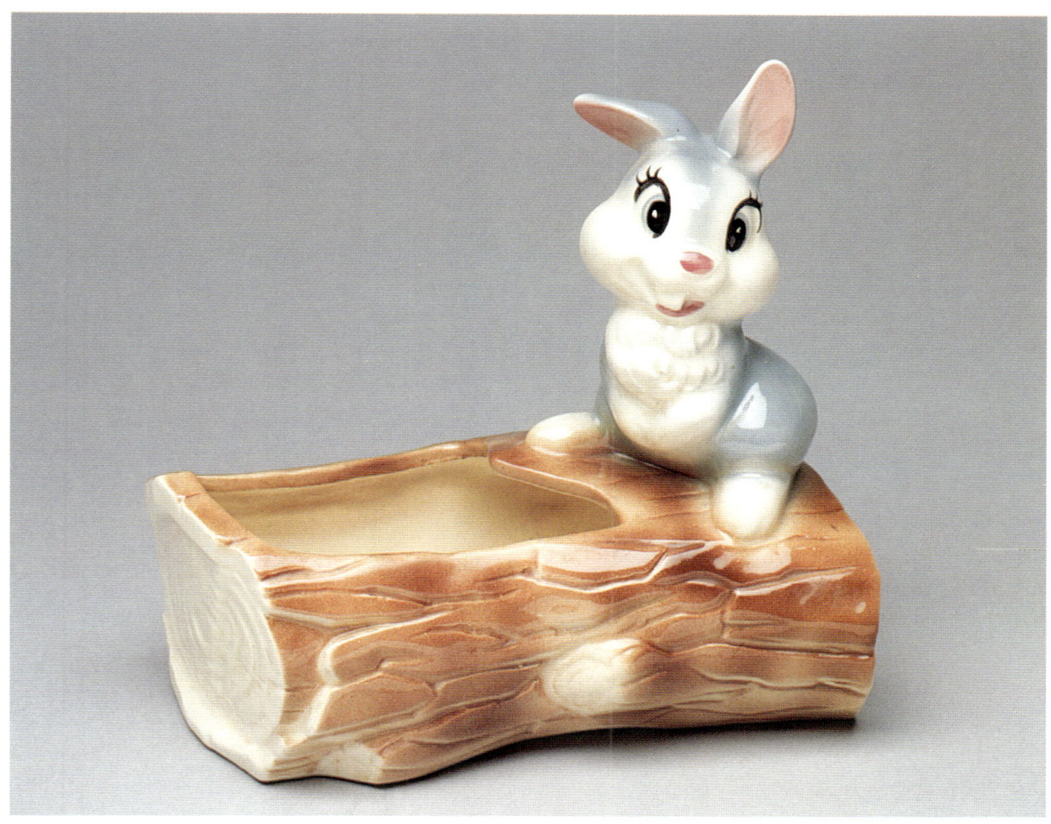

Large Thumper on log (planter) 7 1/2" $300+.

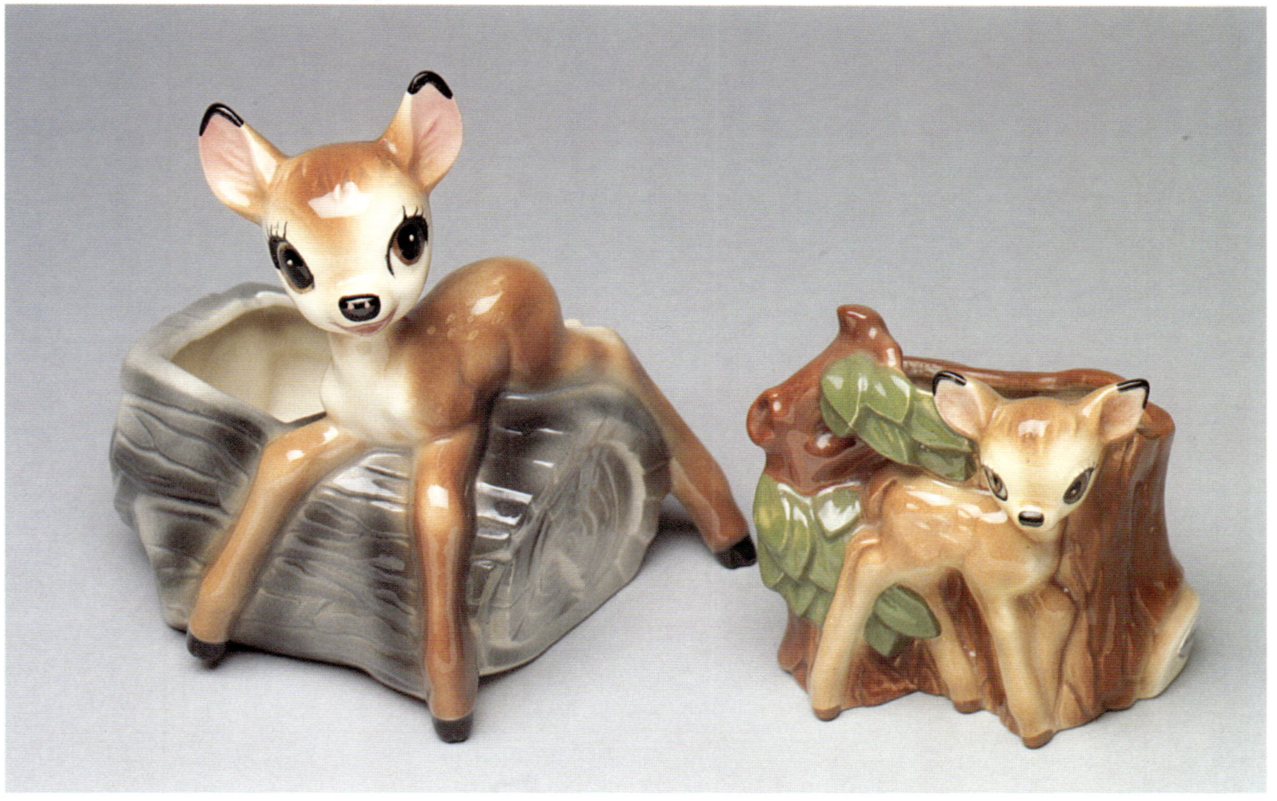

Medium Bambi on log (planter) 6" $300-400, small Bambi next to tree (planter) 4" $145-200.

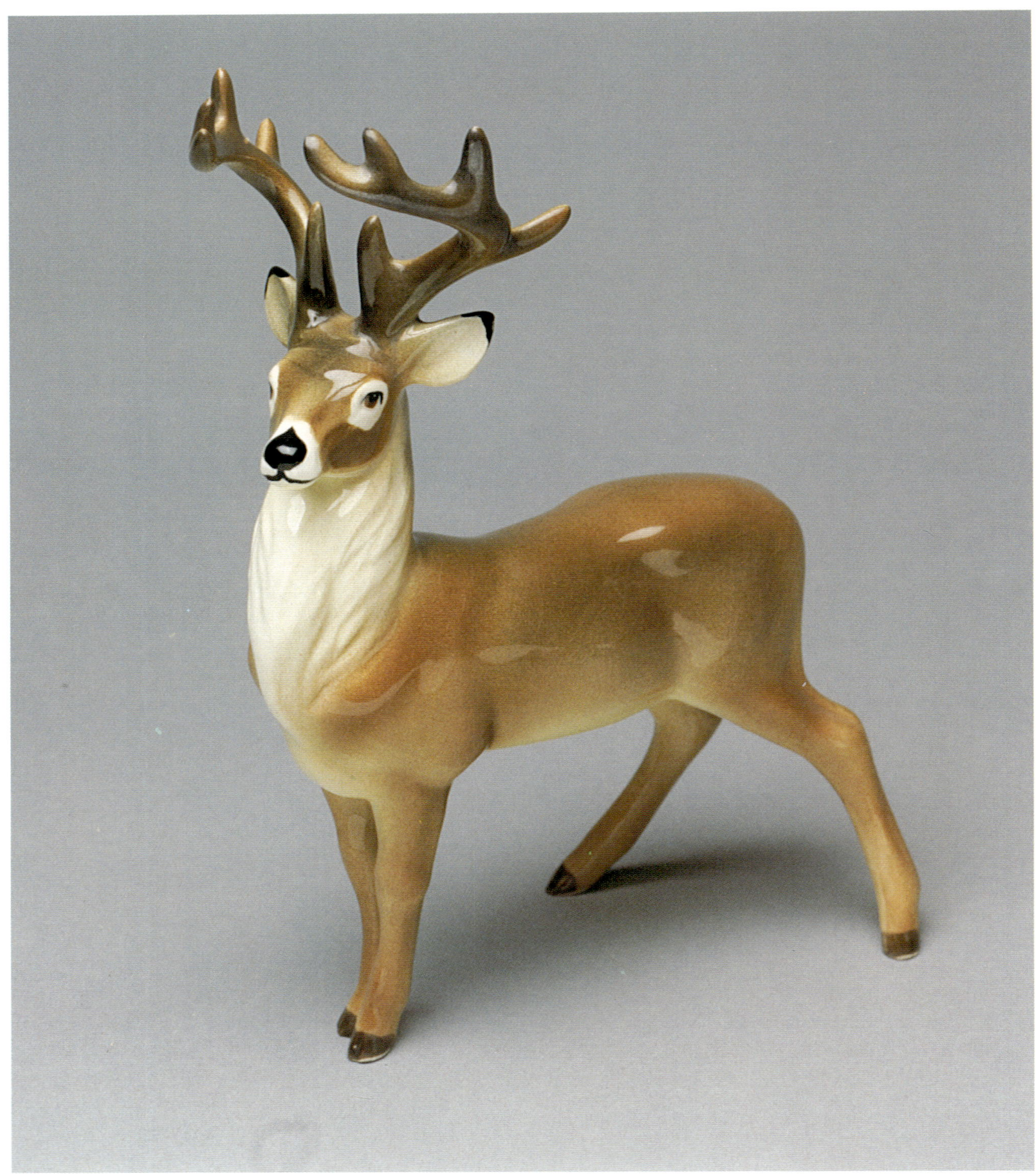

Stag "King of the Forrest" 9" $1000+.

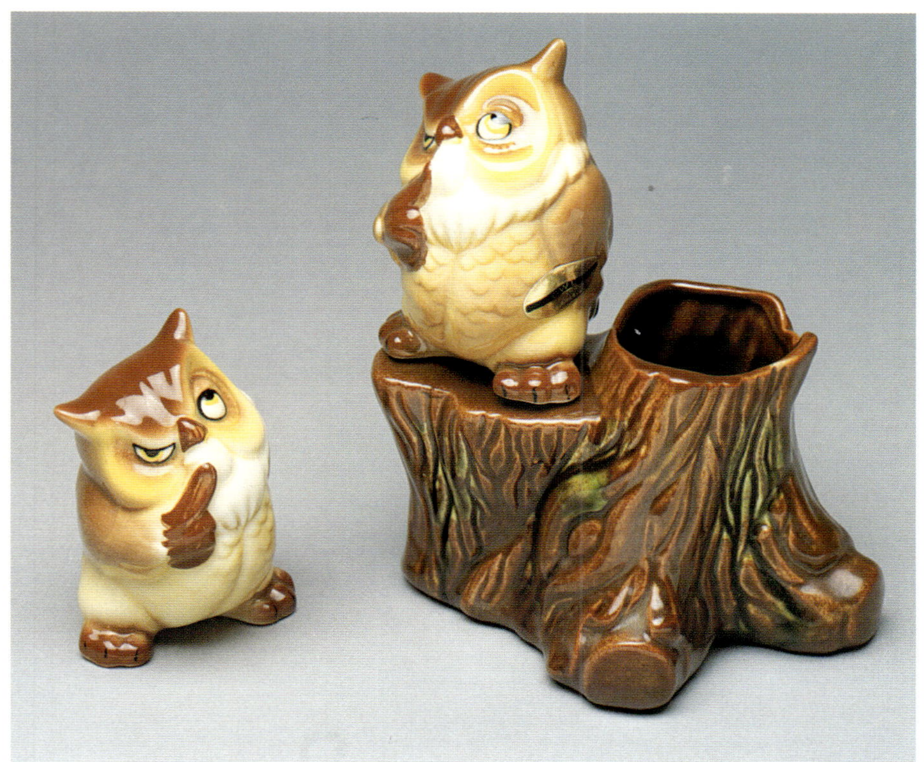

Friend Owl 3 1/4" $195-225, Owl on stump (planter) 6" $NPA

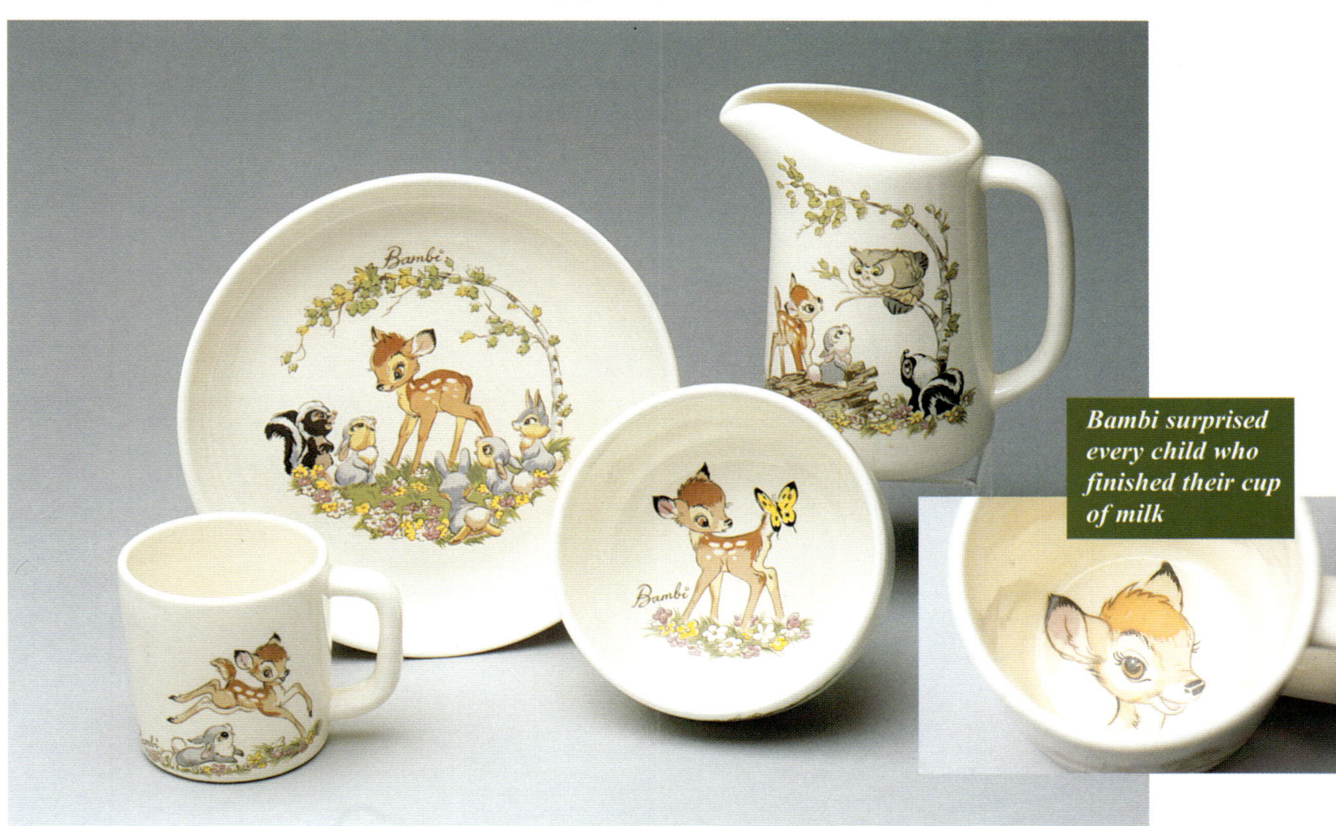

Bambi decal decorated dinner set, cup $65-75, bowl $65-75, plate 7 1/2" $40-60 and pitcher 6" $85-125.

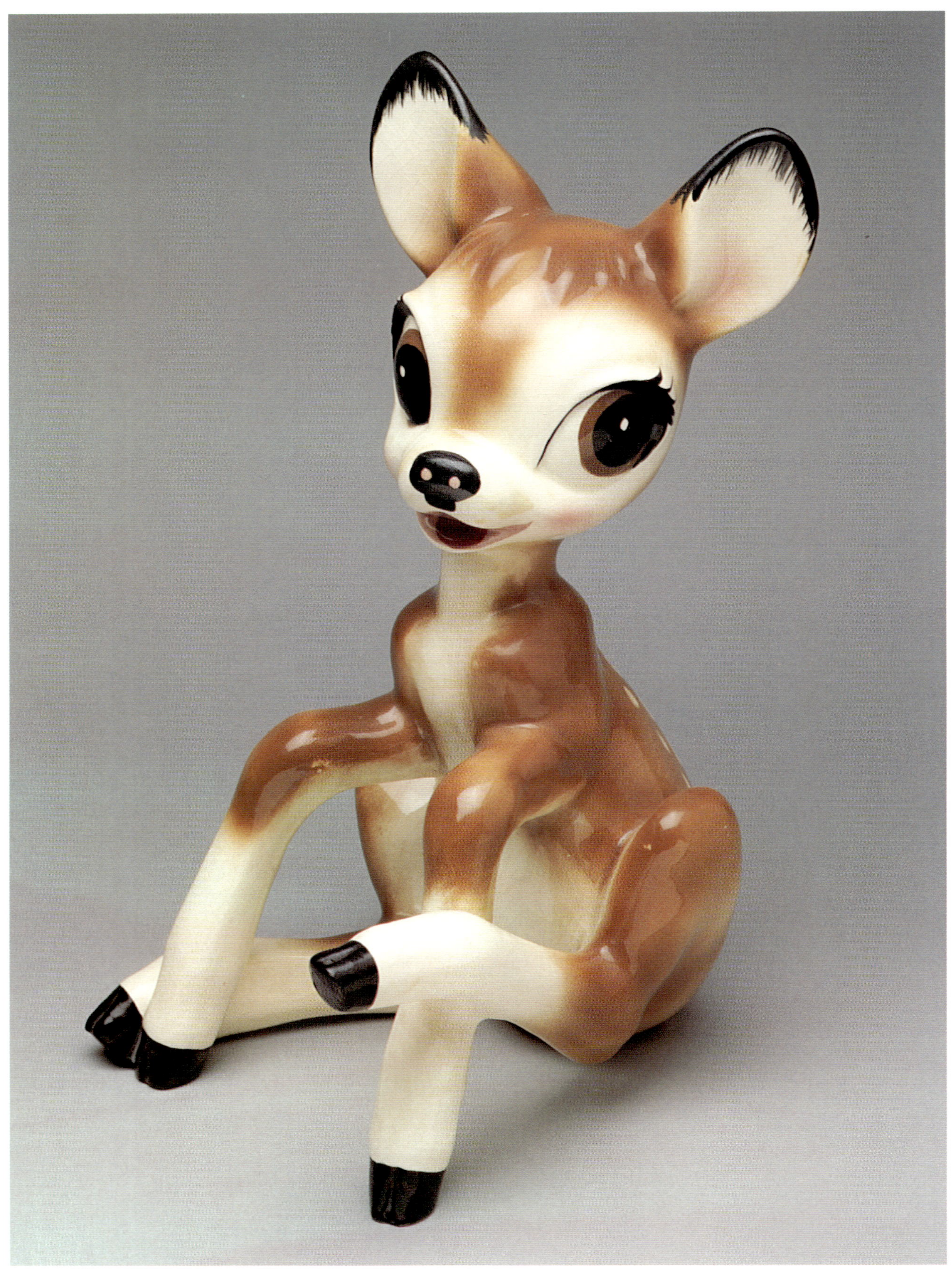

Jumbo Bambi 14 3/4" $2000+

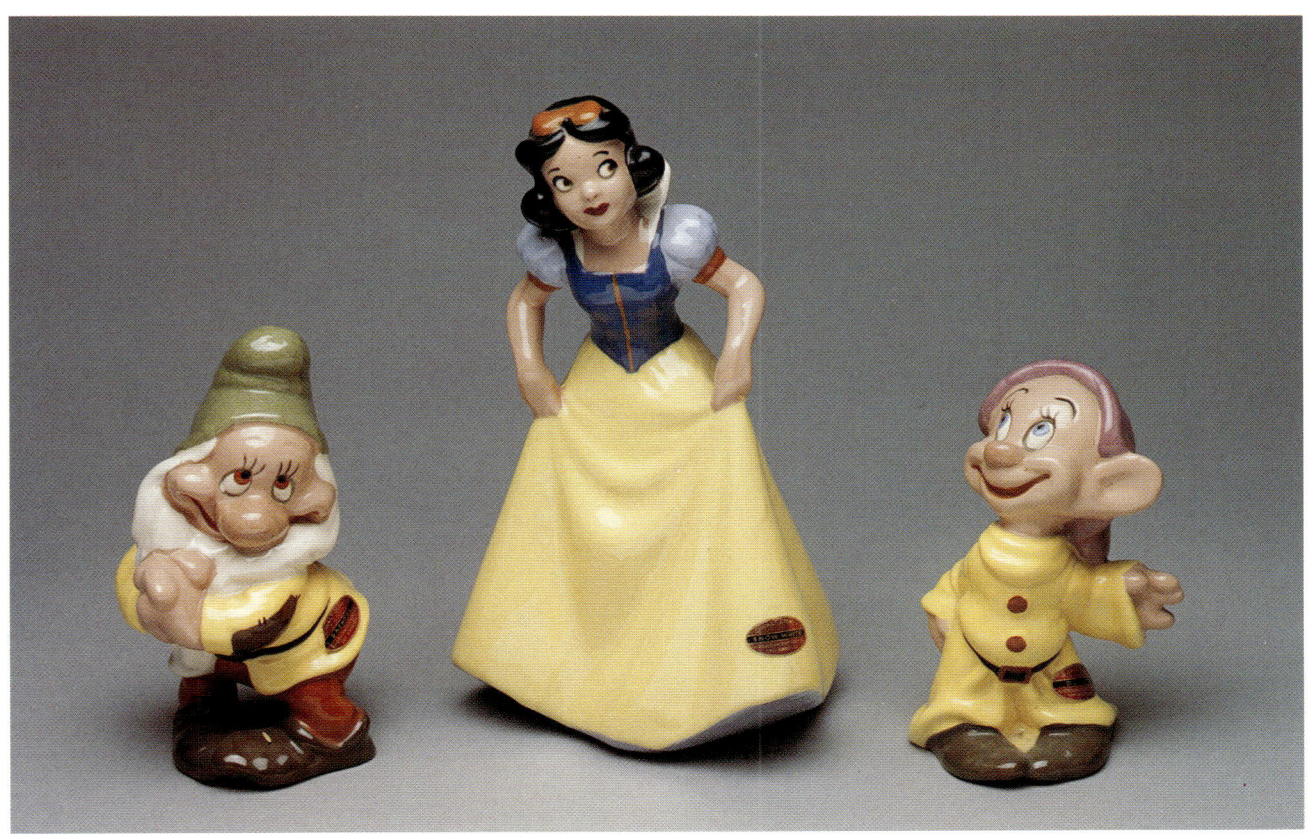

Bashful 6" $185-225, Snow White 9" $295-350, Dopey 5 1/4" $185-225.

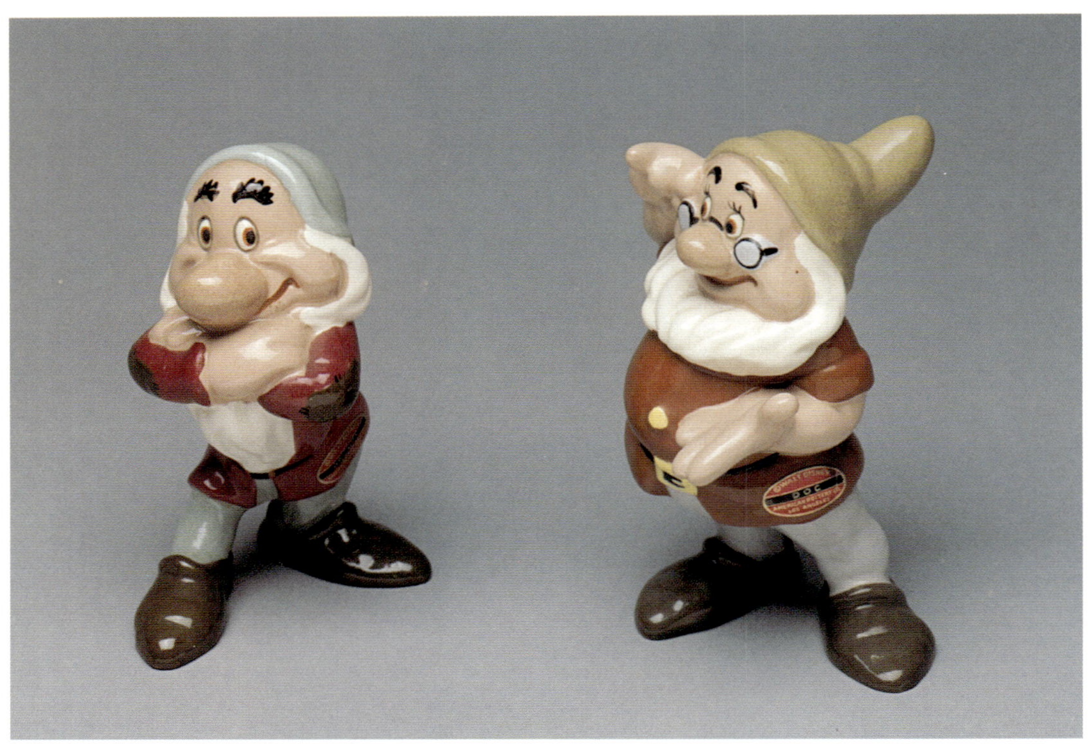

Grumpy 5 3/4" and Doc 6" $200-250 each

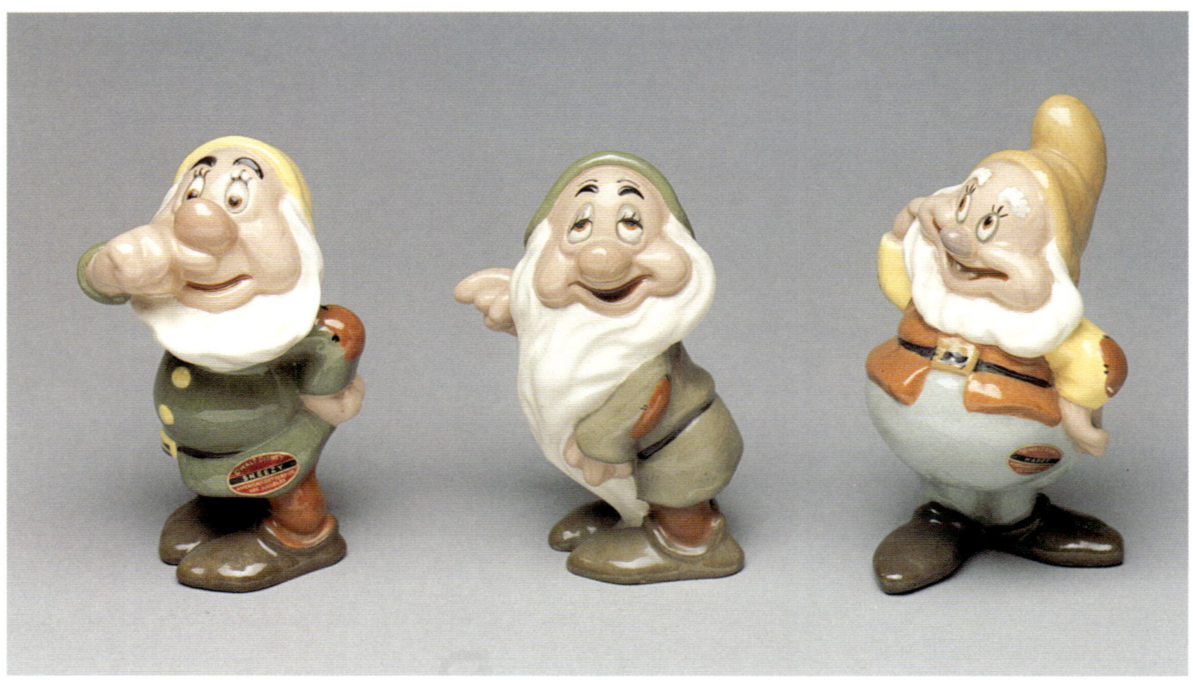

Sneezy 5 3/4", Sleepy 5 3/4" and Happy 6" $185-225 each.

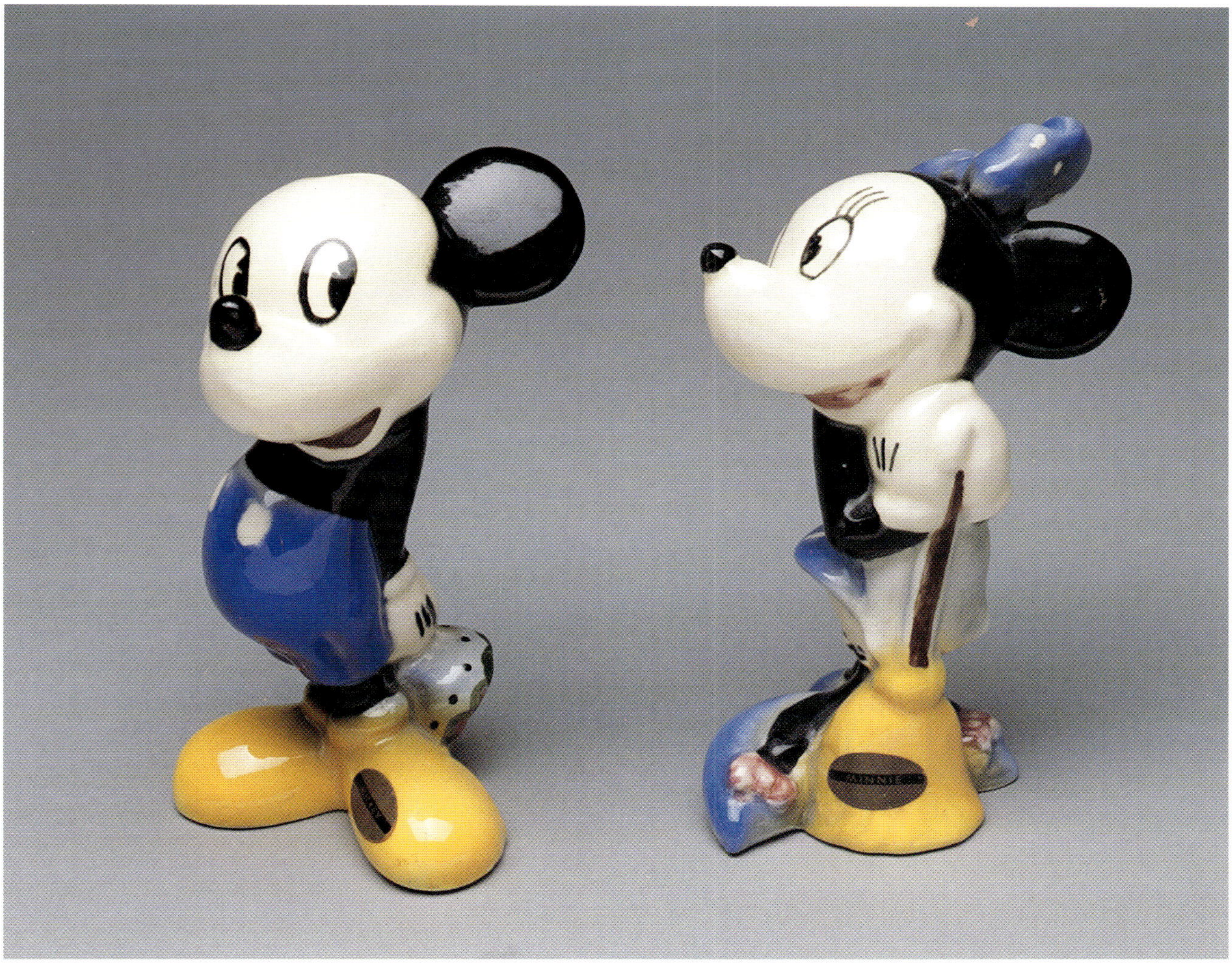

Mickey Mouse 6" and Minnie 6 1/4" $250-300 each

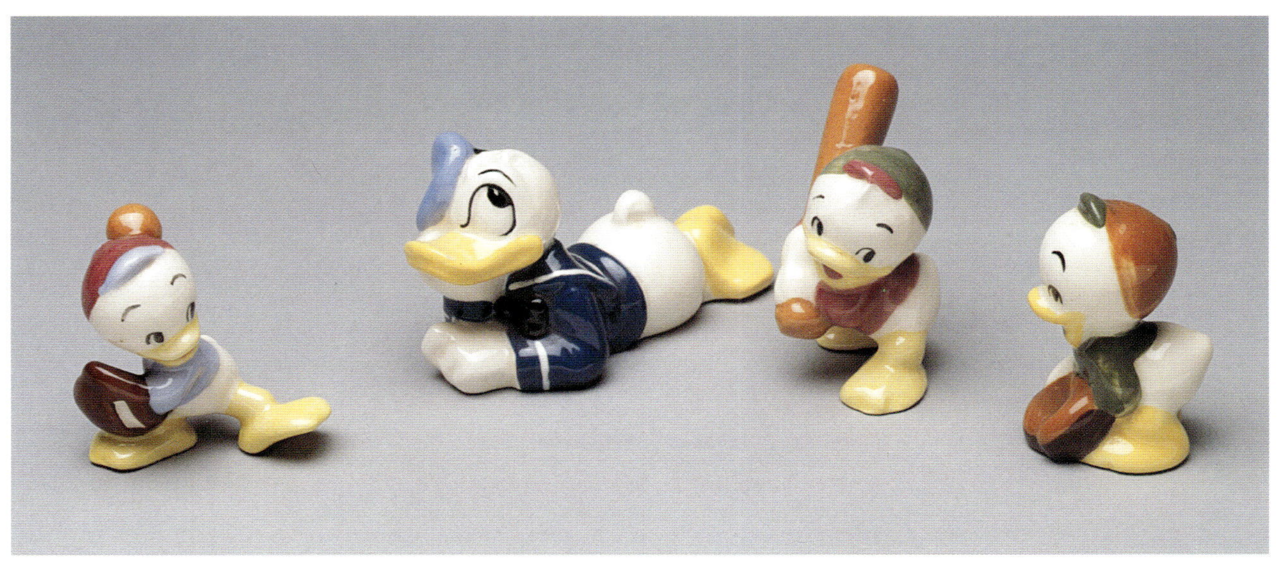

"Play ball!" *Dewey 2 1/2" $75-125, Donald 2 1/2" $150-200, Huey 3" $75-125 and Louie 2 1/2" $60-95.*

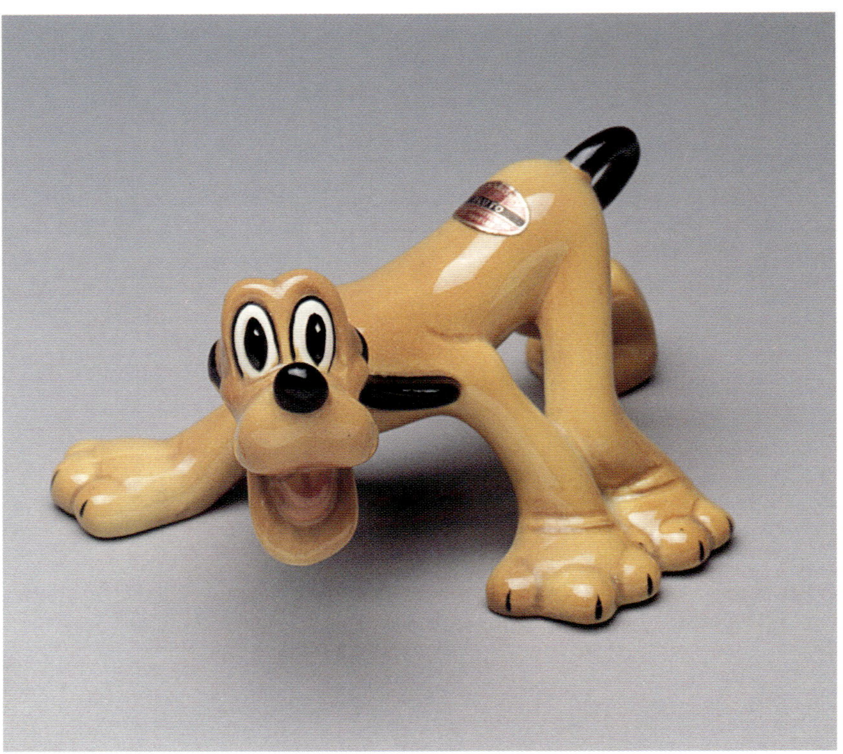

Pluto walking 3 3/4" $225-275.

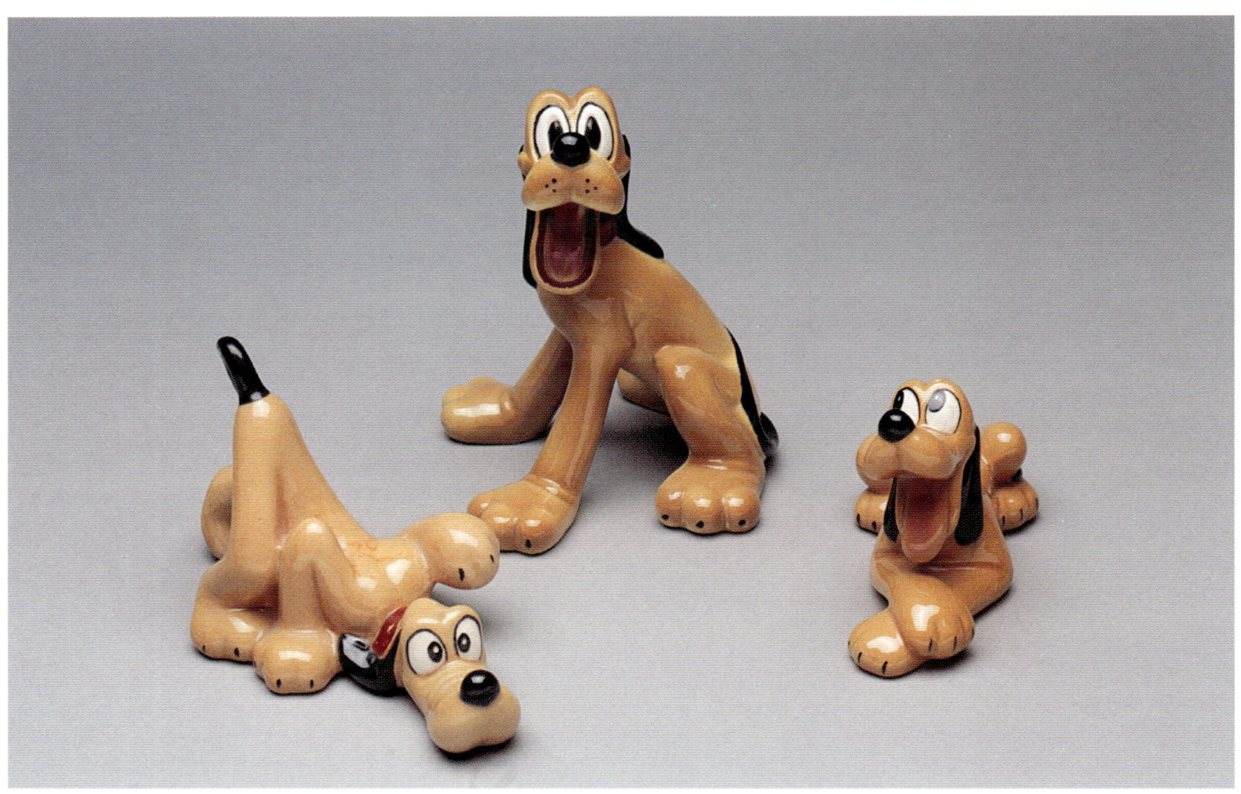

Pluto sniffing 3 1/2", sitting 5 1/2" and lying 3 1/4" $200-250 each.

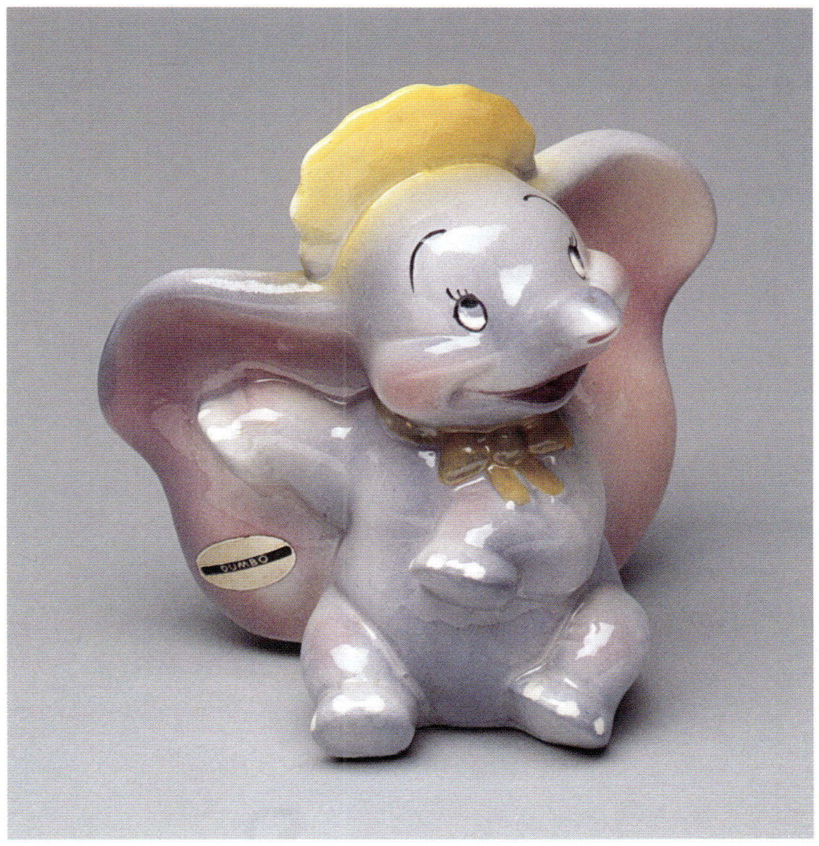

Dumbo with bonnet 5 1/2"
$185-225

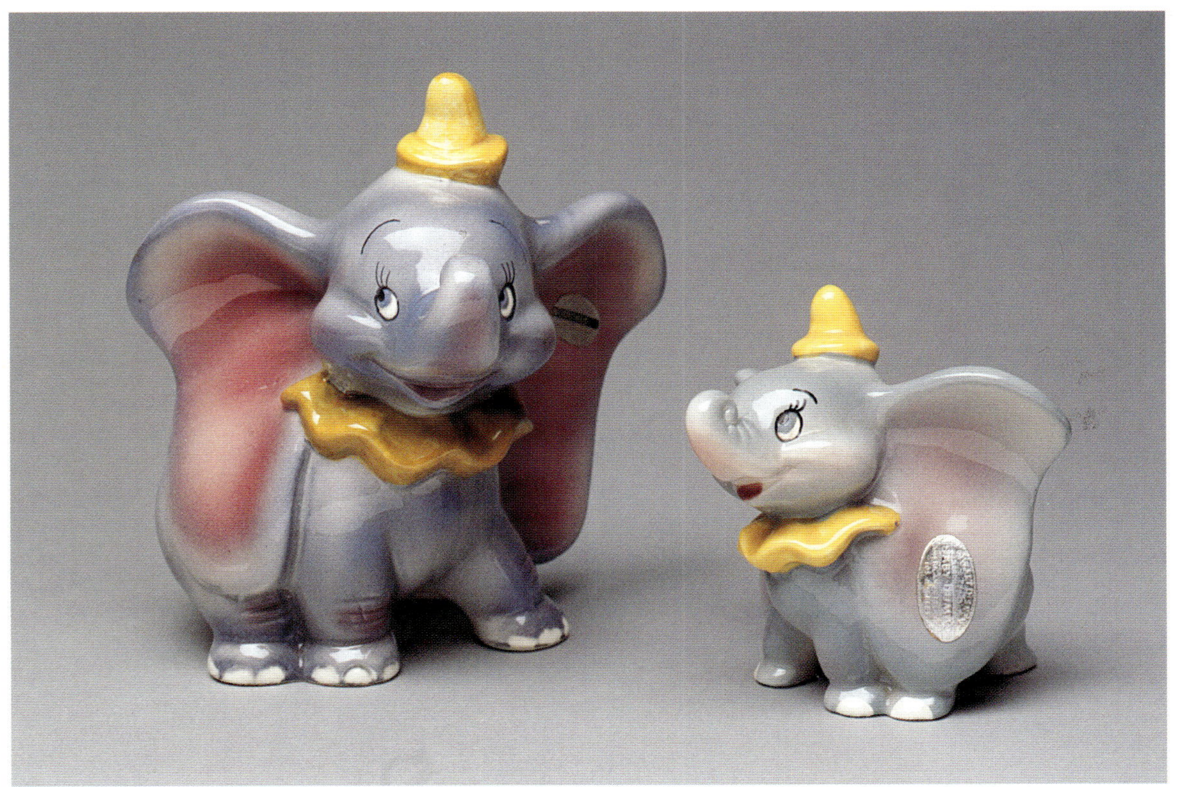

Dumbo standing 5 3/4" $185-225, small Dumbo 3 3/4" $150-175.

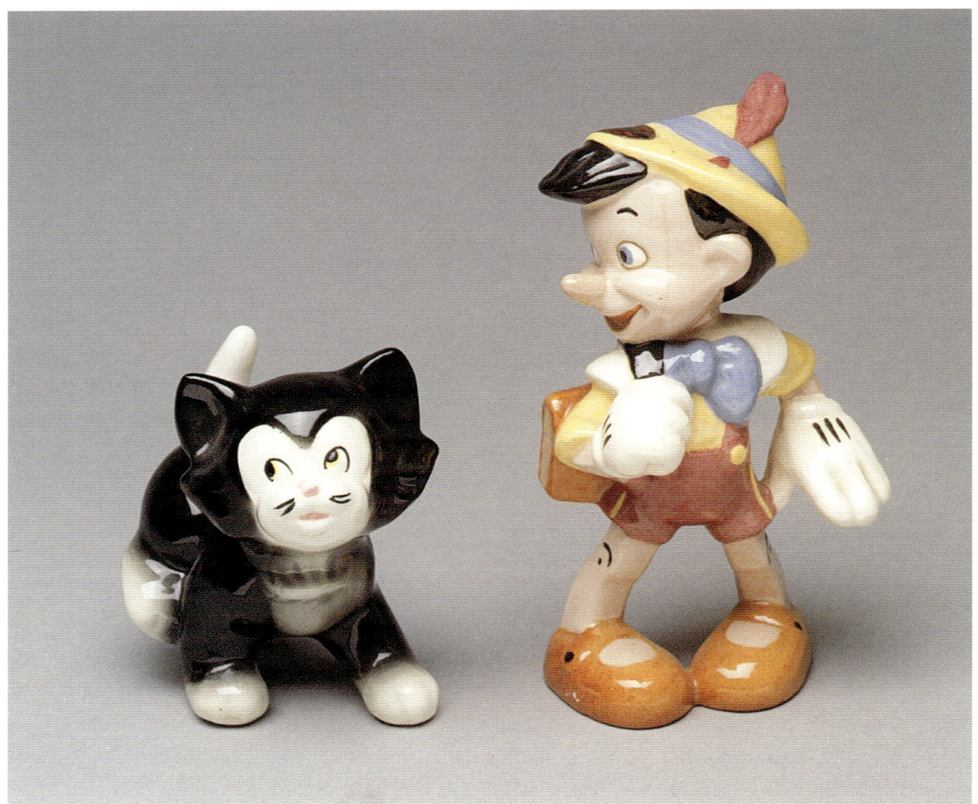

Figaro 3 1/2" $150-200, Pinocchio 6 1/4" $300-400.

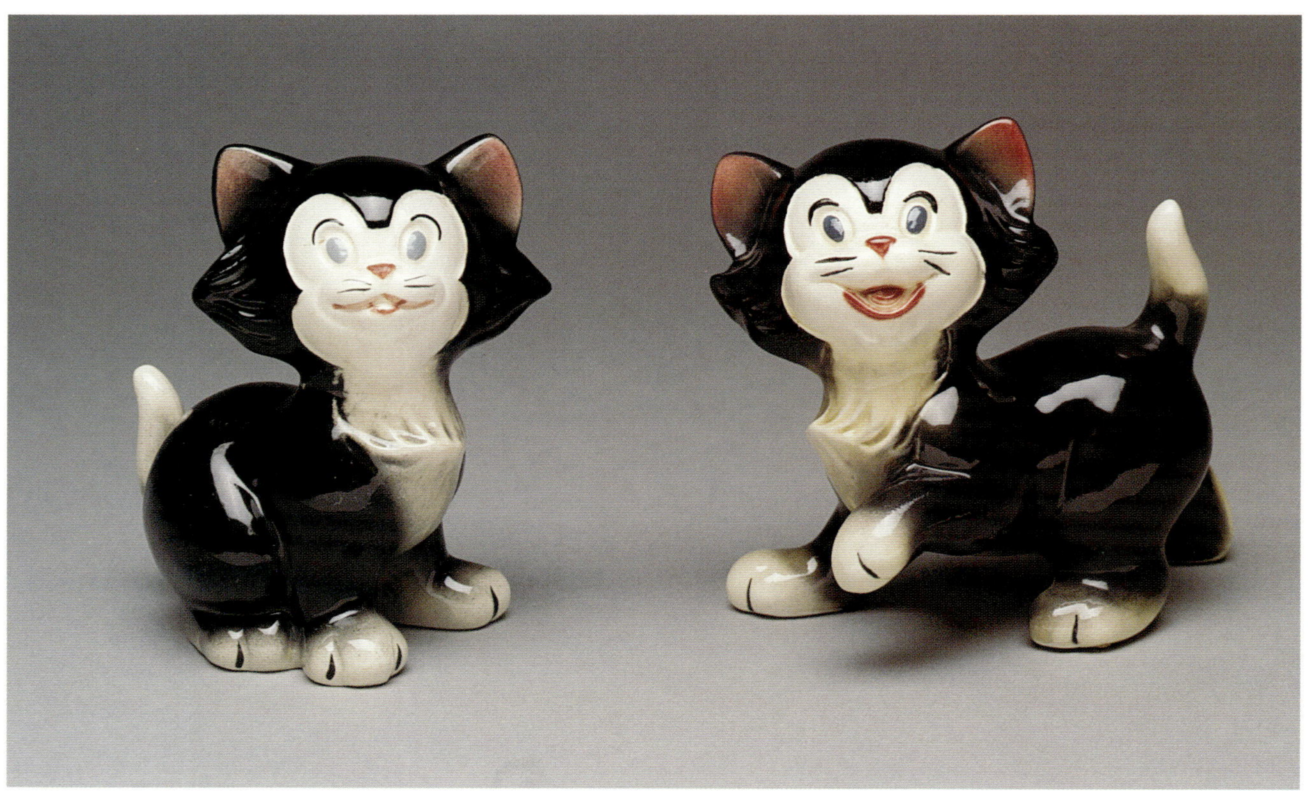

Figaro sitting 4 3/4" $225-300, Figaro standing 4 1/2" $150-200.

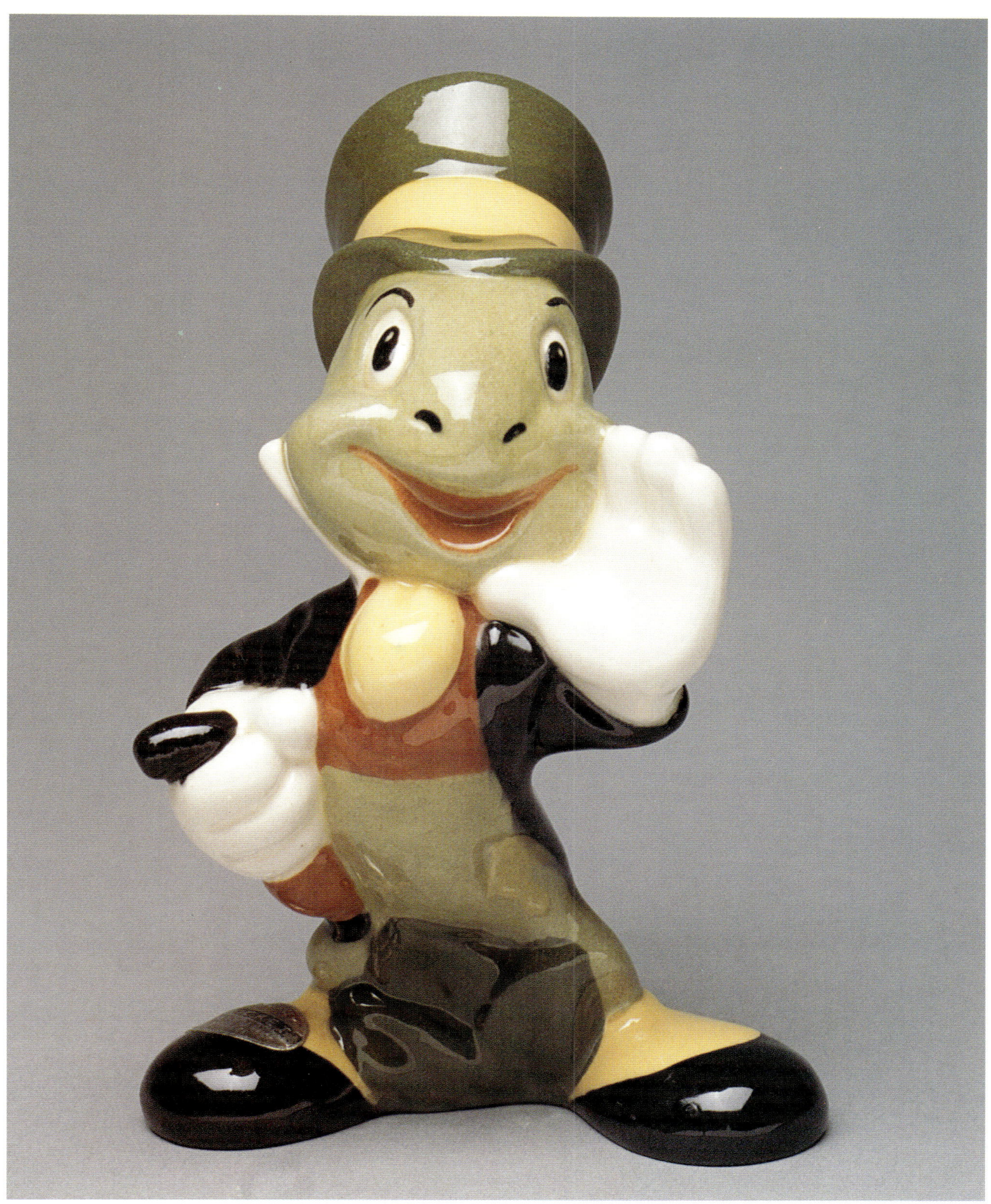

Jiminy Cricket 5 3/4" $2000+

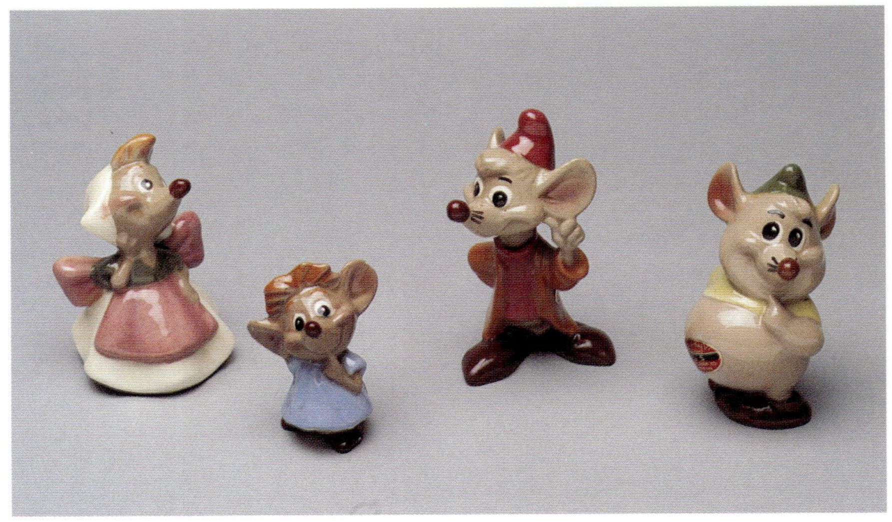

Cindy's mice, Mama Mouse 3 1/4" $200-225, Baby Mouse 2 1/4" $225-250, Jaq 4" and Gus 3 1/4" $225-250 each.

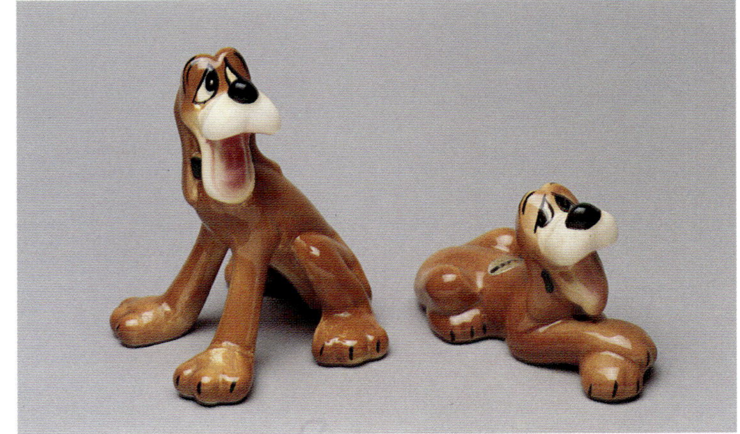

Bruno sitting 5 1/2" $200-275 and Bruno lying 3 1/4" $175-200.

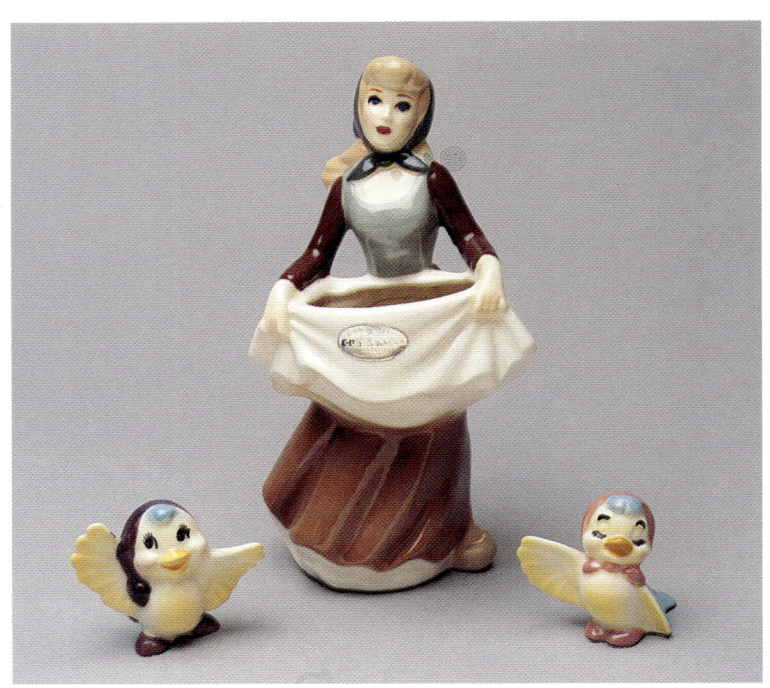

Bobbidi Bird 2" $225-300, Cinderella in rags (planter) 7 1/4" $500+ Bibbidi Bird 2" $250-300.

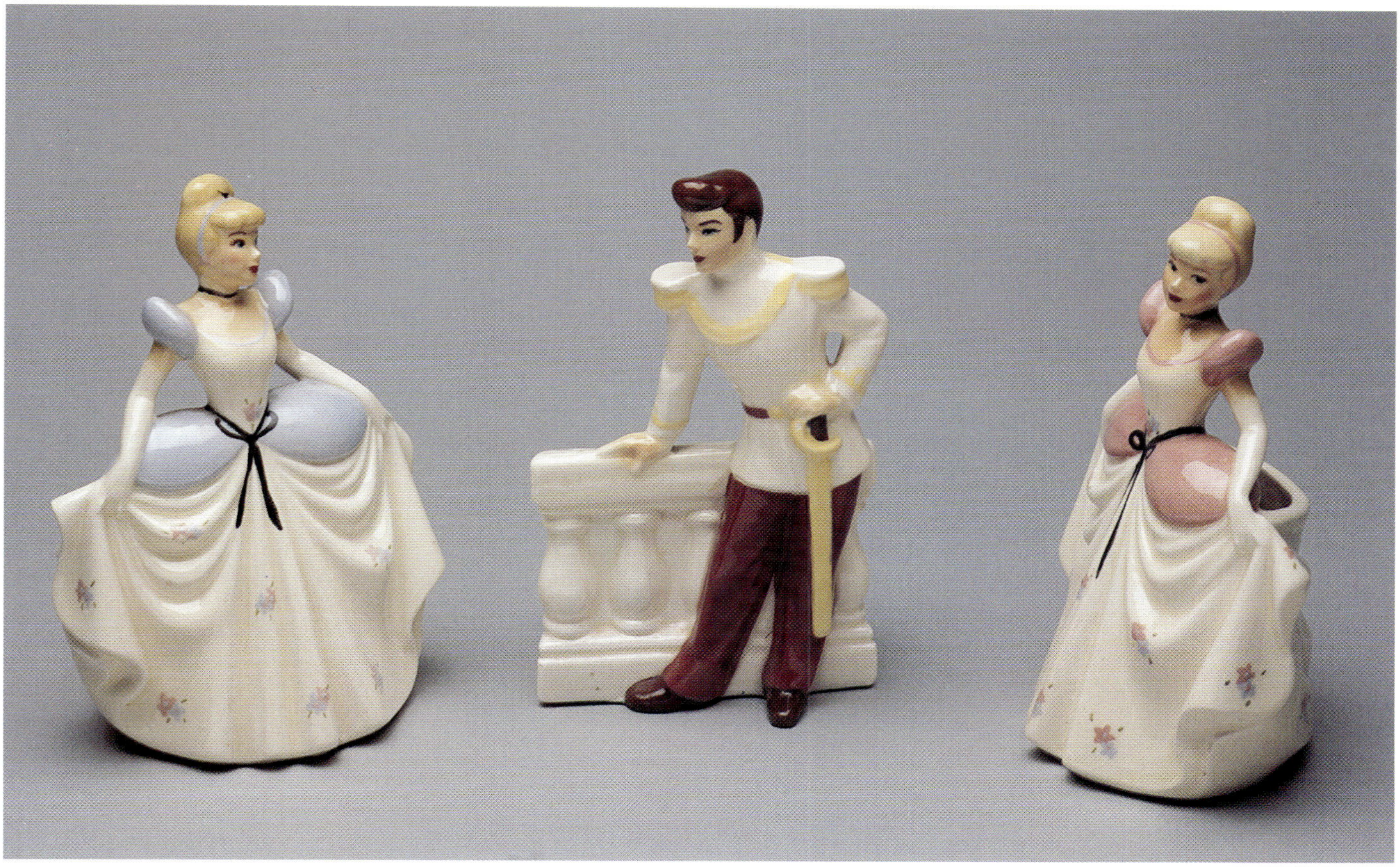

Formal Cinderella in blue 7 1/4" $450-500, Prince 7 1/2" $300-375, Formal Cinderella in pink 7 1/4" $400-450 all planters.

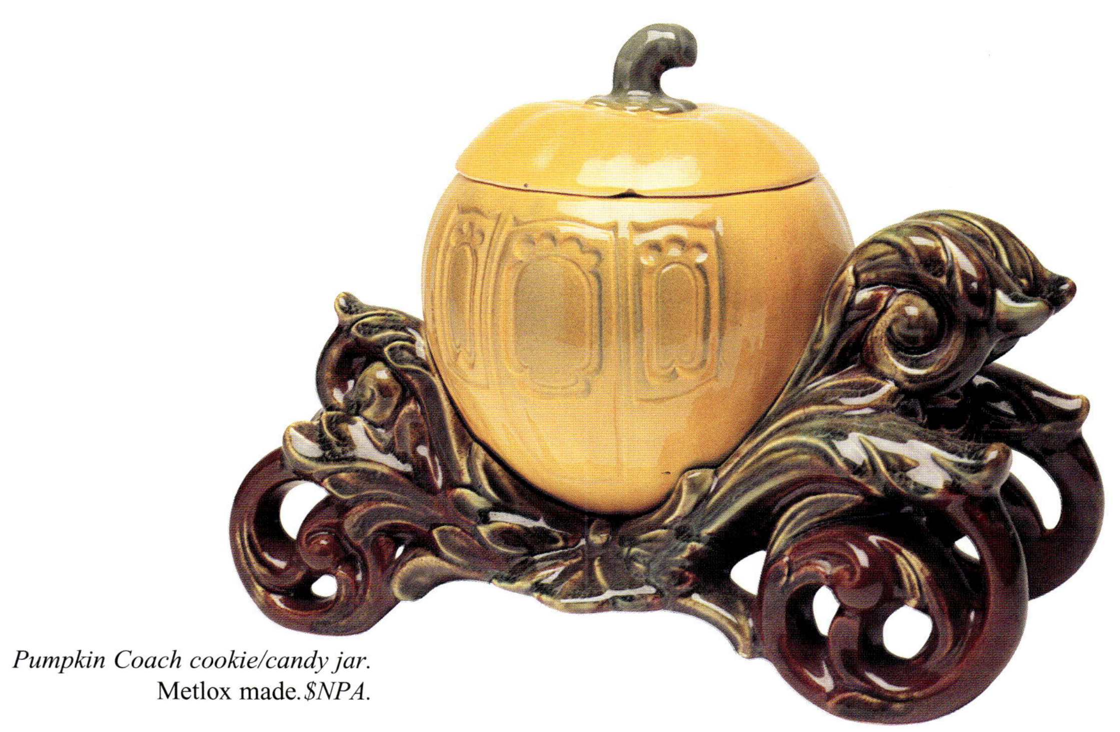

Pumpkin Coach cookie/candy jar. Metlox made. *$NPA.*

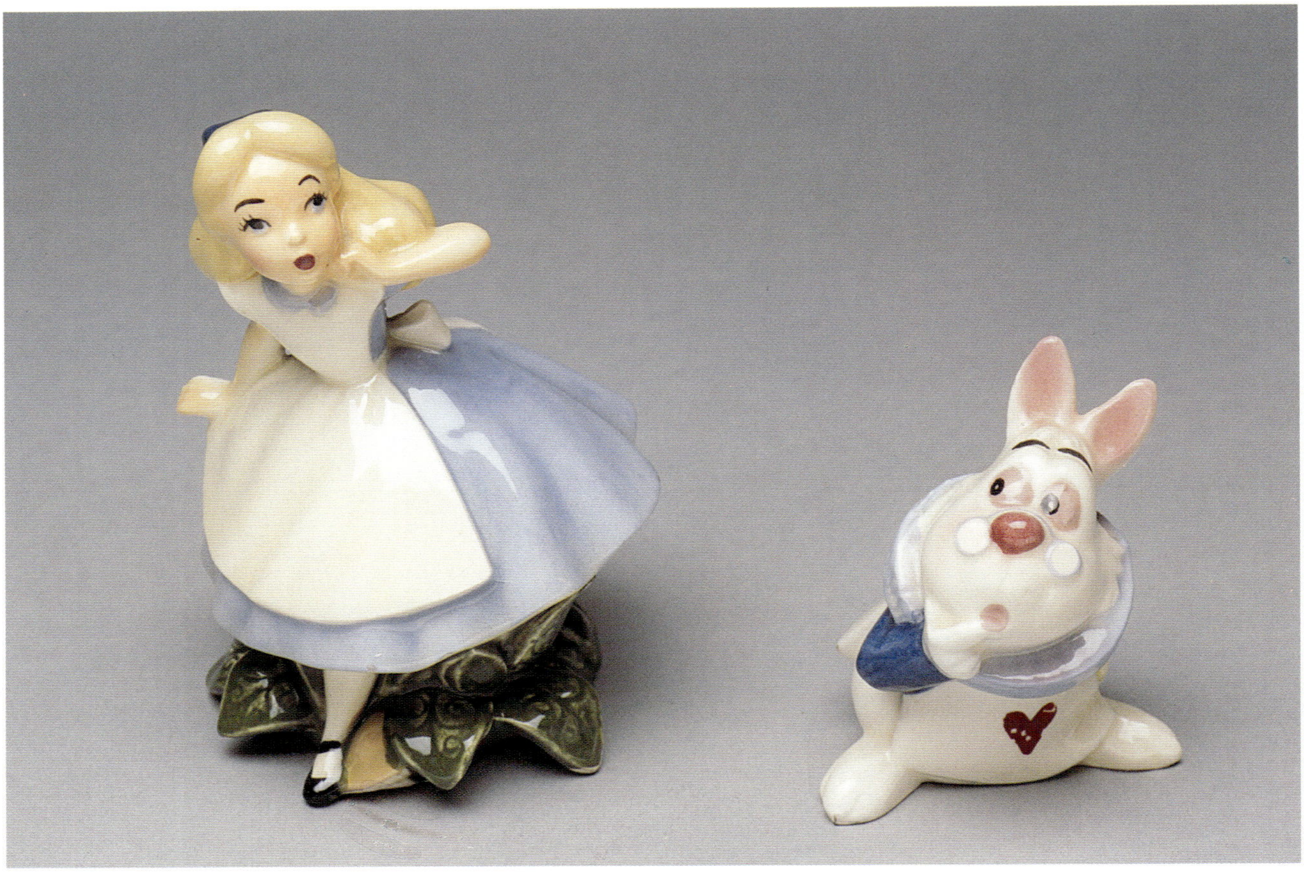

Alice 5 1/2" $350-400 and the White Rabbit 3 1/2" $250-275

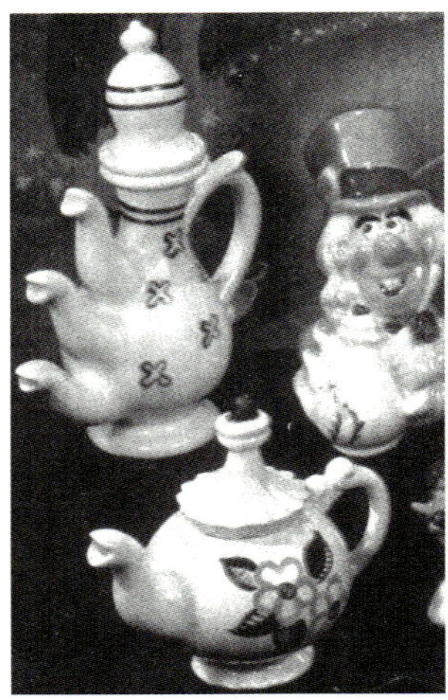

Catalog ad of teapots showing Tea for Three and Tea and Sugar

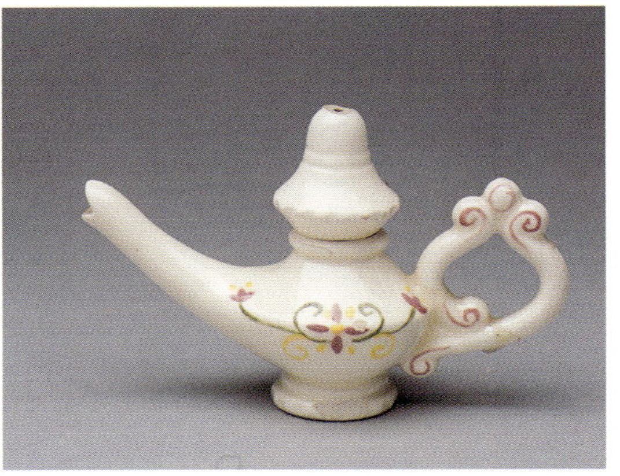

Teapot Magic Tea 3" $500+

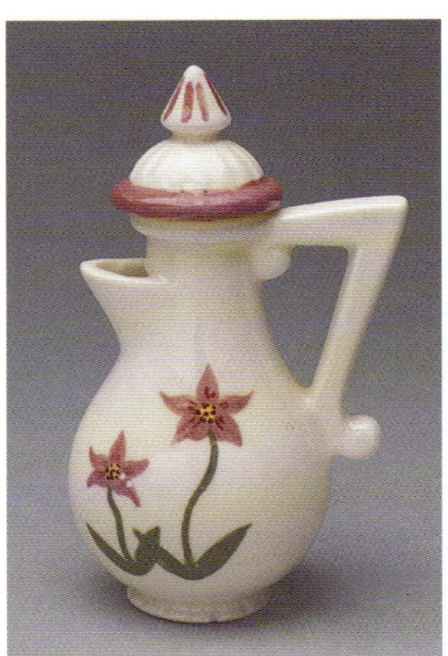

Teapot Tea n' Cream 4" $500+

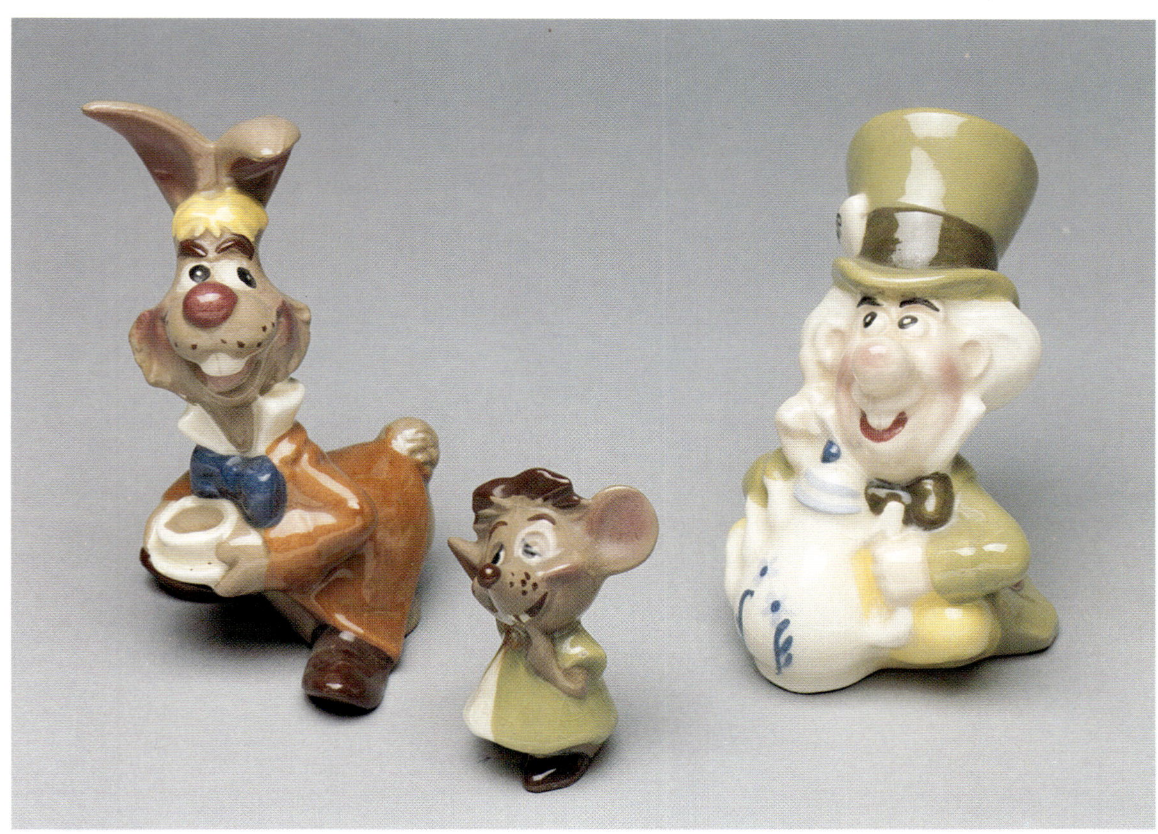

March Hare 4 1/2" $300-350, Dormouse 2 1/4" $350-400, Mad Hatter 4" $250-275.

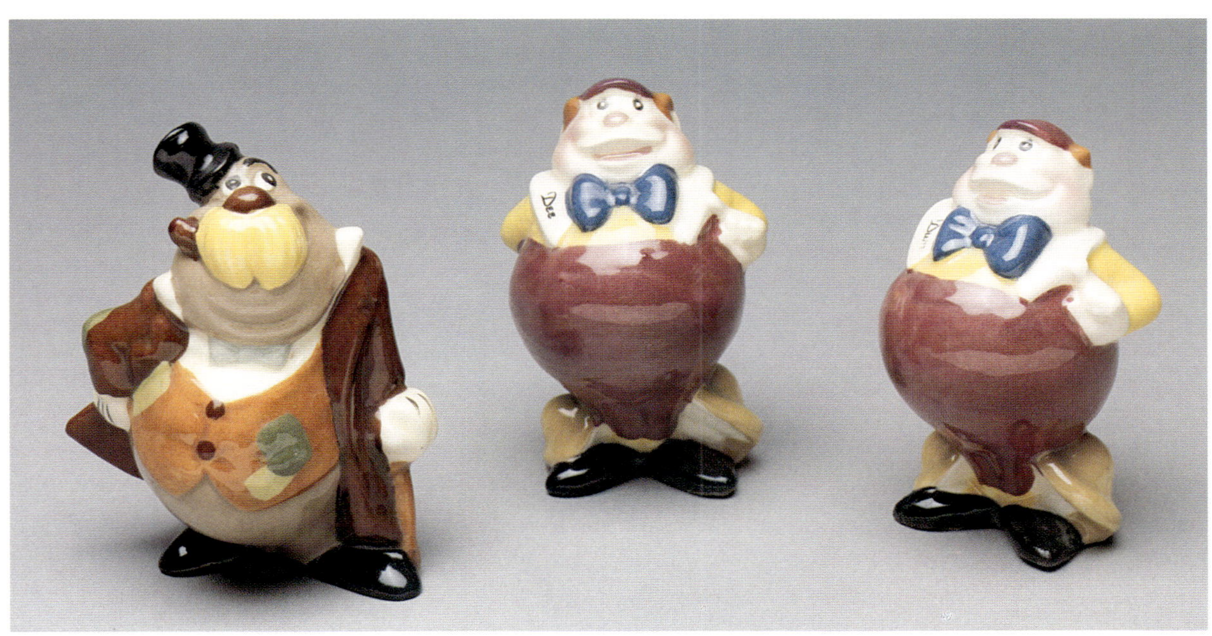

Walrus 4 1/2" $275-325, Tweedle Dee 3 3/4" and Tweedle Dum 3 3/4" $200-250 each.

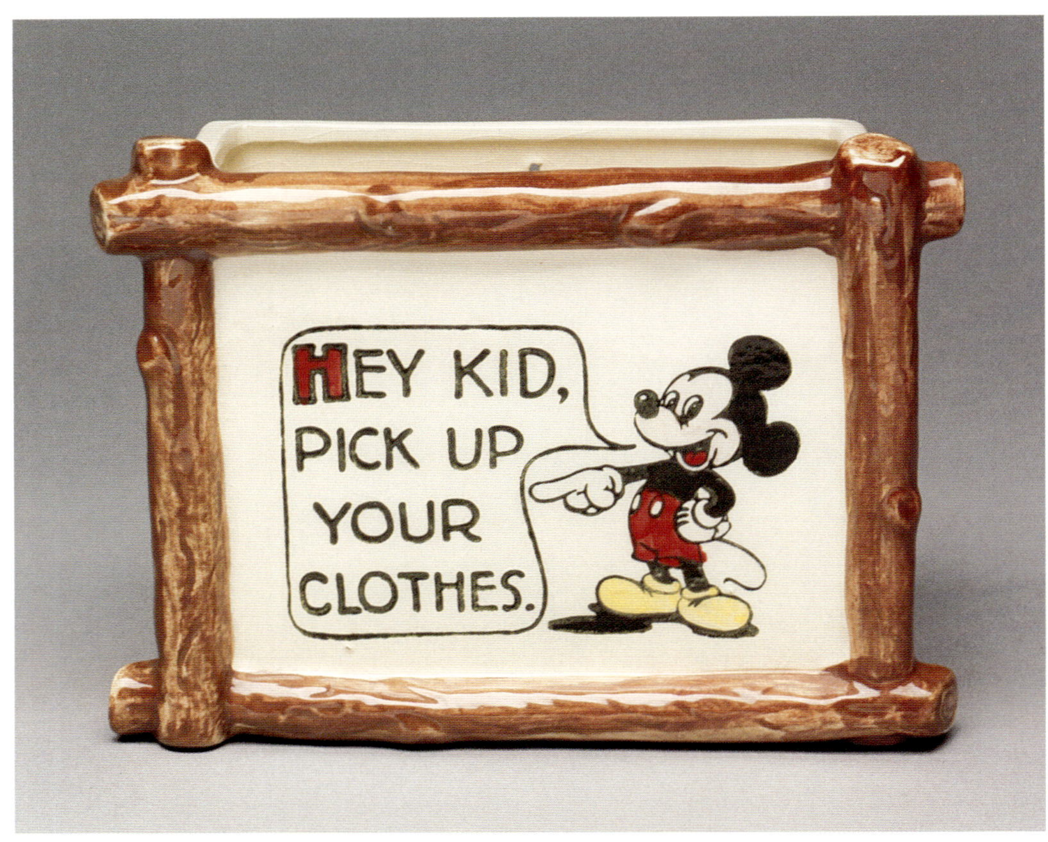

Mickey wall planter 5" $200-300. Not pictured Donald wall planter 5" $200-300

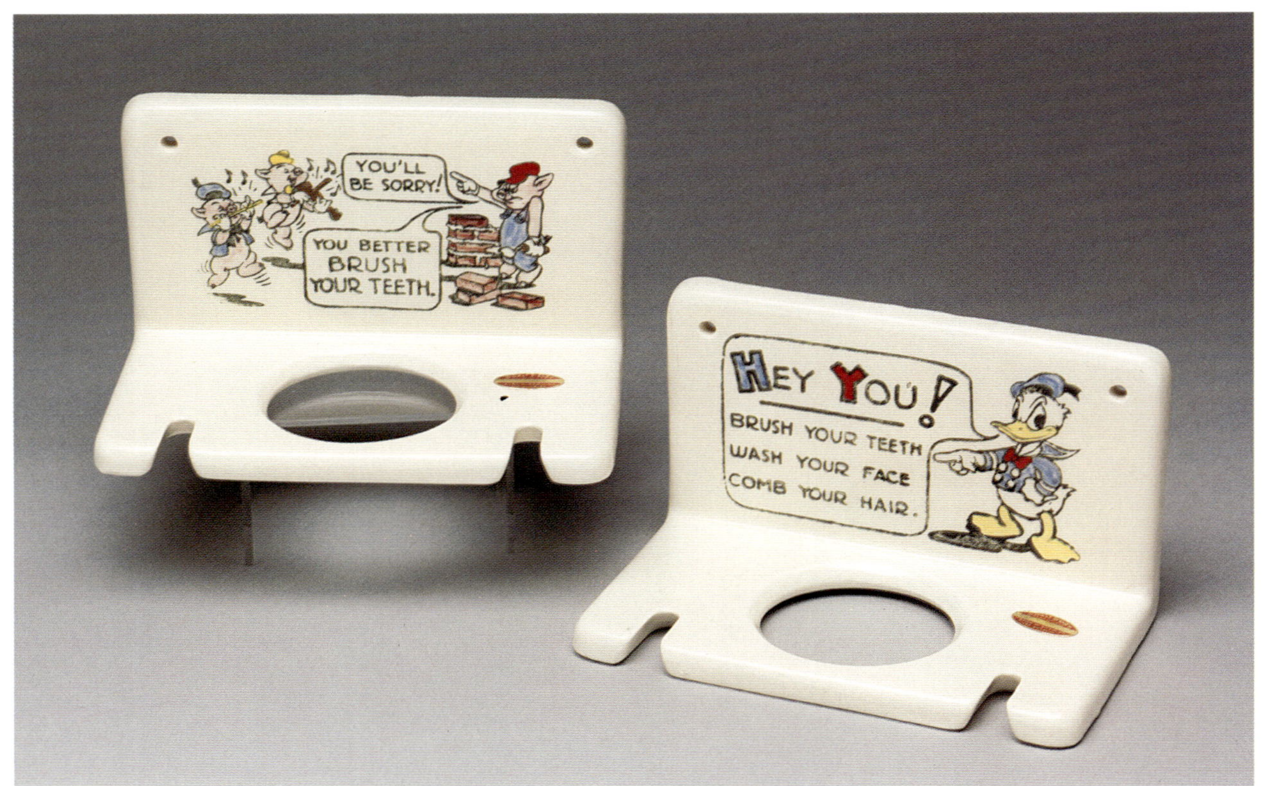

Three Pigs 4" and Donald Duck 4" toothbrush holders $200-300 each

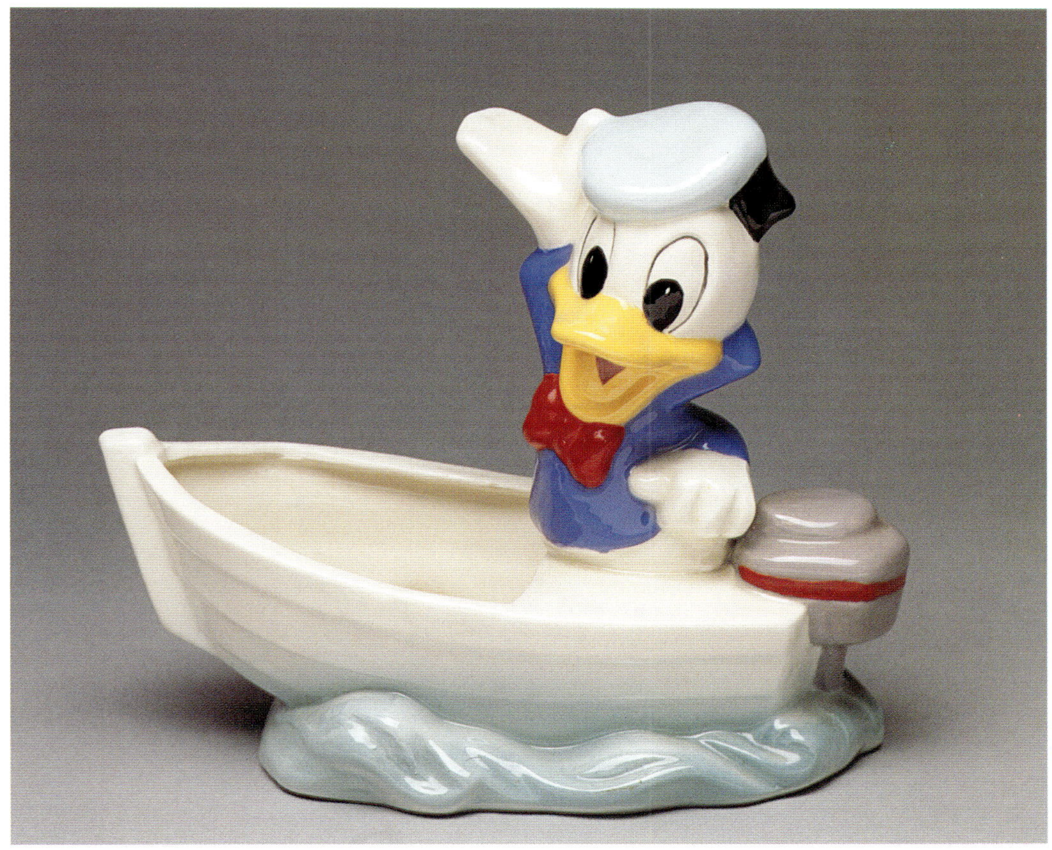

Donald in boat planter 7 1/2" $1000+.

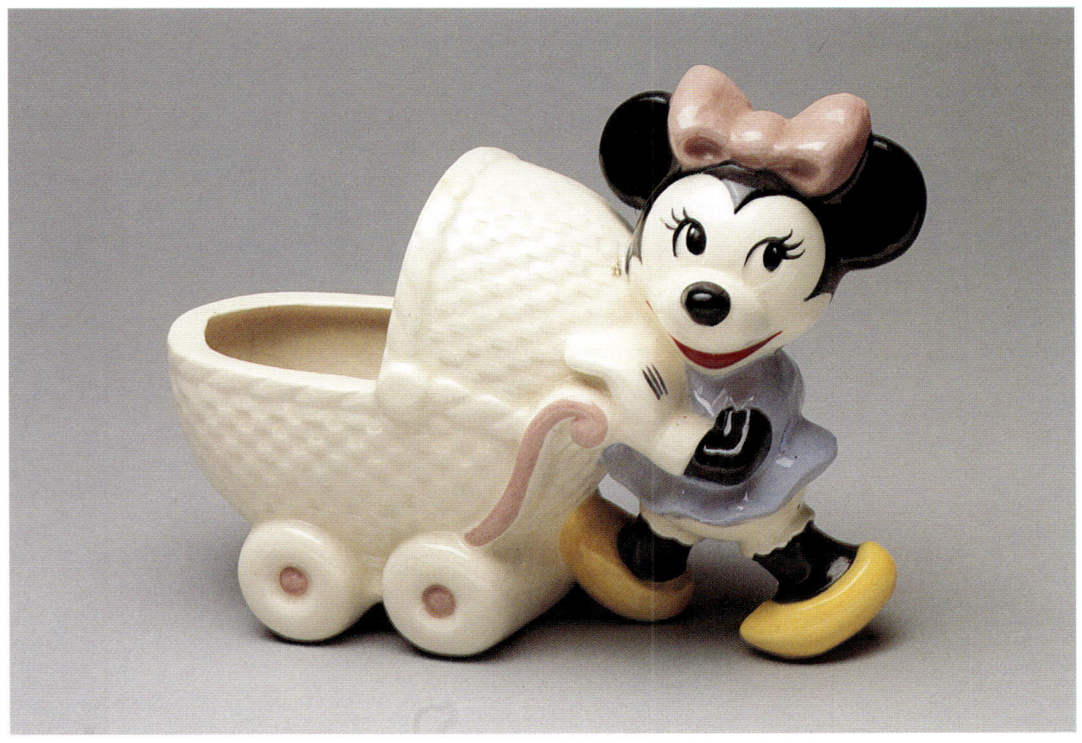

Minnie with baby bassinet planter 6 3/4" $700+.

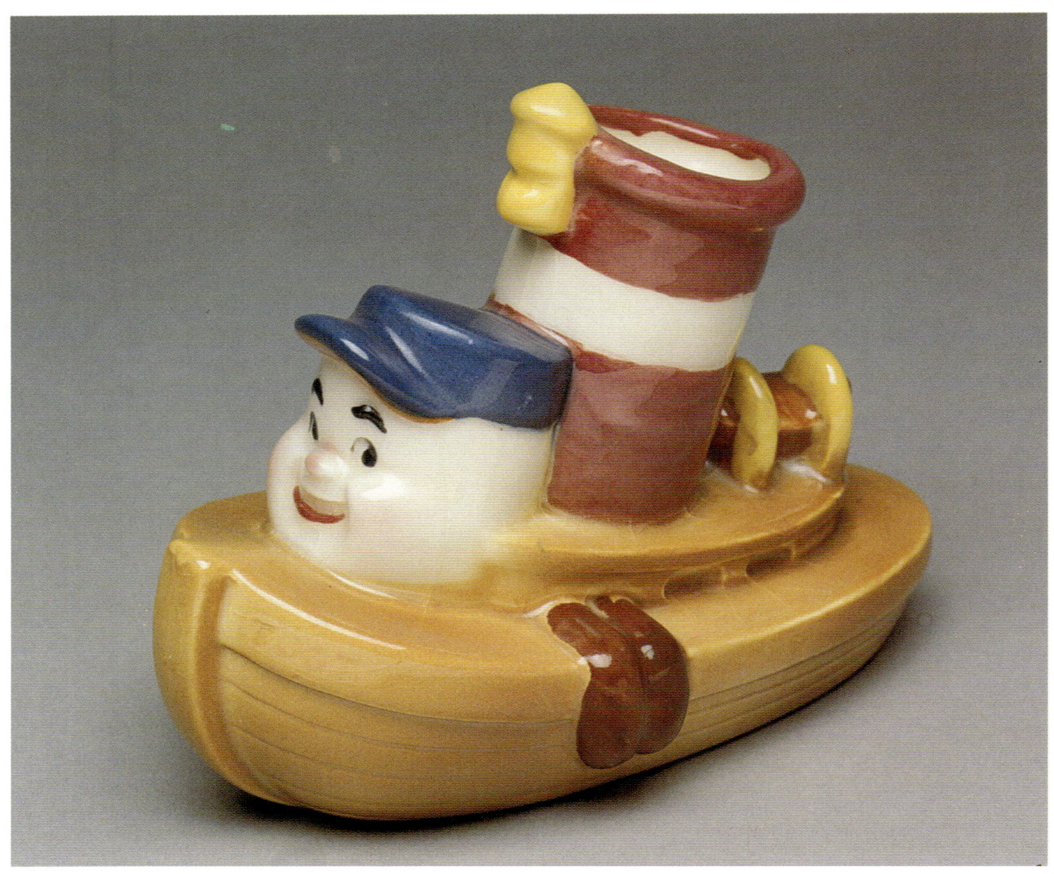

Little Toot planter 5' $2000+.

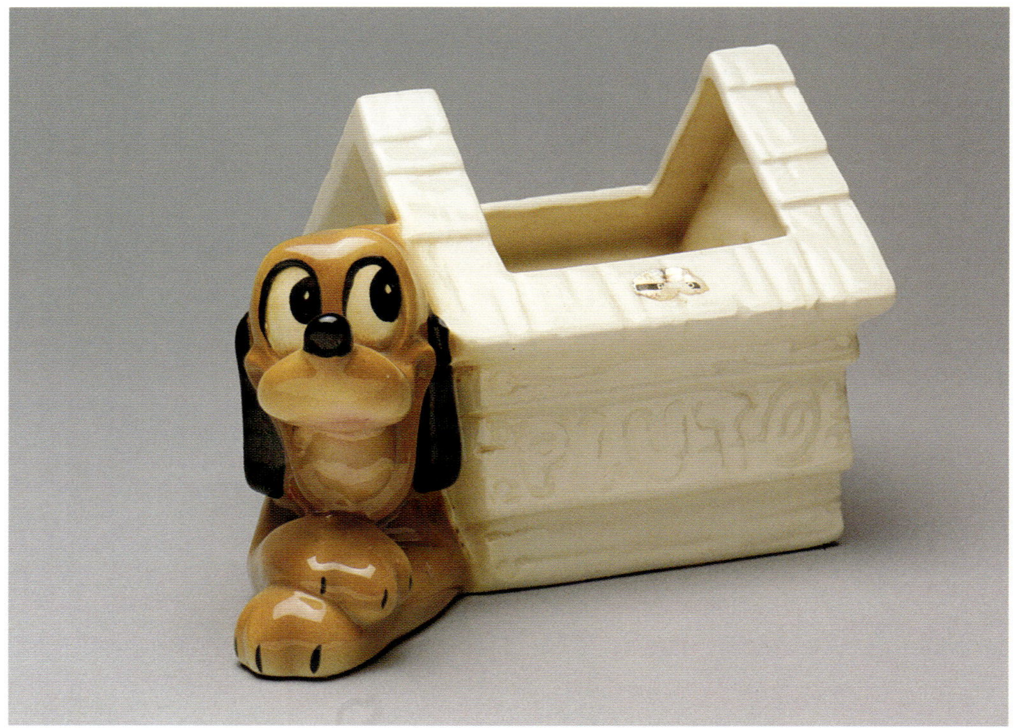

Pluto doghouse planter 5 1/4" $600+.

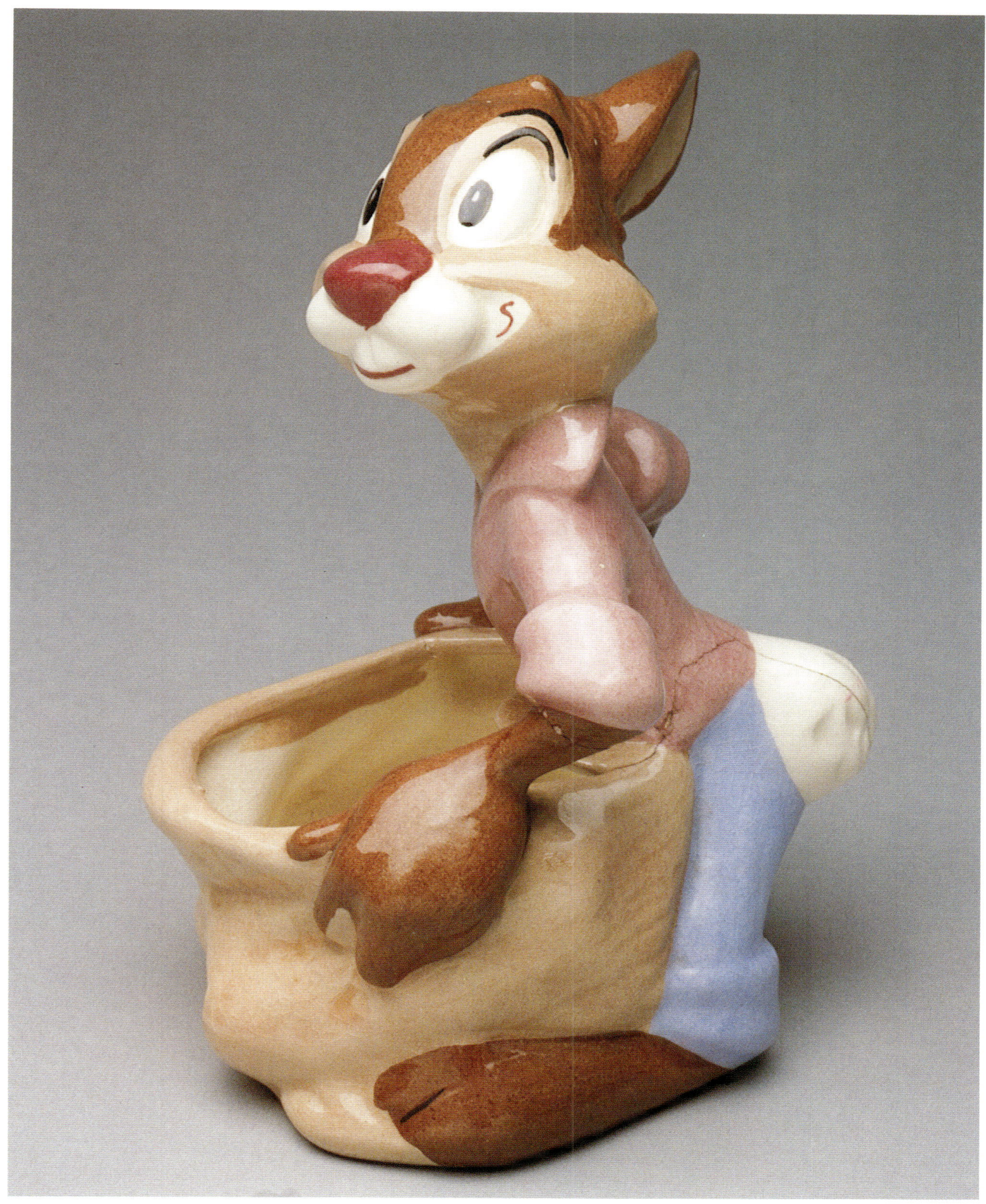

Brer Rabbit planter 6" $2000+. Not pictured: Donald Beehive planter, NPA

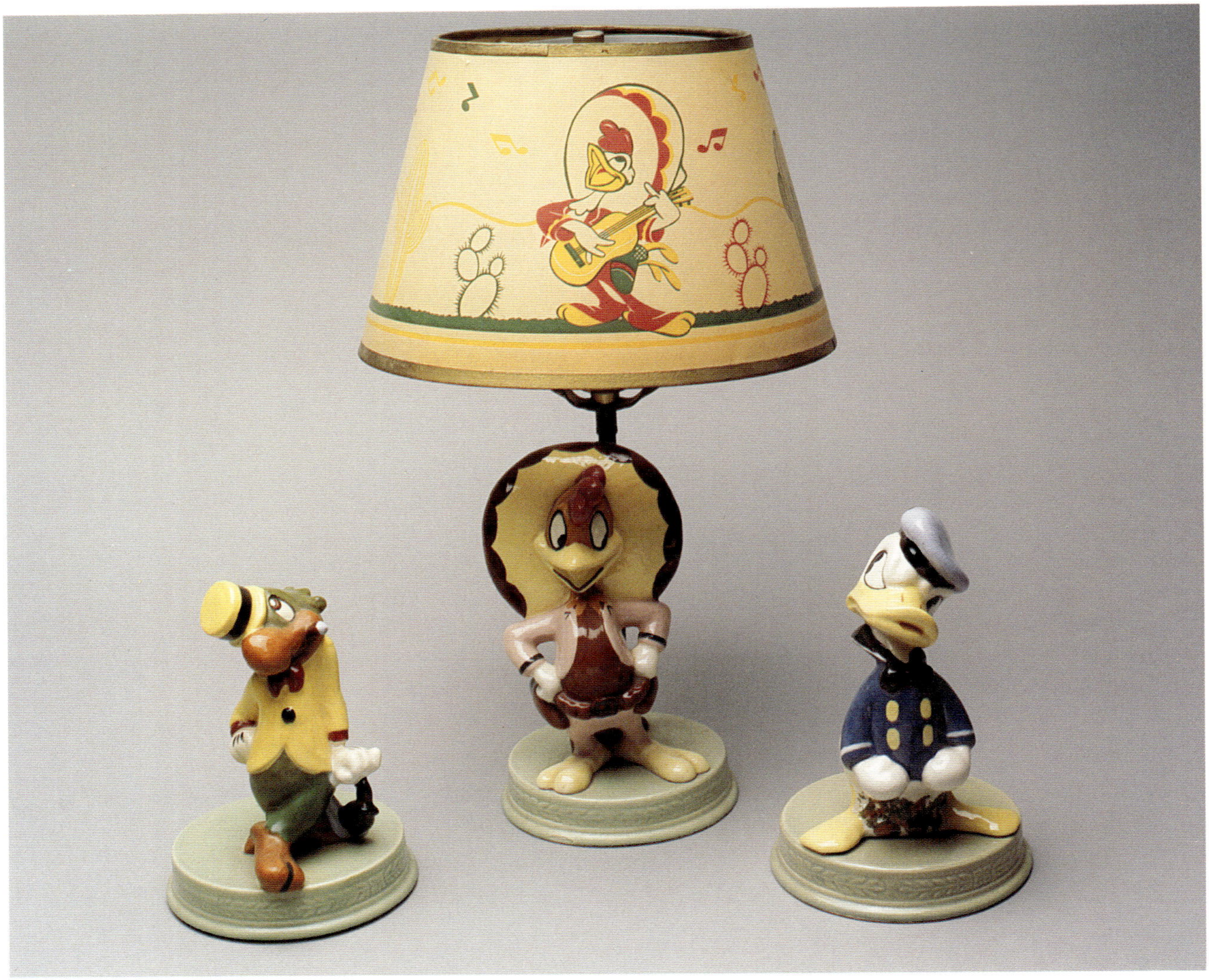

Jose 7 1/2", Panchito 8 3/4" and Donald 8" lamp bases $150-275 each. Lampshade is rare, *$NPA.*

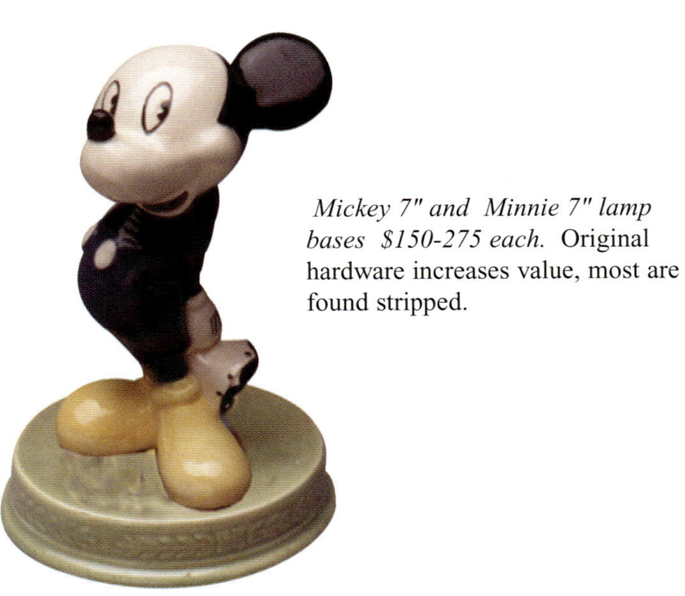

Mickey 7" and Minnie 7" lamp bases $150-275 each. Original hardware increases value, most are found stripped.

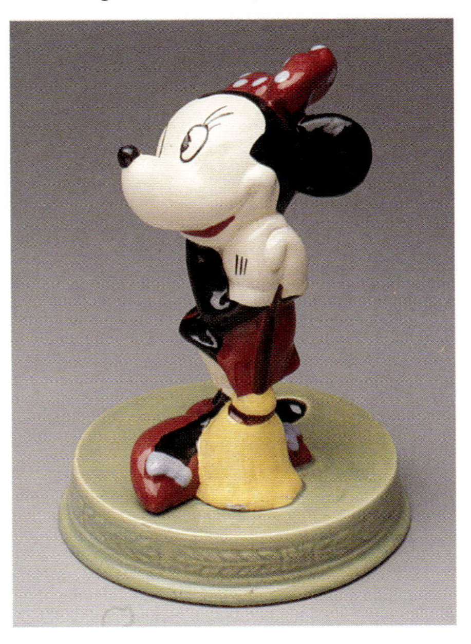

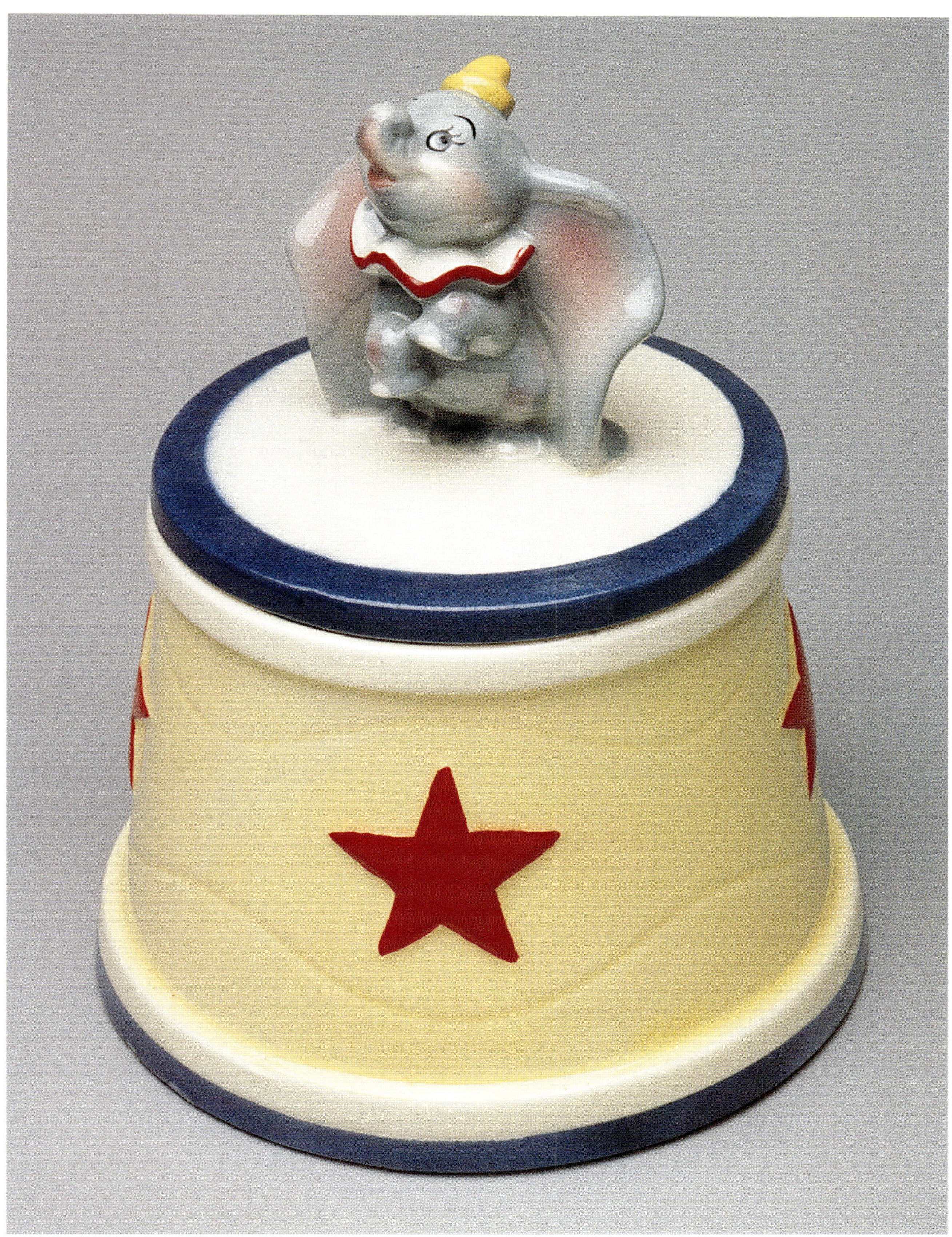

Dumbo cookie jar 10 °" $NPA.

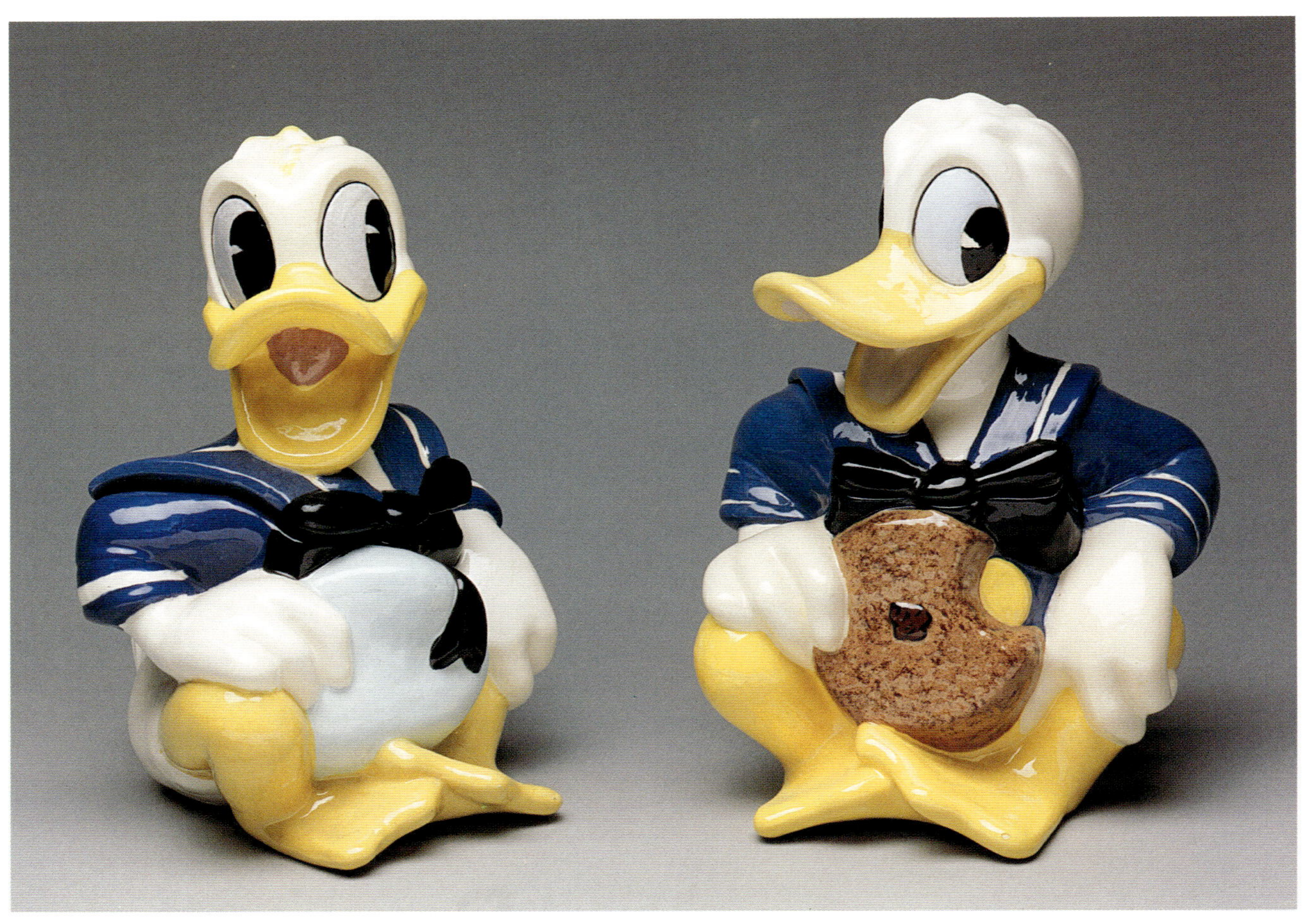

Donald Duck cookie jars, holding hat 11"or cookie 11 1/2" $3000+ each.

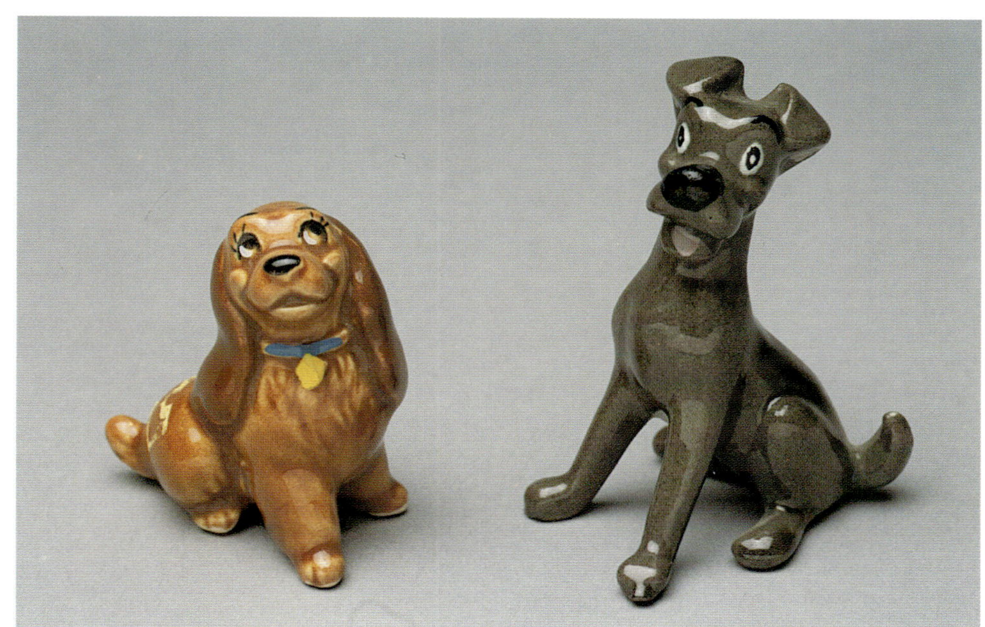

Miniatures Lady sitting 1 3/4" $80-100, Tramp 2 1/4" $150-225.

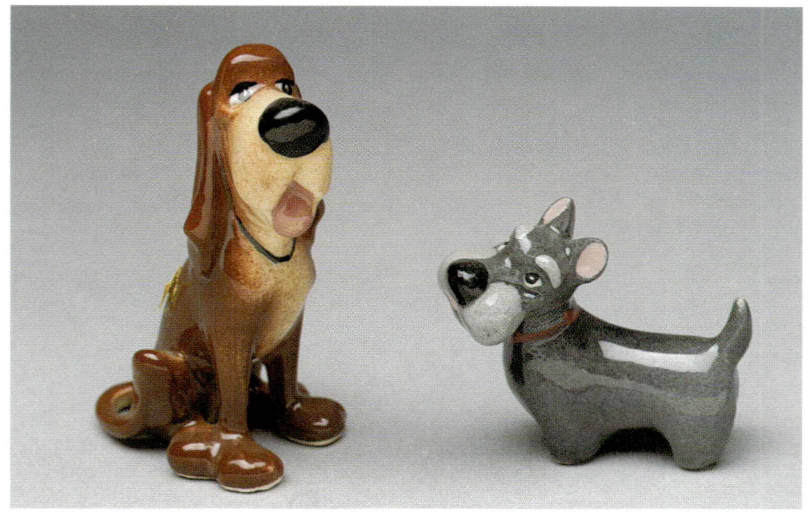

Trusty 2 3/4" and Jock 1 3/4" $80-150 each.

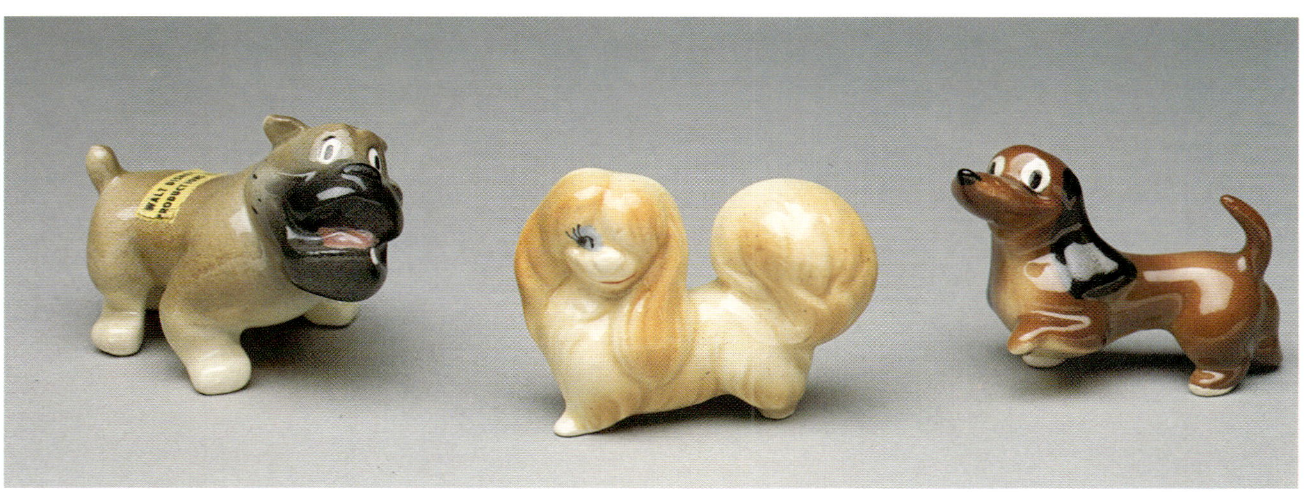

Bull 1 1/2" $80-150, Peg 1 1/2" $150-200, Dachsie 1 1/4" $80-150

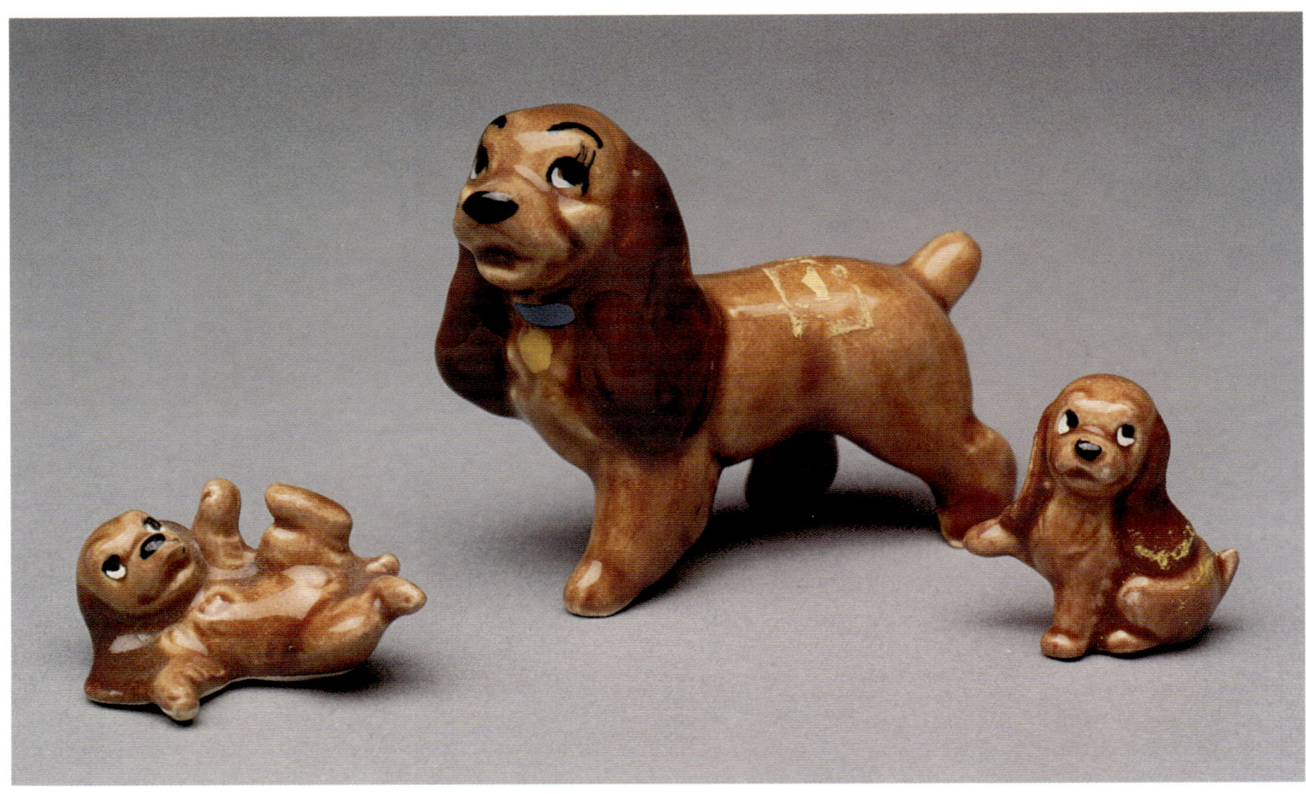

Pup #3, 3/4, Lady standing 1 3/4", Pup #2, 1" $80-100 each. Not pictured, Scamp and Pup #1 $80-100 each.

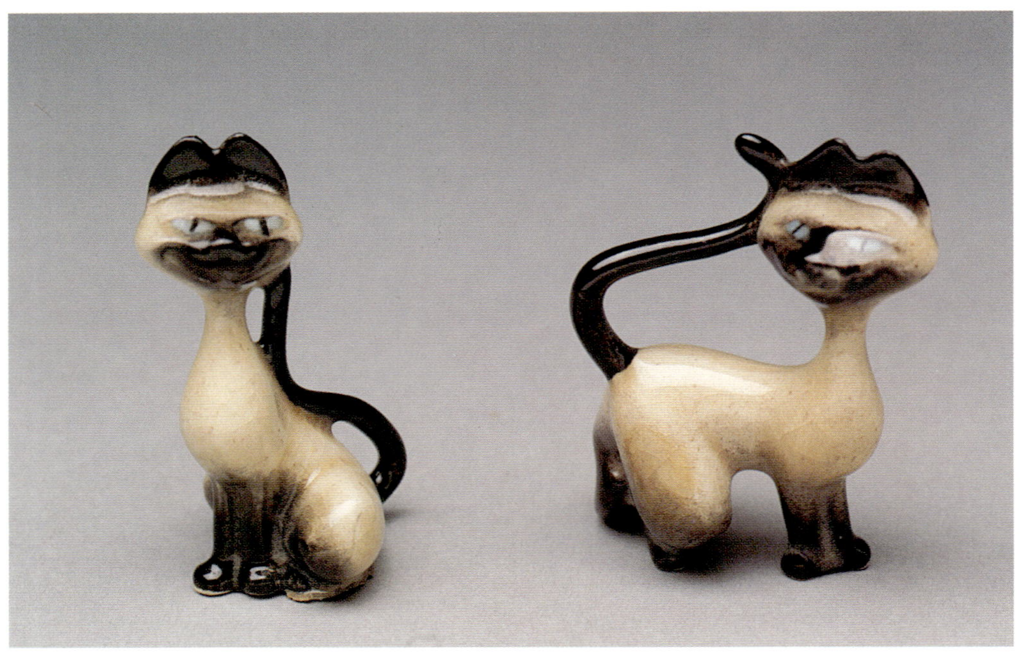

Si (sitting) 2"and Am 2 1/4" $150-200 each

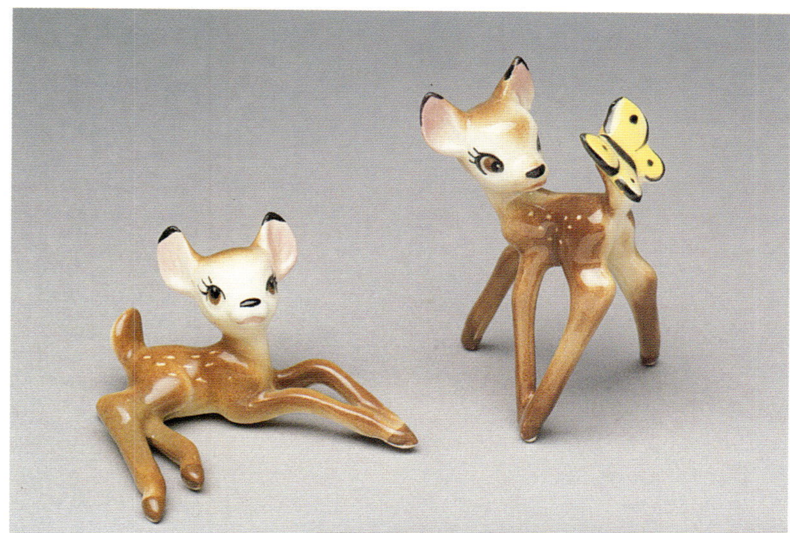

Bambi lying 1 1/2" $150-200,
Bambi w/ butterfly 2 3/4"$175 250.

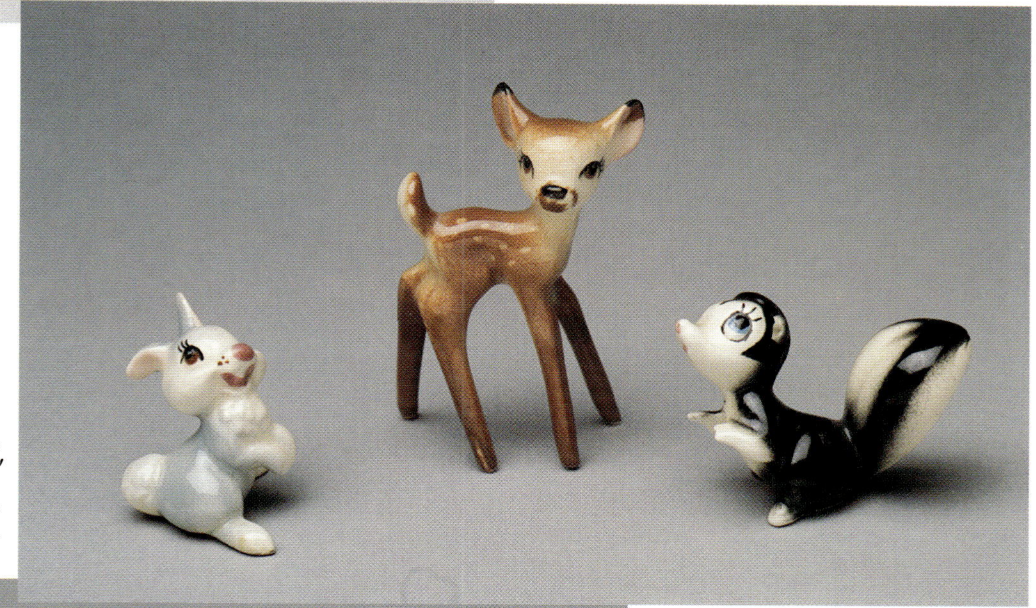

Thumper 1 1/4" $125-150,
Bambi standing 2 1/2" $150-200,
Flower 1 1/2" $125-150.

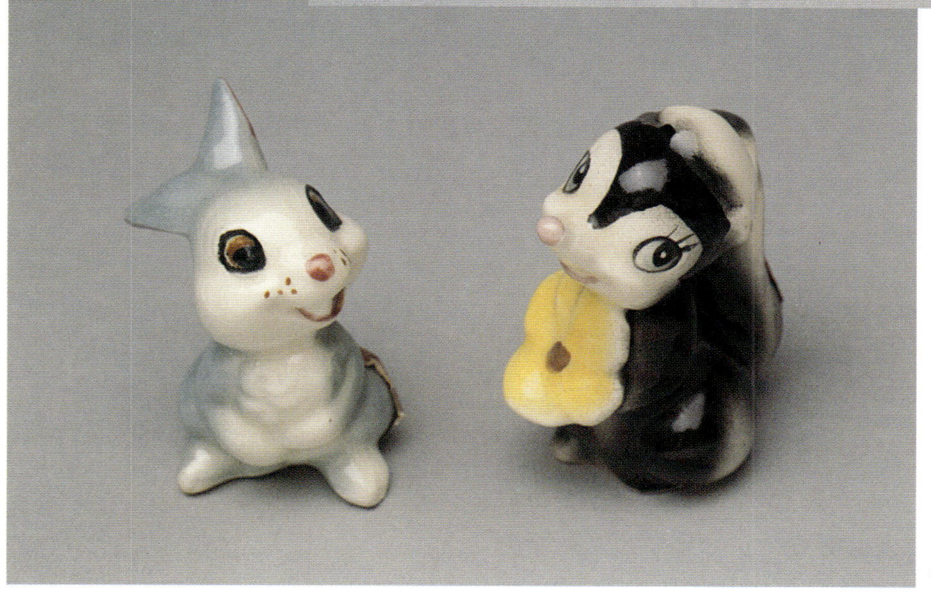

Thumper 1 3/4" and Flower 1 3/4" $125-150 each

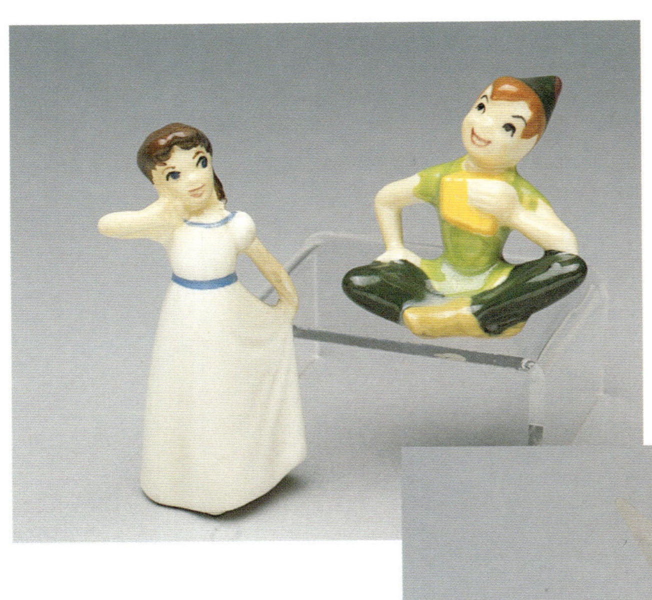

Wendy 3 1/4" $300-350, Peter Pan sitting 2" $350-400

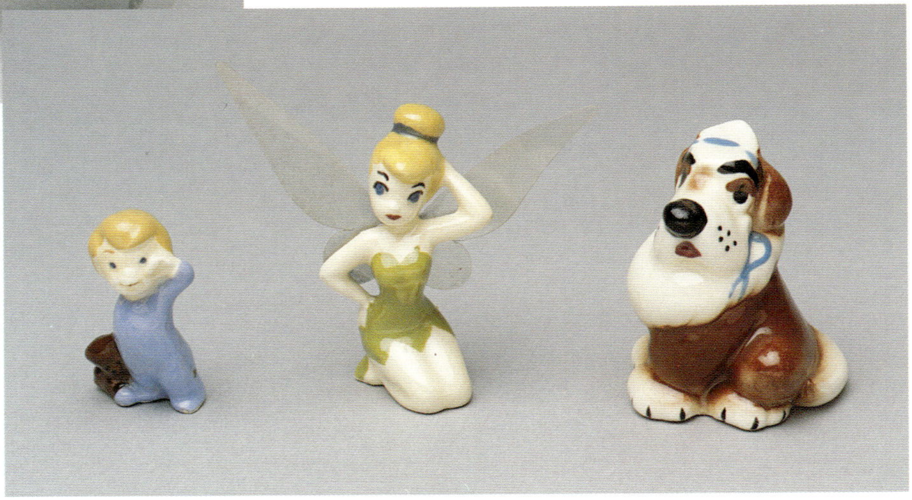

Michael 1 1/2" $150-200, Tinker Bell 2" to head, $400-450, Nana 2" $250-300. Tinker Bell's original celluloid wings are rare!

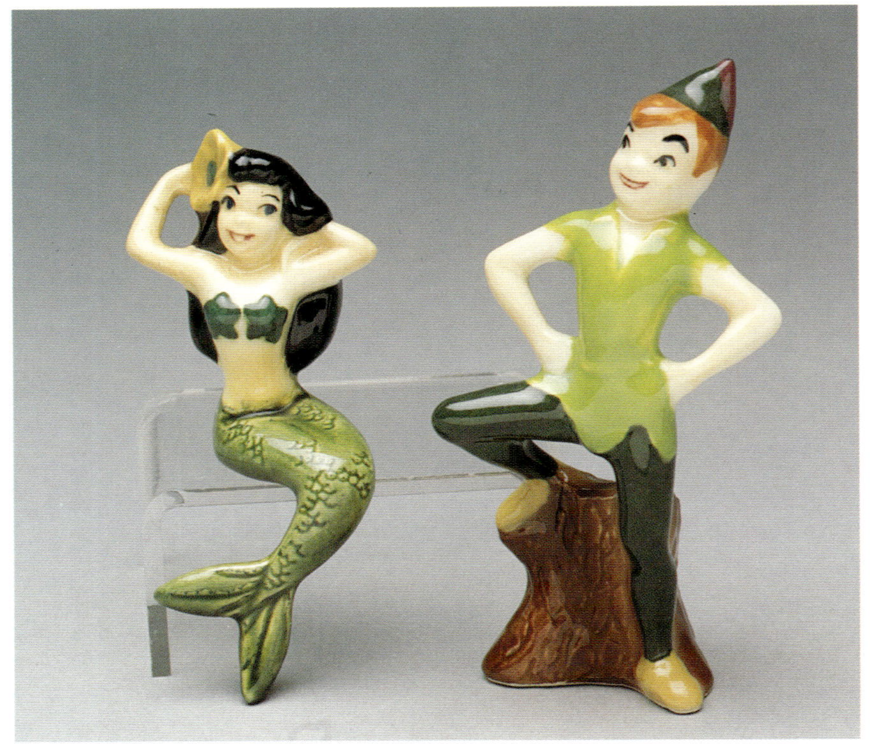

Mermaid 3 3/4" $350-400, Peter Pan standing 4" $350-400.

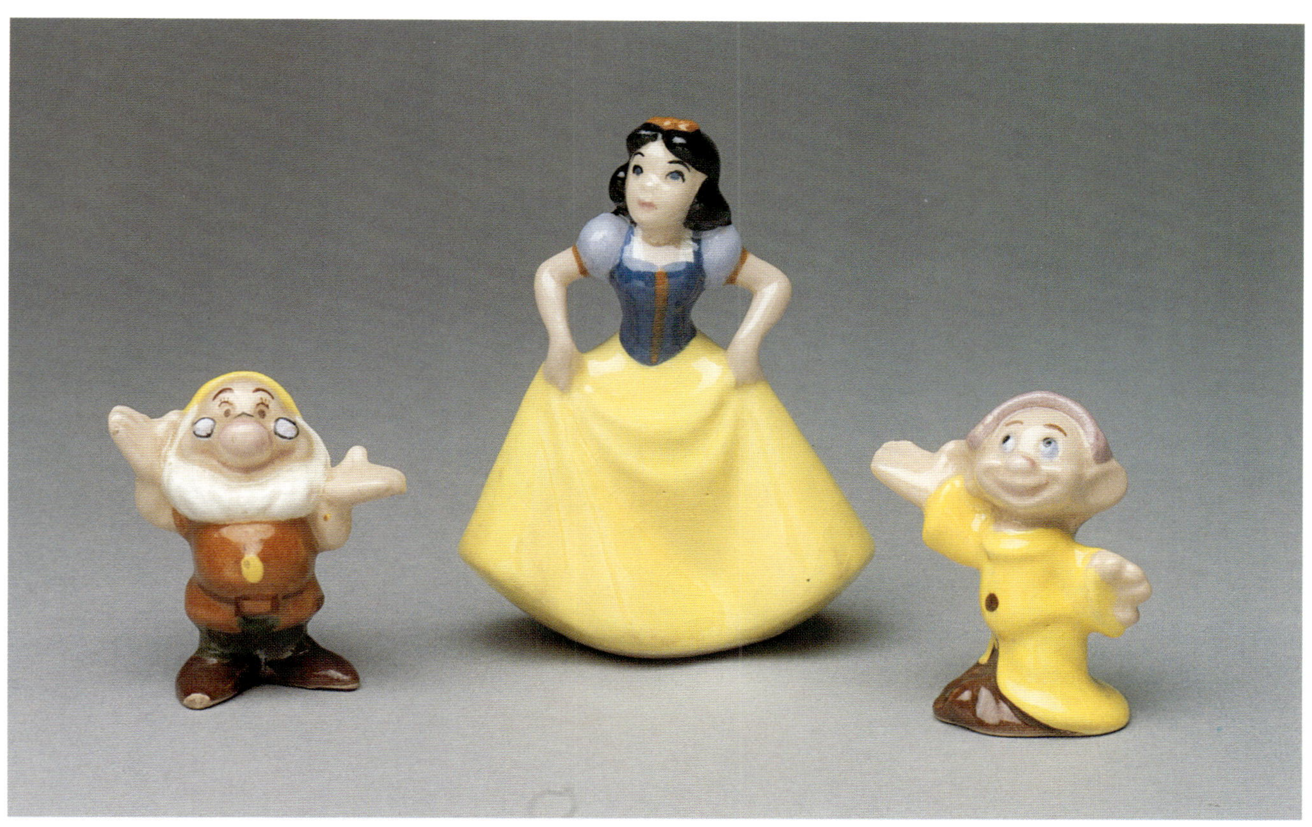

Doc 1 3/4" $100-175, Snow White 3 1/4" $200-275, Dopey 1 3/4" $100-175.

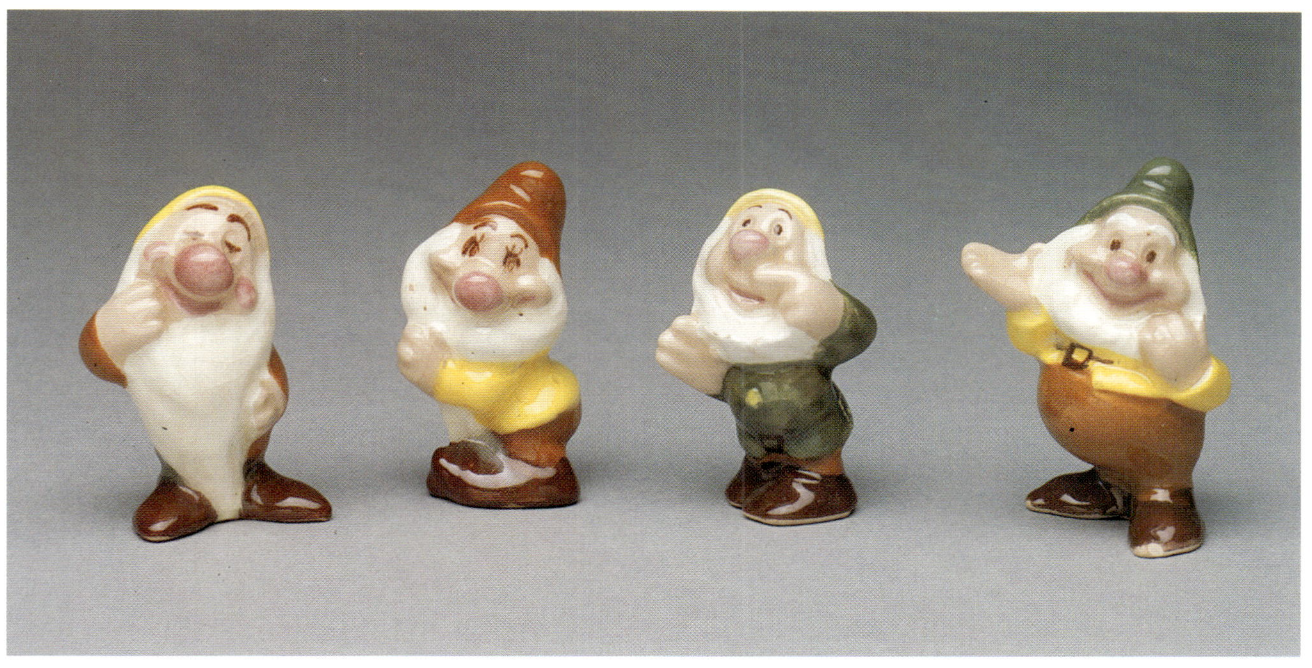

Sleepy, Bashful, Sneezy and Happy 1 3/4" each, $100-175 each. Not pictured, Grumpy $100-175.

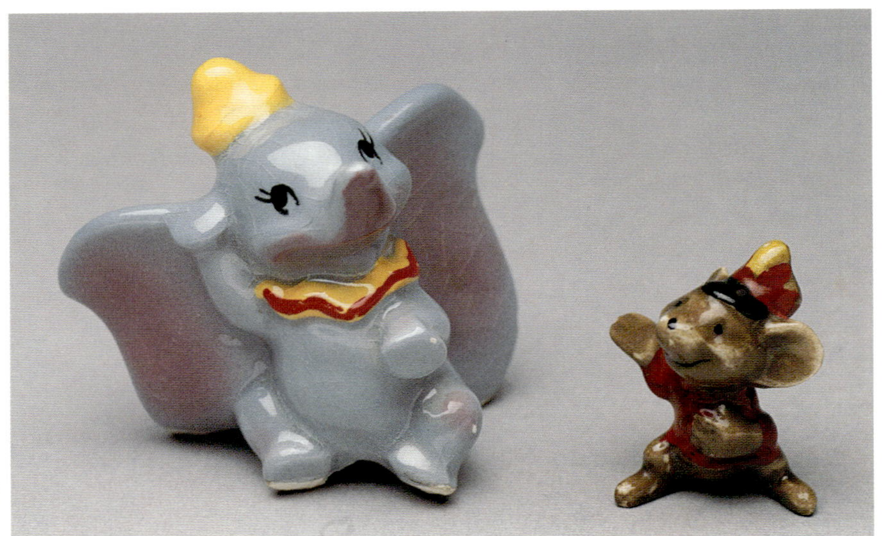

Dumbo 1 3/4" $150-250 and Timothy Mouse 1" $150-200.

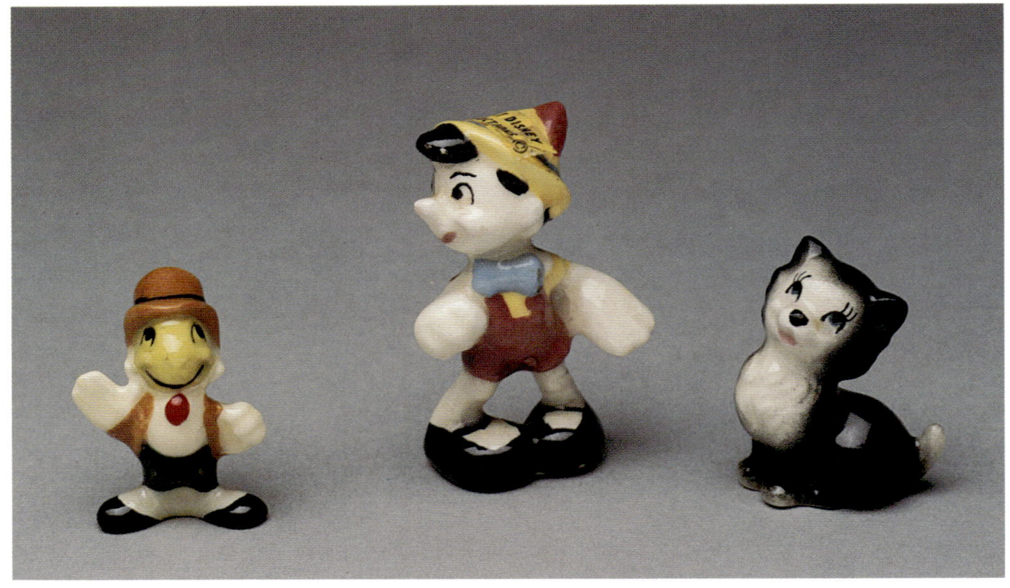

Jiminy Cricket 1 1/4" $225-300, Pinocchio 1 3/4" $175-250, Figaro 1 1/4" $150-200.

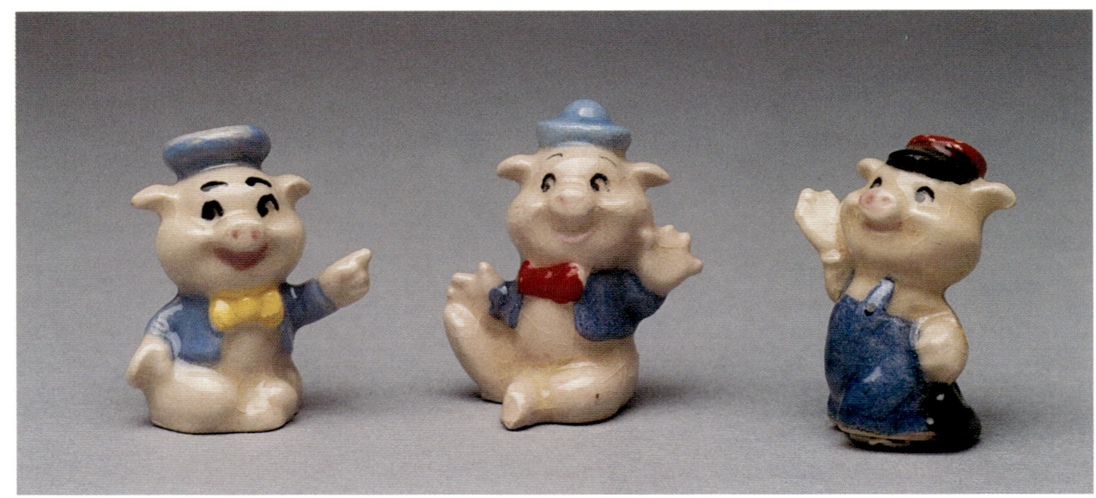

Three Little Pigs 1 1/4" each, $75-100 each.

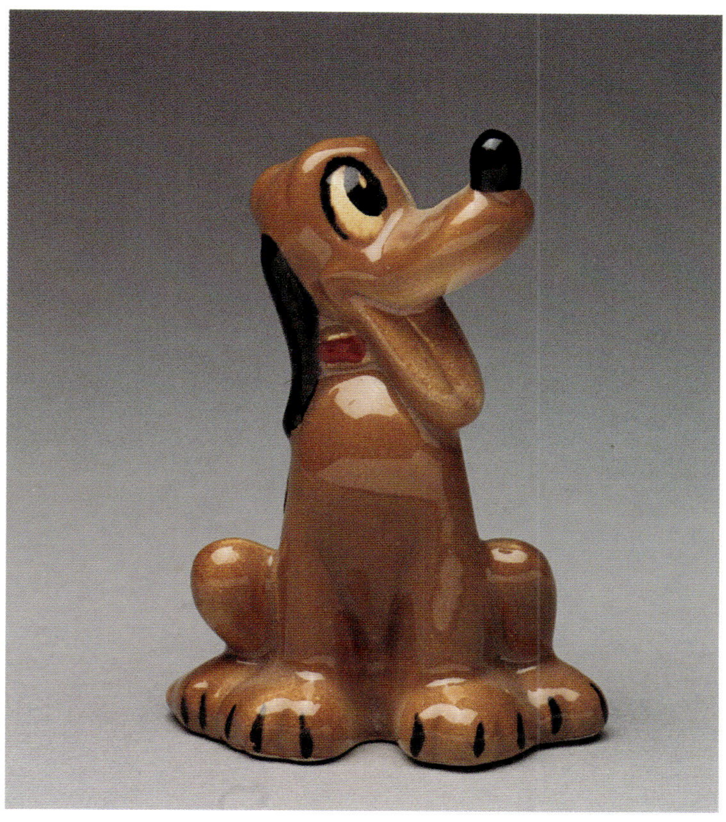

Medium Pluto 3" $100-150.

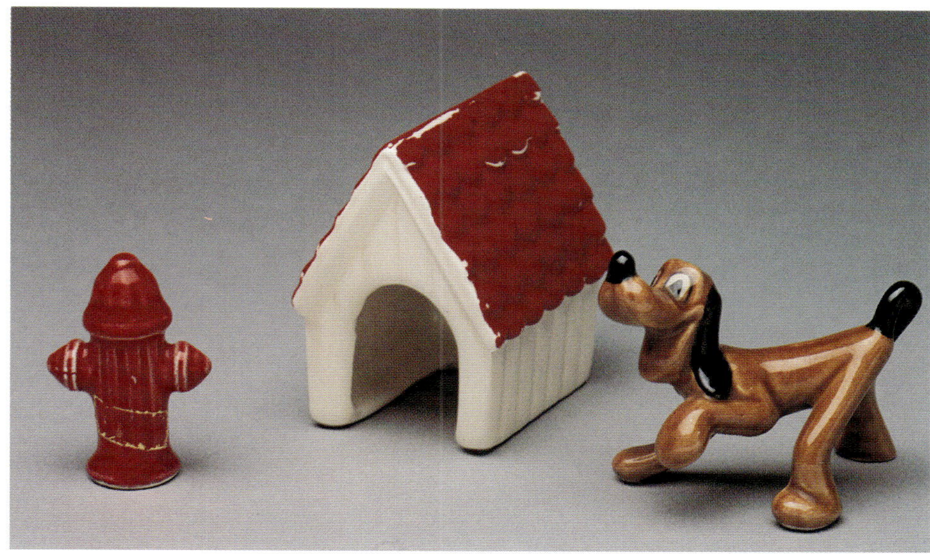

Fire plug 1 3/4" $40-60, Dog House 2 1/4" $50-75, Pluto 1 1/2" $80-150.

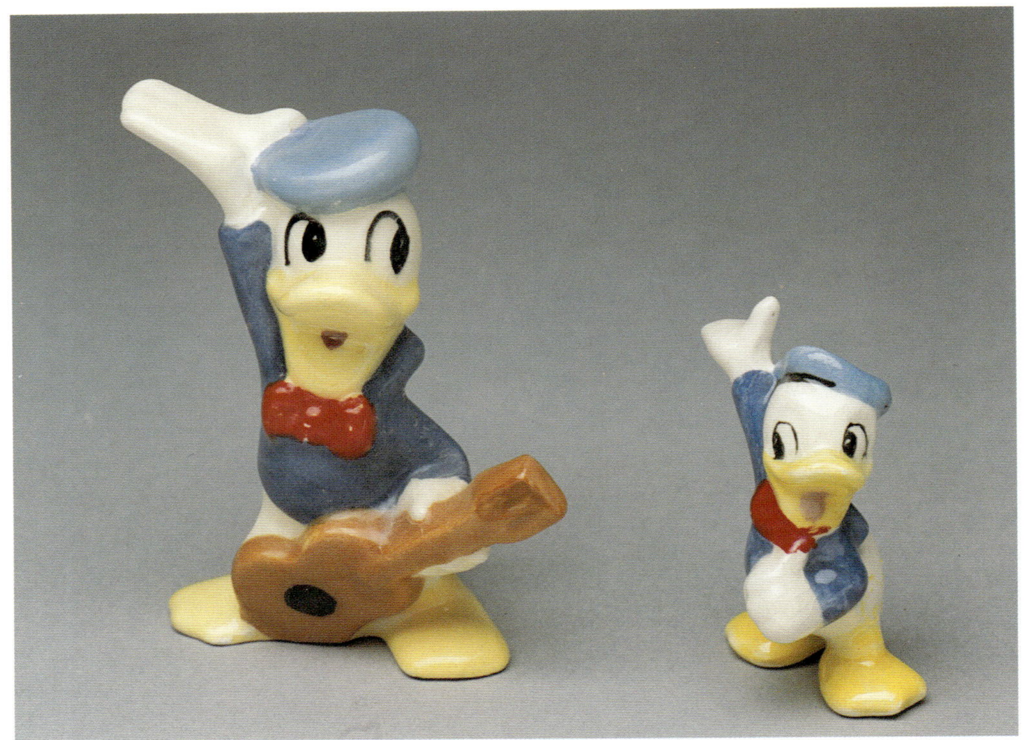

Donald with Guitar 3" $100-150, Donald waving 2" $100-150.

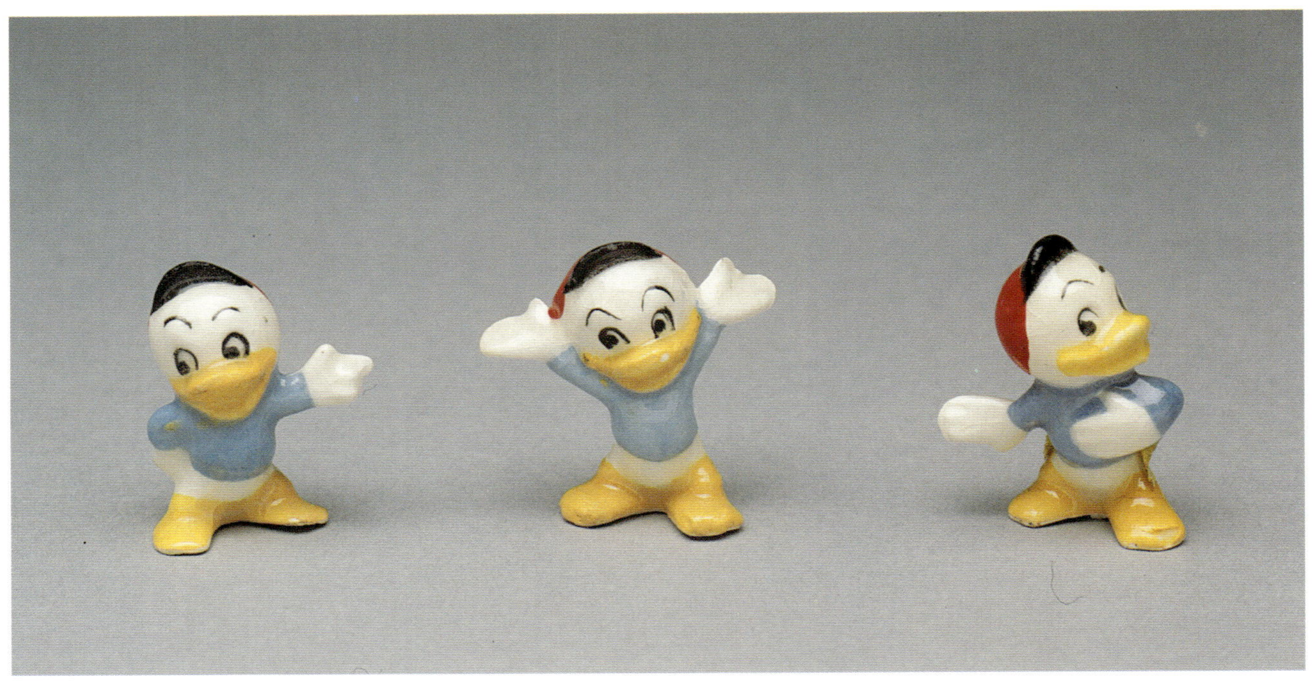

Huey, Dewey and Louie 1 1/4" each, $80-125 each.

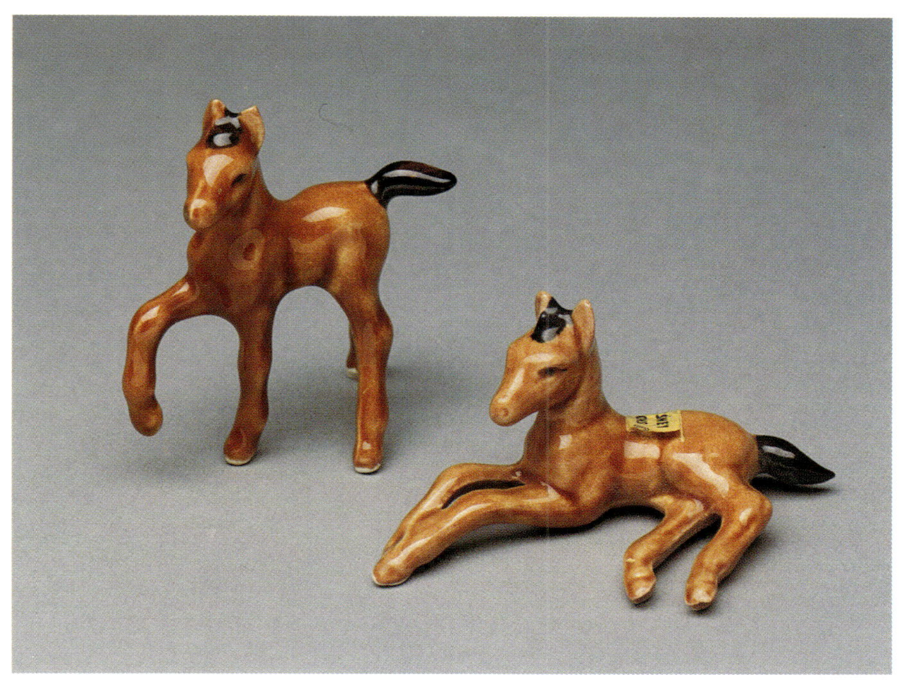

Stormy standing 2", Stormy lying 1 1/4" $50-75 each.

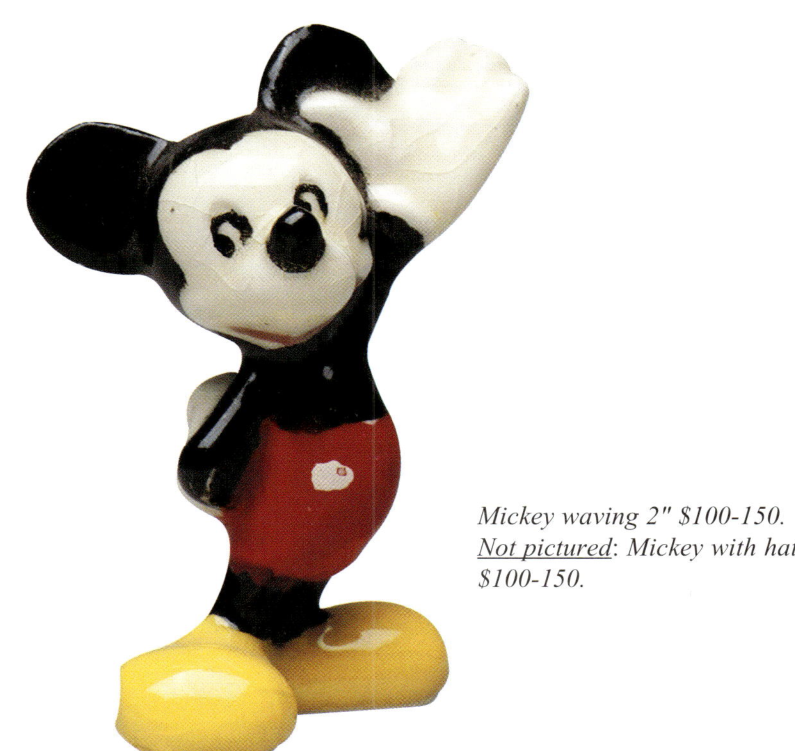

Mickey waving 2" $100-150.
Not pictured: Mickey with hat $100-150.

Hagen-Renaker

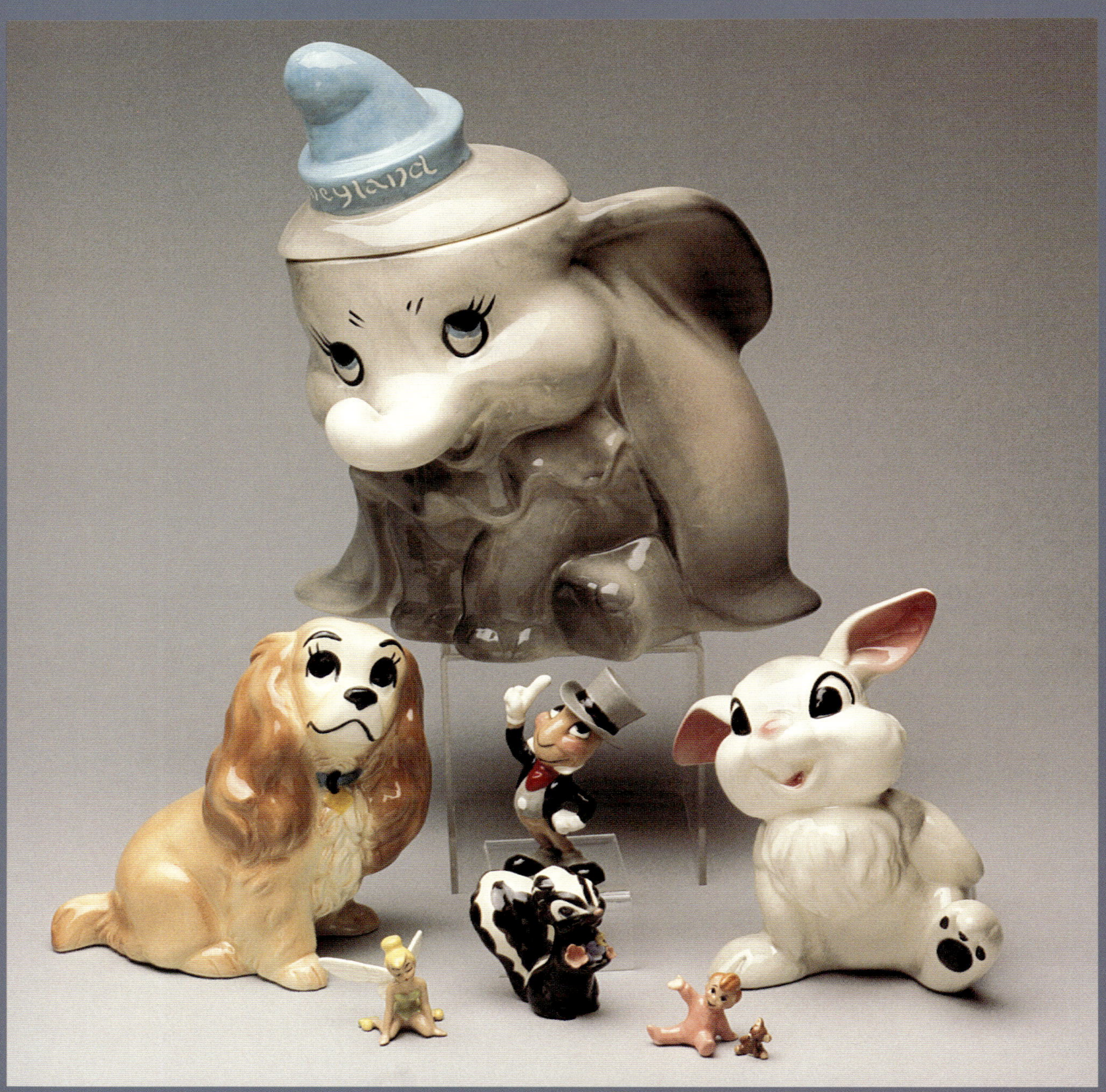

Hagen-Renaker 1955-1961

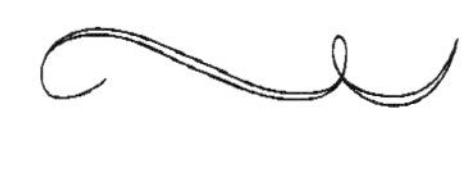

Hagen-Renaker, the company that produces delightful miniature animal ceramics, began its hugely successful operation in Monrovia, California in 1946, founded by the husband and wife team of Maxine and John Renaker and her father Ole Hagen. John Renaker was a local librarian and with the births of his two children, he decided he needed more than the $140 a month salary he was receiving to raise his growing family.

Renaker took a job with Joe Walker of Walker Potteries with the stipulation that he would be taught every aspect of the ceramic business. Renaker learned the art of sculpture, mold making, kilning, and bookkeeping throughout his time at the pottery before striking out on his own. Walker would later team with Renaker on producing a separate line of humorous porcelain miniatures.

The Walker-Renaker division lasted for seven years in the 1950's. The Hagen Renaker company itself began in late 1945 on the idea of producing useful, quality ceramic items for the kitchen table including hand-decorated butter pats, plates and pitchers. It wasn't until a year later that Renaker noticed some of his wife's small hand-formed clay ducks and other water fowl she had made for a Camp Fire event. Renaker began introducing the decorative items to the line.

As local interest spread for the charming diminutive critter creations, the firm began visualizing the possibilities of turning his wife's hobby into part of their ceramics business. By hiring other talented artists and sculptors whose work was exceptionally well adapted in miniatures, Hagen Renaker was to succeed remarkably. Throughout the late 1940's and 50's, Hagen's production output of cute farmland animals, realistic horses, humorous characters, and a dog line became wildly popular sellers. By 1950 the company had found its special market niche and the butter pats, plates and pitchers were gone forever.

Most of the miniatures produced by the company were commonly no more than two inches and the larger figures rarely exceeded six inches in height. The ceramics sold and continue today to sell at popular road-side attractions and souvenir stores across California and in many other states. Visitors and citizens alike could find rows of the ceramics at boutiques and gift shops in the Farmers Market in Los Angeles, Knott's Berry Farm in Buena Park, and in various shops along San Francisco's Fisherman's Wharf. Toy stores, gift shops and local hardware stores were also sales outlets for the diminutive figures.

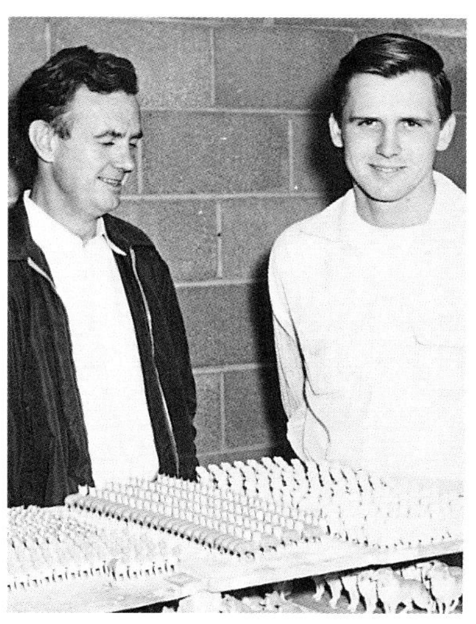

Hagen-Renaker President John Renaker and General Manager Bill Nicely. (Archival photo)

Throughout the years, the company has produced very little in-house advertising for its product as word-of-mouth worked and still works quite well for the firm today. Over the years the ceramics could be found across the United States and today they are exported to many foreign countries including Korea, Australia, England, Germany and France.

Almost every Hagen-Renaker ceramic sold was labeled with a small sticker, glued to a square paper label base or ink stamped under glaze. Most of the Disney banks and cookie jars were not permanently marked and have been found with gold foil labels.On July 25, 1955 Hagen-Renaker signed a one year exclusive license contract with Walt Disney Productions Character licensing division that would be re-newed on a yearly basis until 1961. During this time Hagen-Renaker would be the only American company licenced to produce ceramic sets of Disney's most colorful characters after the Shaw contract expired in December 1955. That same year, Eleanor Welborn Art Products in Seaside, California was licensed for the production of decal and hand decorated ceramic souvenir plates and small trinkets for the new Disneyland park.

Walt Disney himself personally labeled the Hagen-Renaker ceramic representations of his animated characters "the finest three-dimensional reproductions of (the animated) drawings that he ever saw". Walt Disney had always had a fondness for miniatures so it seemed justly appropriate for Hagen-Renaker to produce ceramic likenesses of his beloved characters.

For many years Walt had a tiny train and locomotive tracks running through and around his Holmby Hills home. Often on his extensive world travels, Disney would collect miniatures of animals, dolls, furniture and toys in their native land, displaying the selections in his studio office. He even personally had crafted diminutive appliances such as an iron pot-belly stove for a small cabin scene but his most popular and viewed labor of love was the Disneyland Lilliputian attraction, the Storybook Land Canal boat ride.

Sculptress Martha Armstrong-Hand, Nell Bortells and Helen Farnlund were the artists considered responsible for designing most of the intricately detailed representations of the Disney animated characters. Hand was so proficient in producing three-dimensional replicas that her creations developed the personalities they represented. Hand and the other sculptors would be sent animation drawings from the artists at the studio. The art would be used as references while sculpting in modeling clay and Hand became very adept at achieving the individual character's personality, expressions and nuances in such extreme detail. The Sleeping Beauty set is of special note in that the tiny detail right down to the rings on the characters fingers are visible. According to the Renakers, the ceramics with human attributes were the hardest to create in that scale and proportion from facial expression to body size had to be accurate to achieve life-like qualities. Cartoon-like animals on the other hand had more leeway in their execution in that they didn't always have to anatomically correct.

Hagen-Renaker was required to send its product in the development stages to the artists and consumer products people at Disney for approval. The artists would make suggestions as to color of paint used on a figure or the re-sculpting of a particular subject to get its appearance perfectly matched to the film version.

The first Disney set sold was from the concurrent 1955 CinemaScope film *Lady and the Tramp*. These first canine figures featured most of the cast including Lady, Tramp, Jock, Trusty, Dachsie, Pedro, the Siamese cats, Si & Am and the pups. The individual ceramics were souvenirs sold at the newly opened Disneyland Park in Anaheim and were also displayed as a promotion for the film at the May Company department stores in Southern California. The petite, intricate creations could be found on Main Street in the large turn-of-the-century Emporium of OrangeCounty and in the china shop, and at the Art Corner in Tomorrowland among other souvenir locales. So popular was the Lady set that two more figures, Peg and Bull were added in 1957.

The company continued producing the most popular sellers and added new sets every year until 1960. Also these ceramics were sold in retail outlets outside the park beginning in 1956 through a sales representative firm, George Good of Los Angeles. In 1956 characters from Alice in Wonderland, Bambi, Cinderella, Dumbo, and bandleader Mickey, Goofy, Donald, Scrooge, Pluto,Chip & Dale, and Donald's three nephews were introduced. In 1957 some Peter Pan and Fantasia figures were added. 1958 saw Snow White and her Seven Dwarfs arrive and in 1959 the beautiful Sleeping Beauty set completed the ceramic line.

A "Shaggy Dog" figure also known in the standard HR Designers Workshop pedigree line as Mops, an English Sheep dog in color variant was added at this time. It was not uncommon for a child growing up in the 1950's to collect these tiny but beautifully decorated and detailed ceramics along with the fables accompanying story and comic books as the tiny ceramics sold initially for the reasonable price of about a dollar each.

The ceramics were produced with the best possible materials and quality control was evident throughout the entire production process. More than a dozen steps were involved in the production of the ceramics from the original character inspiration to clay sculpture to mold making, slip casting, firing, finishing, decorating, glazing and final firing to labeling and packaging. Once the sculptor finished the original sculpt, it was approved by the head artist at Hagen-Renaker and a two piece plaster mold was made.In the production process, the small slip cast clay figures fresh from their molds would be carefully cleaned of mold lines and any imperfections and after air drying, sent through the kiln for their first firing. Because of the size of the figures, many could be sent through the kiln at one time. However, their small size and delicate nature contributed heavily to their breakage once in a new owner's home.

Some of the Disney ceramics required special clay oxide tinting and some of the Sleeping Beauty pieces required round bases to keep the figures vertical. Many exhibit an added amount of mixed media in their production. Cinderella's broom handle, Mickey's baton and Maleficent's staff with the perched Diablo the raven were metal dowels applied to the figure before its first firing while it was still moist. Peter Pan's Nana dog had a hand-applied clay nursemaid's bonnet while Cinderella's Gus and Jaq each have pearl beads on their tails and hands and Uncle Scrooge's cane is attached to a tiny printed paper dollar bill. The bright paints employed in the production were closely matched but not precise to animated character's original coloring with few exceptions.

One decorator recalled the amount of fine painting detail on each figure. "You had to be very careful painting for one wrong stroke of the brush and you would have to start all over again. But you got pretty good fast". Once sprayed with silica glaze, they would receive the second firing. If gold or silver decoration were applied over-glaze, a third firing was necessary. Then each piece was marked with a small round gold sticker or their base glued to a card and carefully packed and sent to their retail destination.

In the mid 1950's a separate division devoted to larger ceramics was created entitled Designers Workshop. This department created larger figures, cookie jars and banks generally six inches or larger. Sculptress Helen Farnlund was one of the artists responsible for the creation of this line. Artist Don Winton designed all of the 30 plus Designers Workshop Disney ceramics starting in 1956 (not all of the sculptures went into full production). Figures included Bambi, Jiminy Cricket, Figaro, Dumbo, and Snow White. Cookie jars included Dumbo, Figaro, Thumper and Practical Pig. Banks were representations of Thumper, Dumbo, Figaro, and Lady.

Winton had started the Twin Winton ceramics studio with his brothers Ross and Bruce in 1936 in Pasadena, producing slip cast figures of humorous cartoon inspired forest creatures. By the 1950's Winton worked on a freelance basis for several pottery concerns. In his work for Hagen-Renaker, Winton received model sheets from the Disney Studio on how the finished figures were to appear.

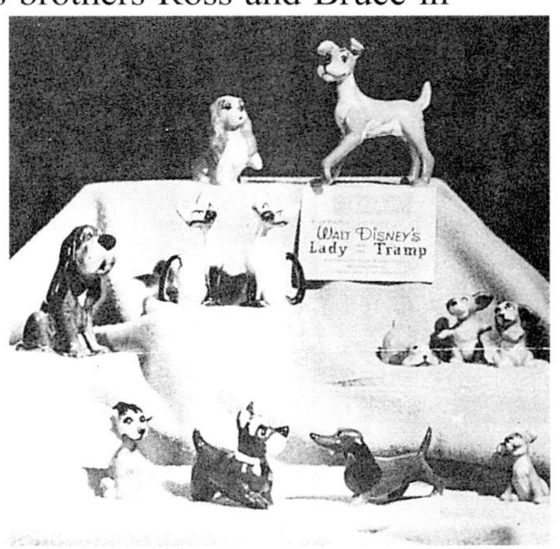

A set of Lady and the Tramp figurines were given as "Mousketreasure"on the February 3, 1956 Talent Roundup segment of the Mickey Mouse Club.

Don remembers his most complex piece for the company was the 6" detailed Snow White. Winton later sculpted many non-ceramic pieces for Disney including Dell Publishing Squeeze Toys and a popular late 1970's icon, the first Mickey Mouse telephone. In May of 1960, the company produced 100 miniature chambers pots at a cost of

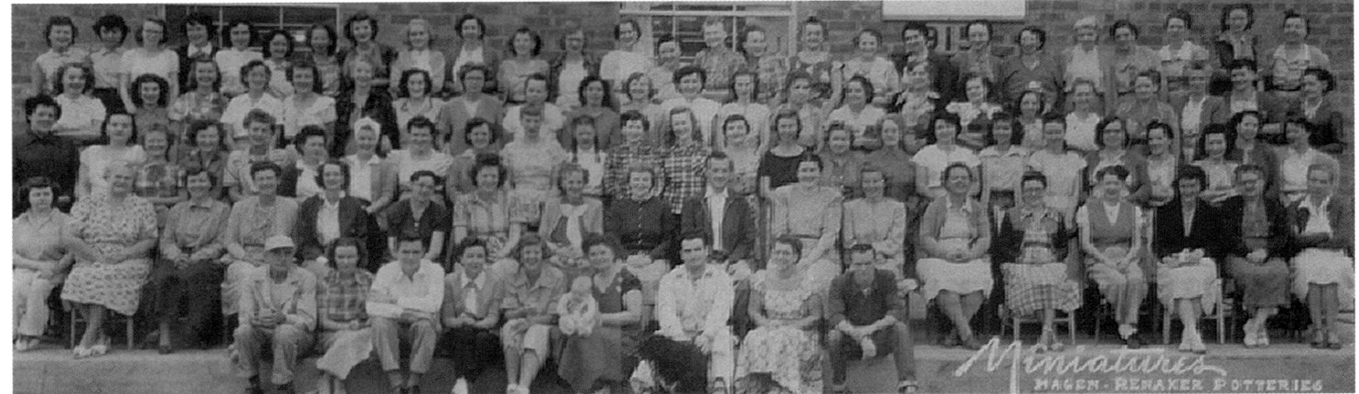

1950's Hagen-Renaker employee group photo at Monrovia plant. John and Maxine Renaker pictured 2nd. row center. Also pictured designer Nell Bartells (lst. row, 5th. from left) Bill Nicely (1st. row, 3rd. from left) and Ole Hagen (lst. row, far left).

$2.50 each. These potties, similar to the ones produced by Shaw ten years earlier, were personally given by Walt Disney as baby gifts to members of his staff and were never made available to the retail trade.

In 1961 the Hagen Renaker company finished its last Disney ceramics on the contract and began selling off the remainder of the figures through Disneyland until the mid 1960's. Hagen went on to build a larger plant in Monrovia, then in 1966 moved to San Dimas. In 1980 the company purchased the Freeman McFarlin plant in San Marcos, California.

In 1984 Hagen-Renaker sold a set of Fantasia figures designed by Disney artist Russell Schroeder. Sold only at shops in Disneyland and Walt Disney World Resort, these ceramics, though miniature, were larger than the Fantasia set produced in the 1950's. Sorcerer Mickey, bucket broom, Bacchus, baby Pegasus decorated in three different colors, tiny mushrooms, and an ostrich completed the set. In company correspondence, it was discovered that a Sorcerer Mickey was discussed as a possible production piece in the line as early as 1955. Other characters and an additional Country Bear Jamboree set were proposed in model form but never put into production.

Today Hagen-Renaker still operates out of its San Dimas plant, one of the last of California's "Golden Era" potters to continue its profitable longevity. Although the Disney designs are no longer produced, some of the molds made for their initial production are still used in ceramics with variant decoration such as some of the dog designs like (Lady), Mamma Cocker. Today there are over 150 people on staff at the facility producing thirty to forty new designs each year. Along with the past favorites, the pottery produces and sells close to 4 million pieces each year. The company's long history of outstanding design is still showcased by the many individually skilled designers with its "Specialties" line of Ceramics featuring humorous and detailed animal groupings. All the company's product of miniature animals and humorous characters produced today are of the same dedicated craftsmanship and quality as the ones produced some fifty years ago.

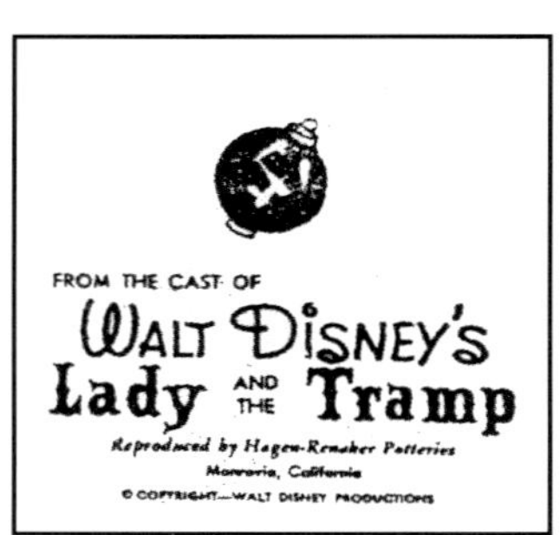

Paper Base

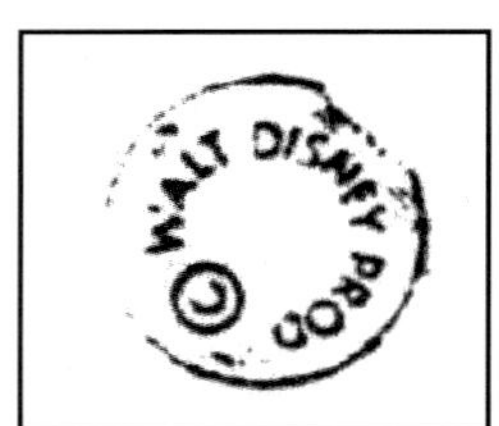

Circular gold foil label

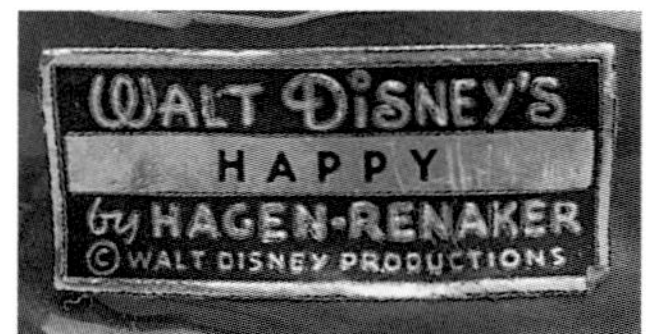

Gold foil label (Designers Workshop)

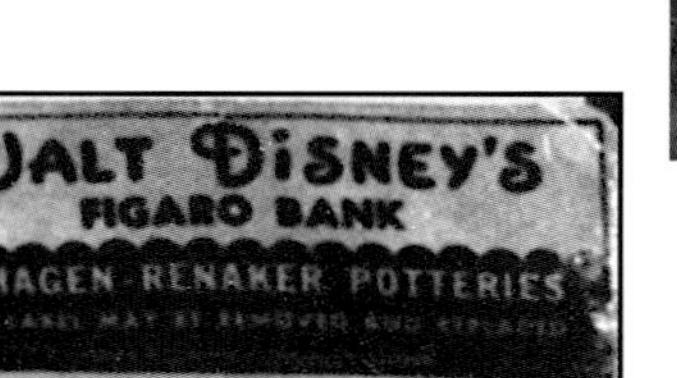

Bank paper label
Seals bank hole on underneath

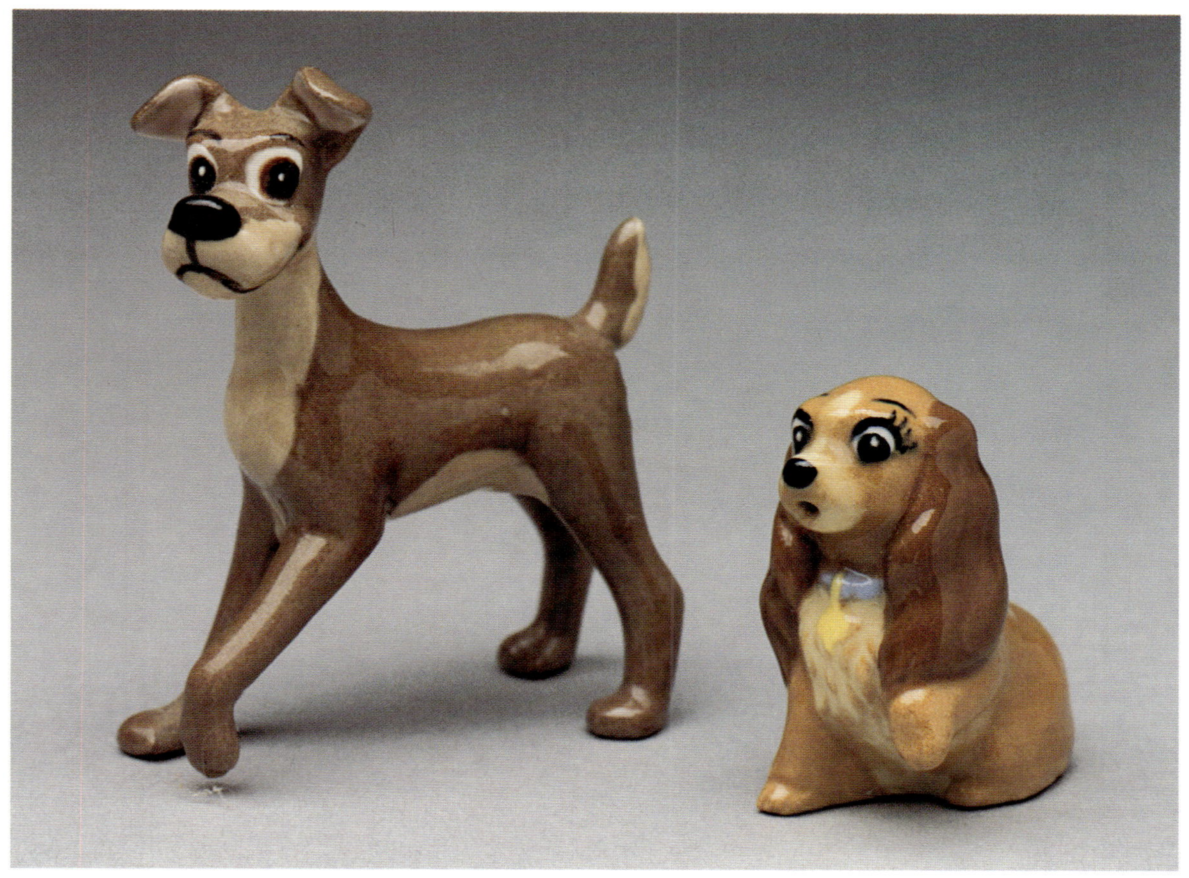

Tramp 2 1/4" $125-250, Lady 1 1/2" $40-80.

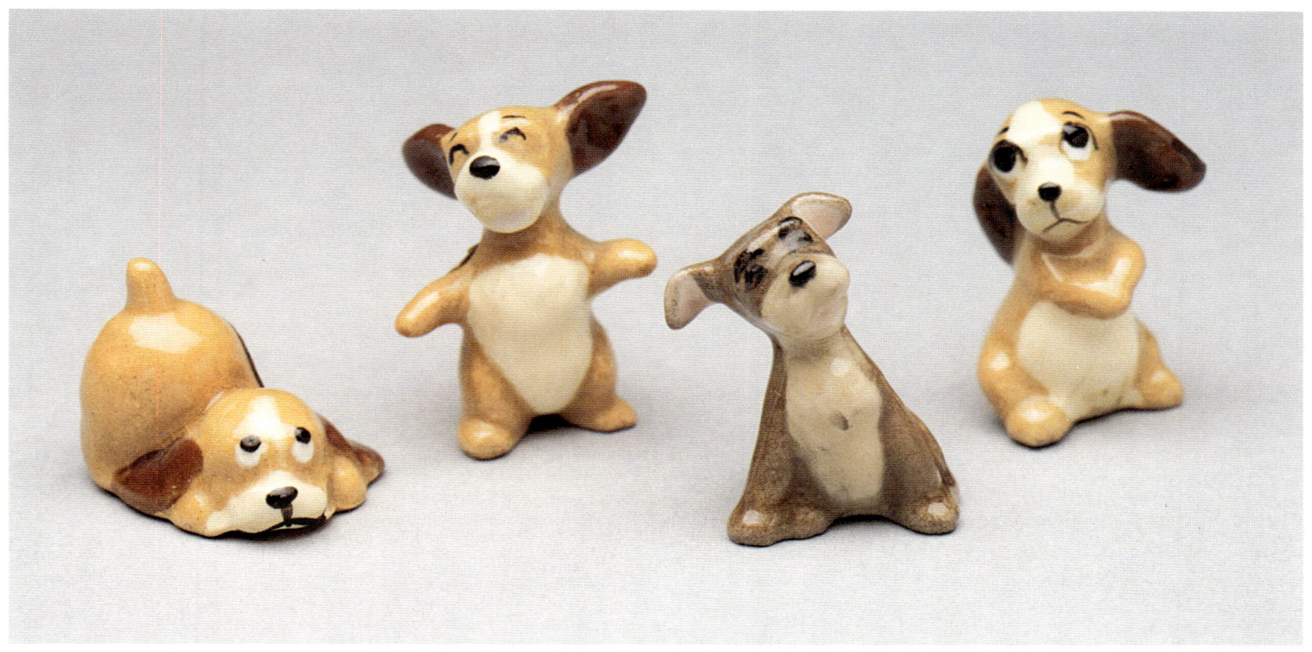

Fluffy 3/4", Scooter 1" , Scamp 1" or Ruffles 1" $50-95 each.

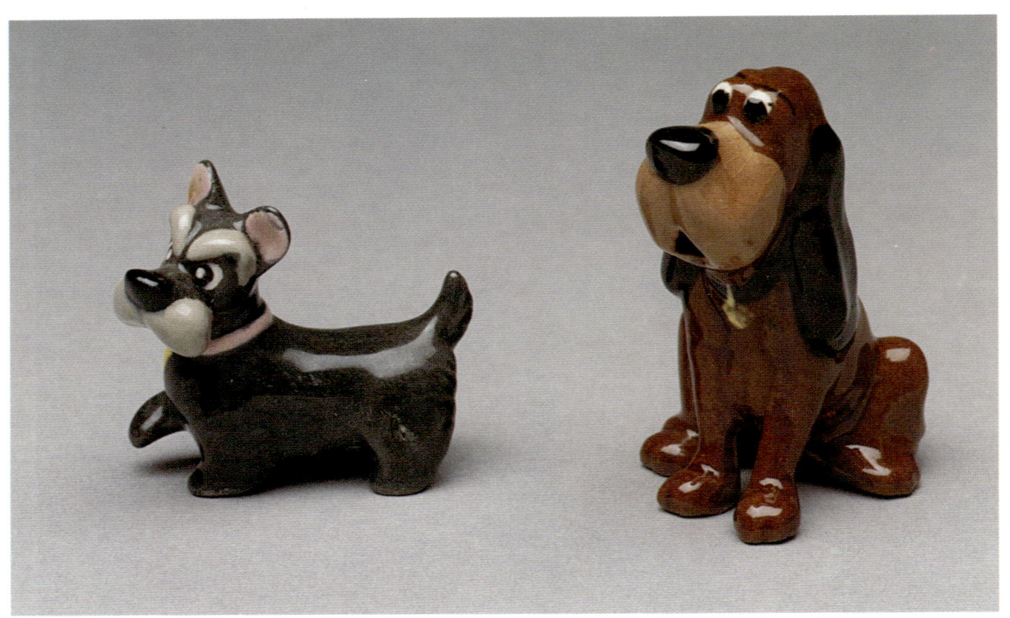

Jock 1 1/2" and Trusty 2" $65-125 each.

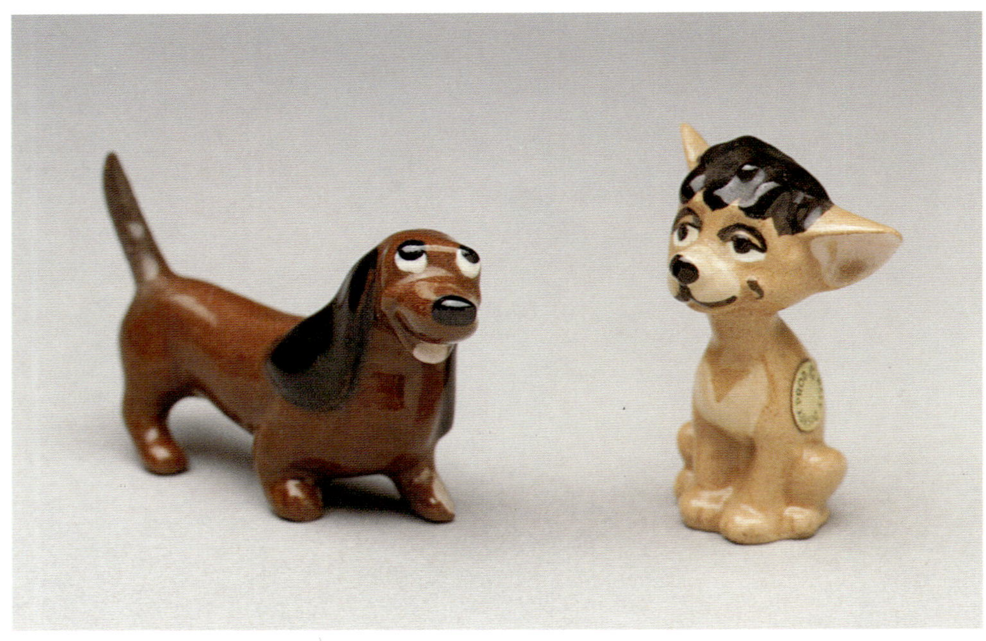

Dachsie 1 1/4" $90-180, Pedro 1 1/4" 75-150

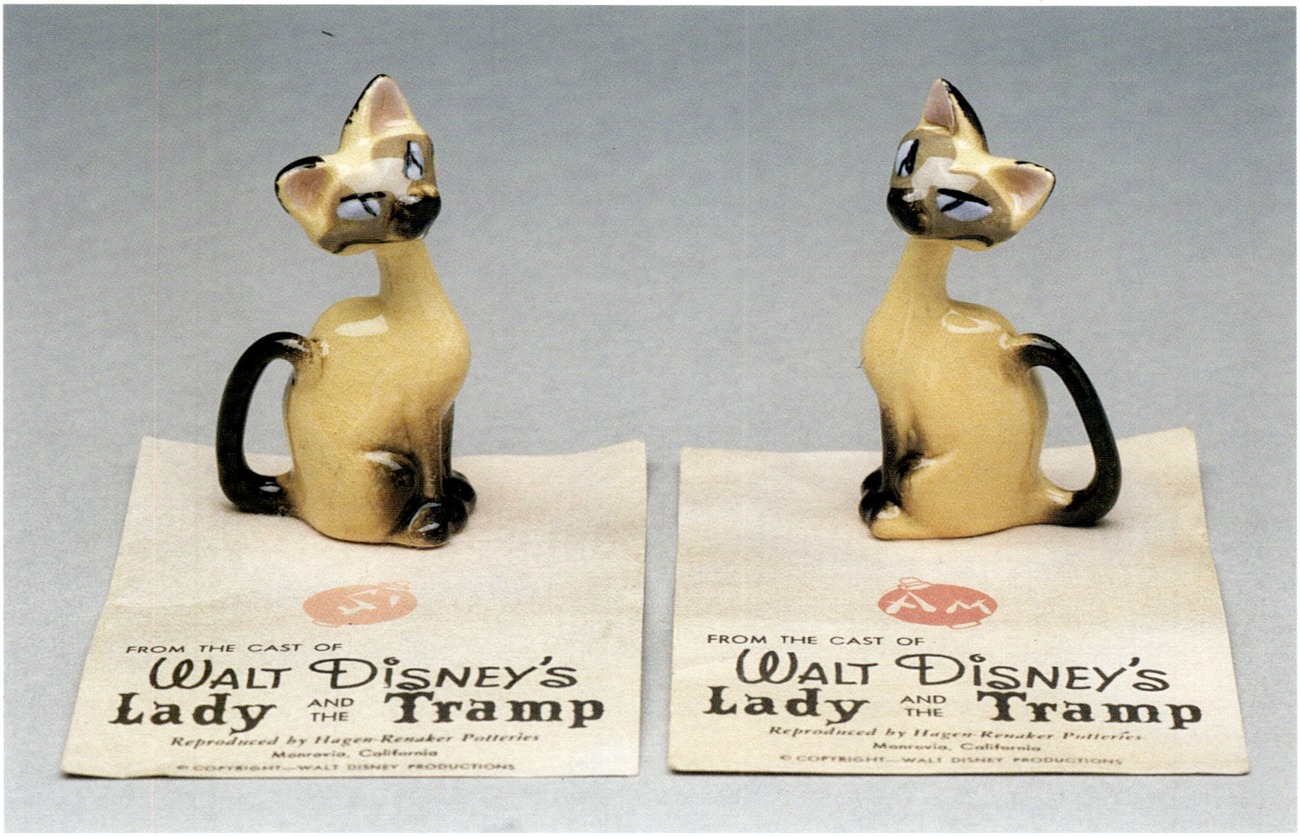

Si and Am 1 3/4" each. on original cards. *$95-175 each.*

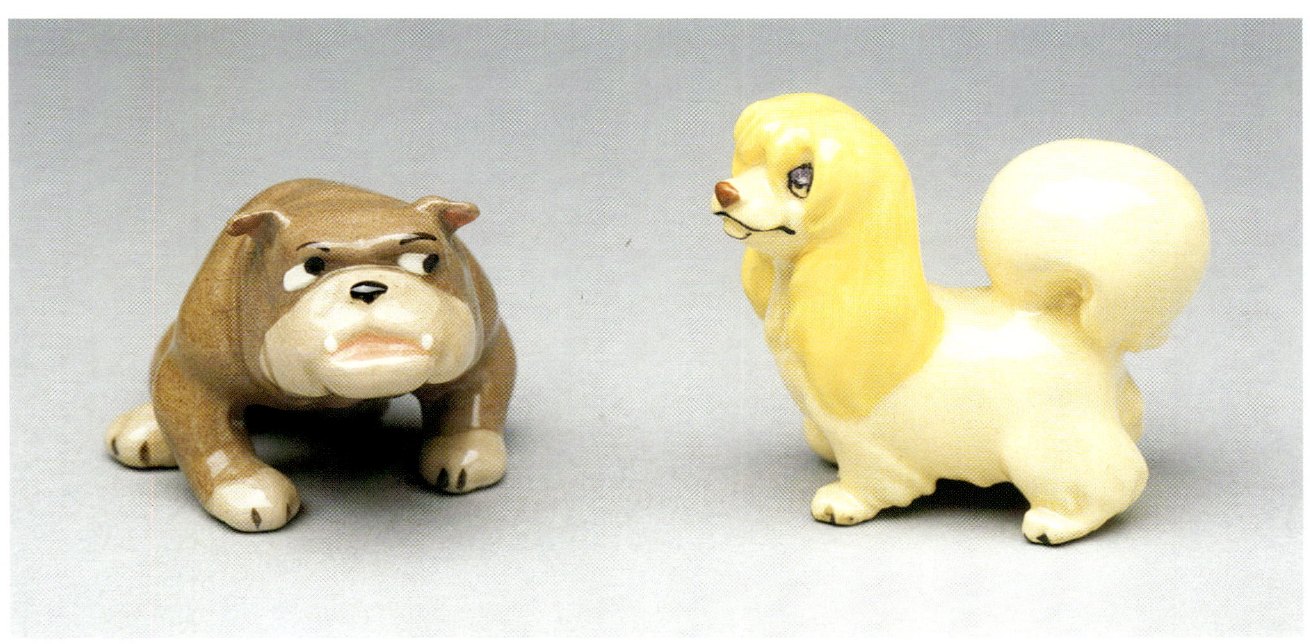

Bull 1 1/4" $100-190, Peg 1 1/2" $125-200.

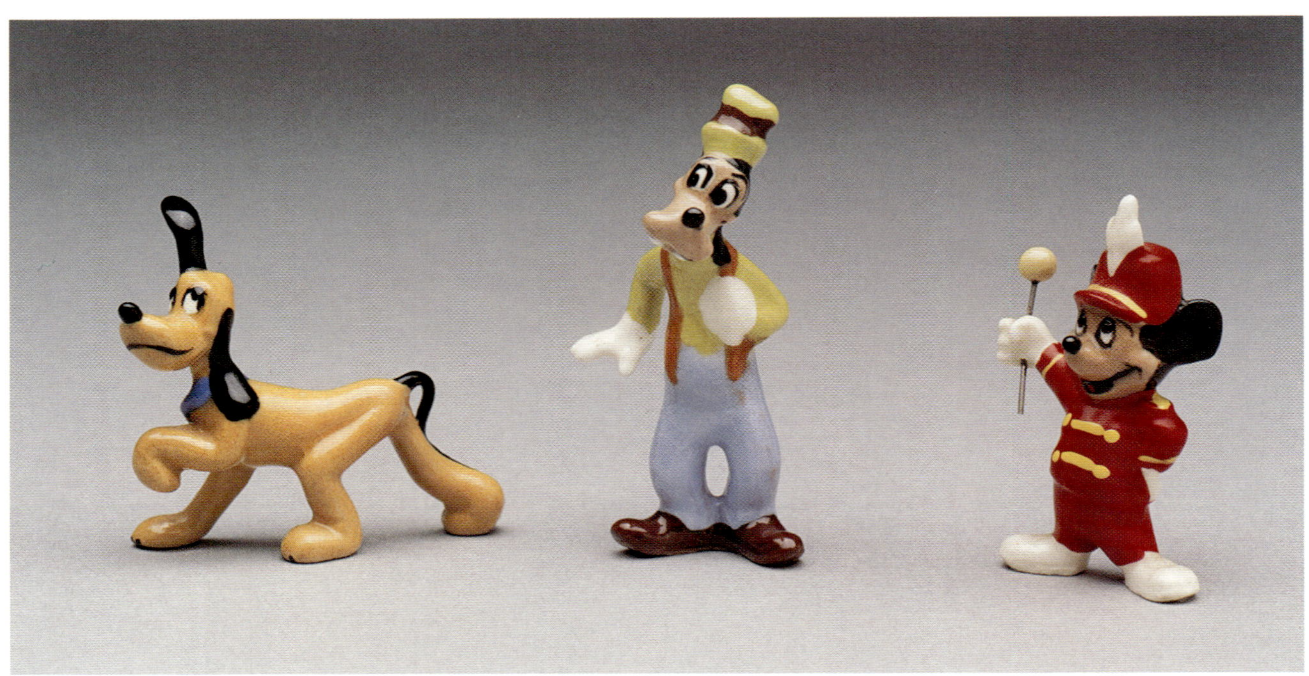

Pluto 1 1/2" $125-200, Goofy 2" $150-250, Bandleader Mickey 1 1/2" $150-250.

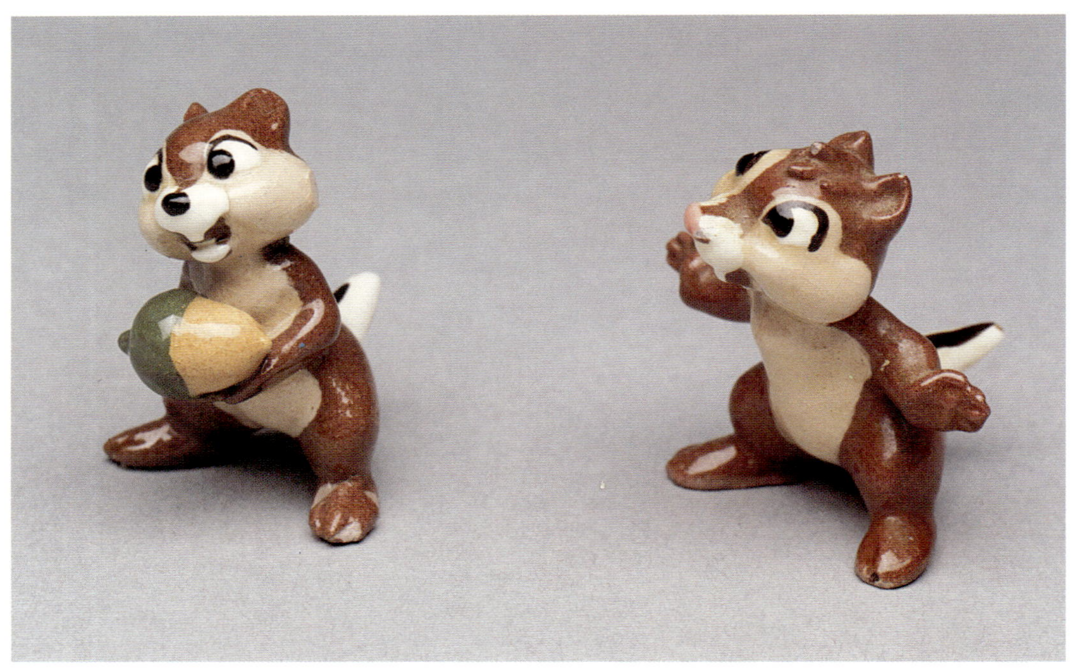

Chip 1 1/4" and Dale 1 1/4" $100-175 each.

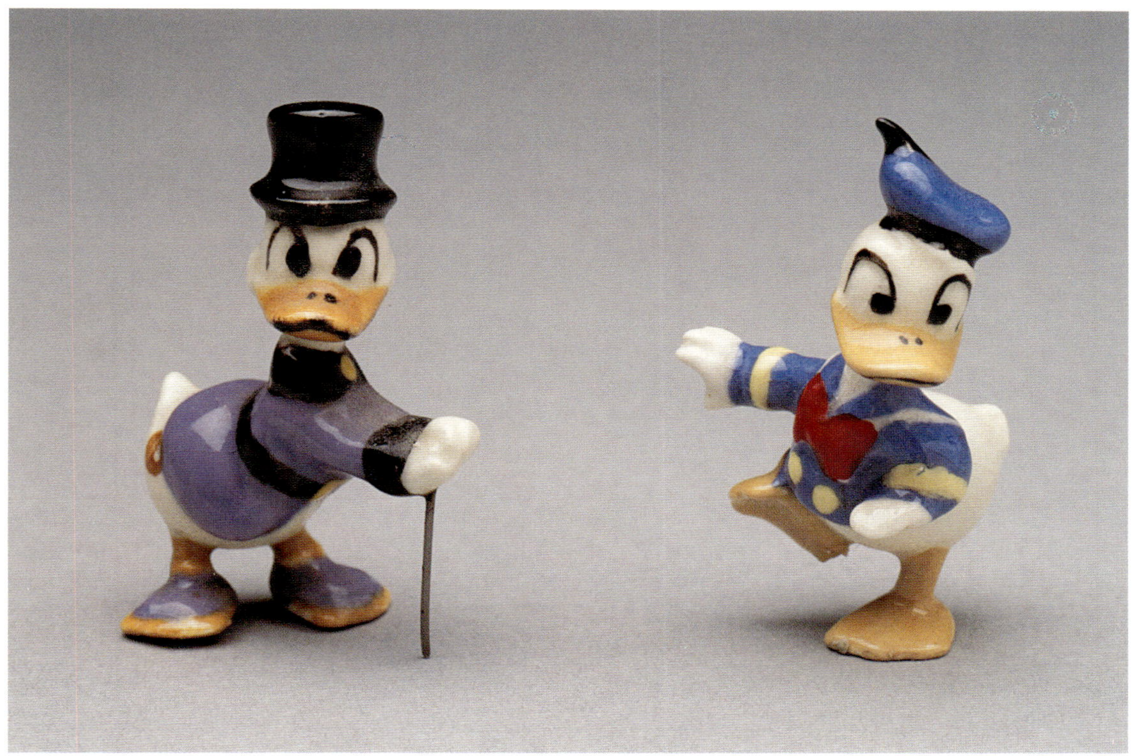

*Uncle Scrooge 1 1/2"*missing dollar *$175-300, Donald Duck 1 1/2" $150-250.*

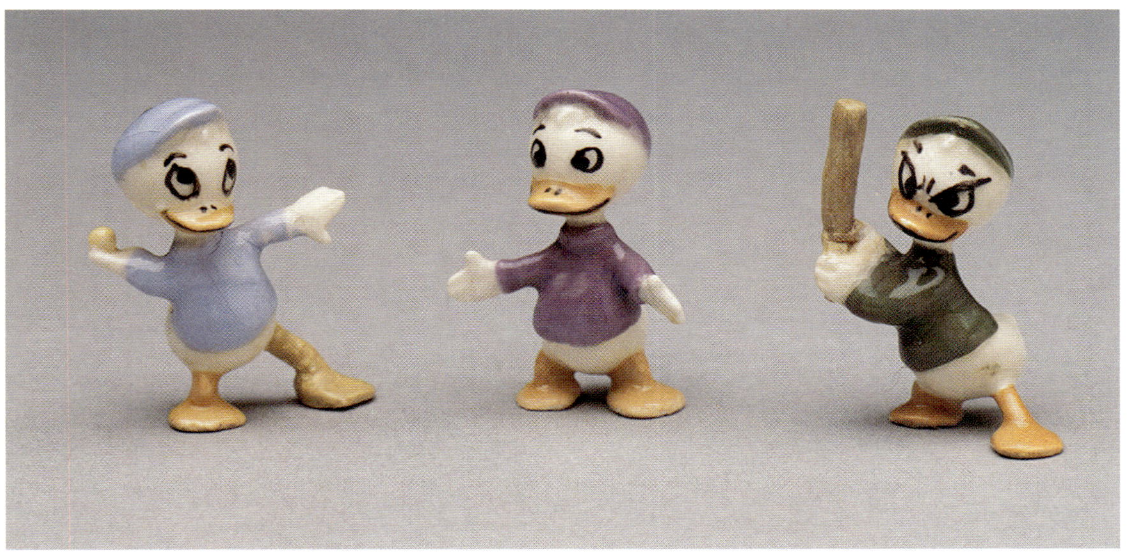

Huey Dewey and Louie 1" each, $80-150 each.

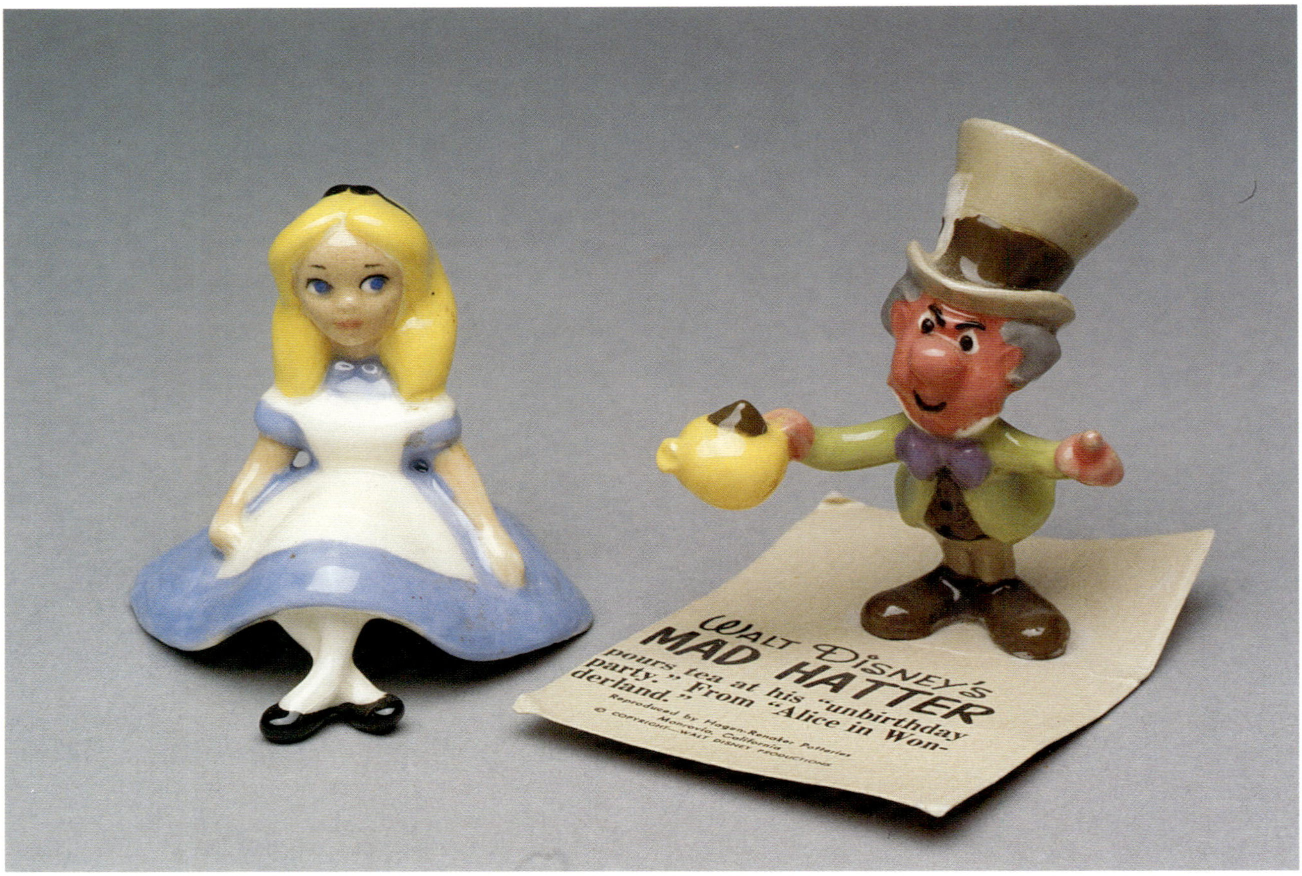

Alice 2" $200-400, Mad Hatter 2 1/2" $300-450
Not pictured: Caterpillar $500+ and March Hare $350-450

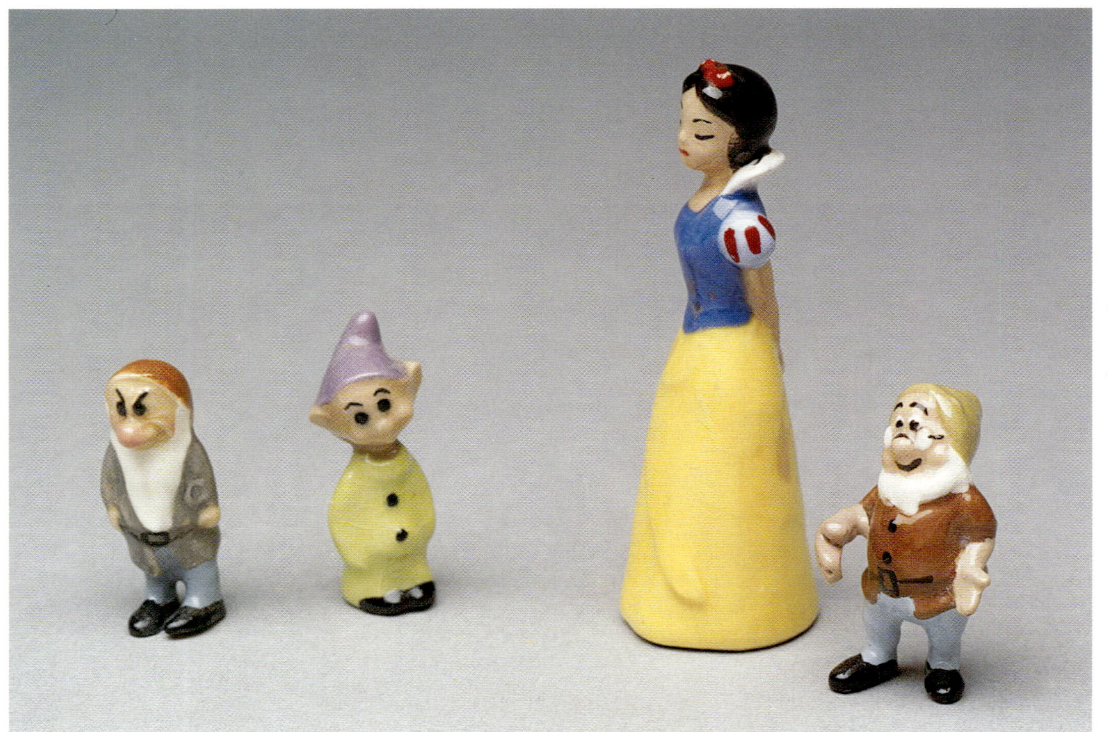

Grumpy 1", Dopey 1", Snow White 2 1/4" $150-225, Doc 1"

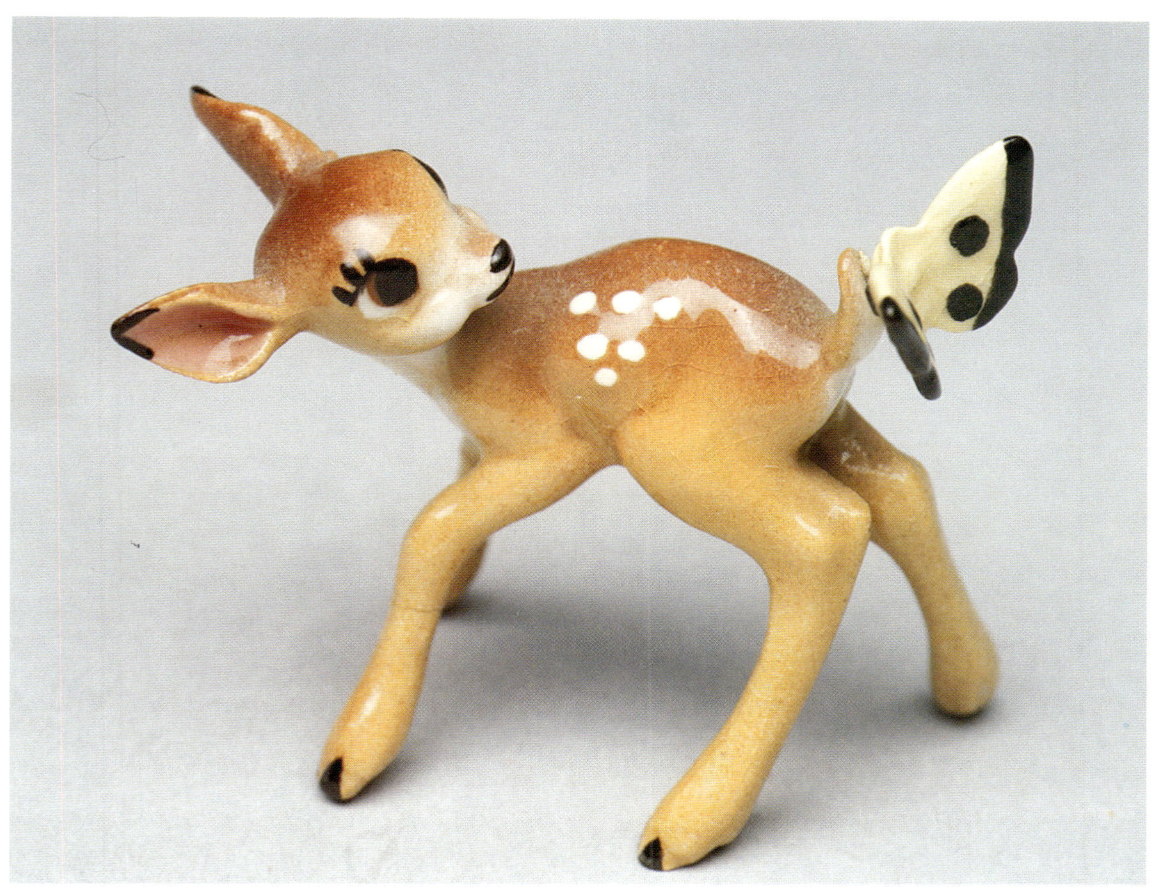

Bambi with Butterfly on tail 1 1/2" $200-300. Not pictured Faline and Bambi without butterfly $150-250 each.

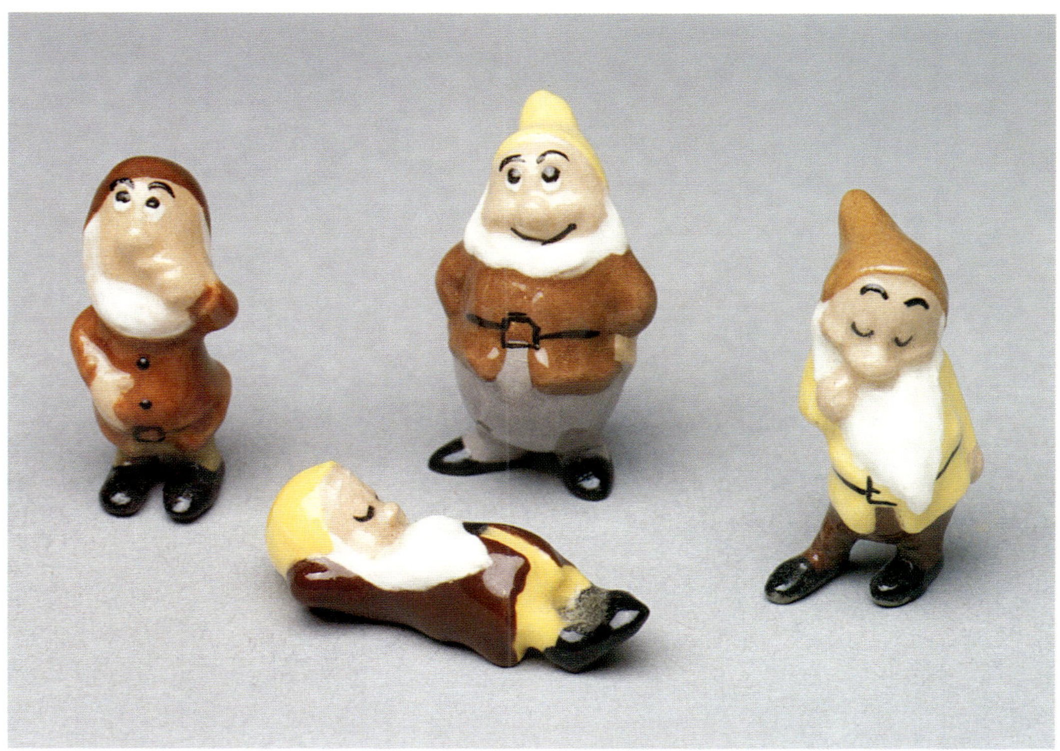

Sneezy 1", Sleepy 1/4", Happy 1" and Bashful 1". All Dwarfs $80-125 each

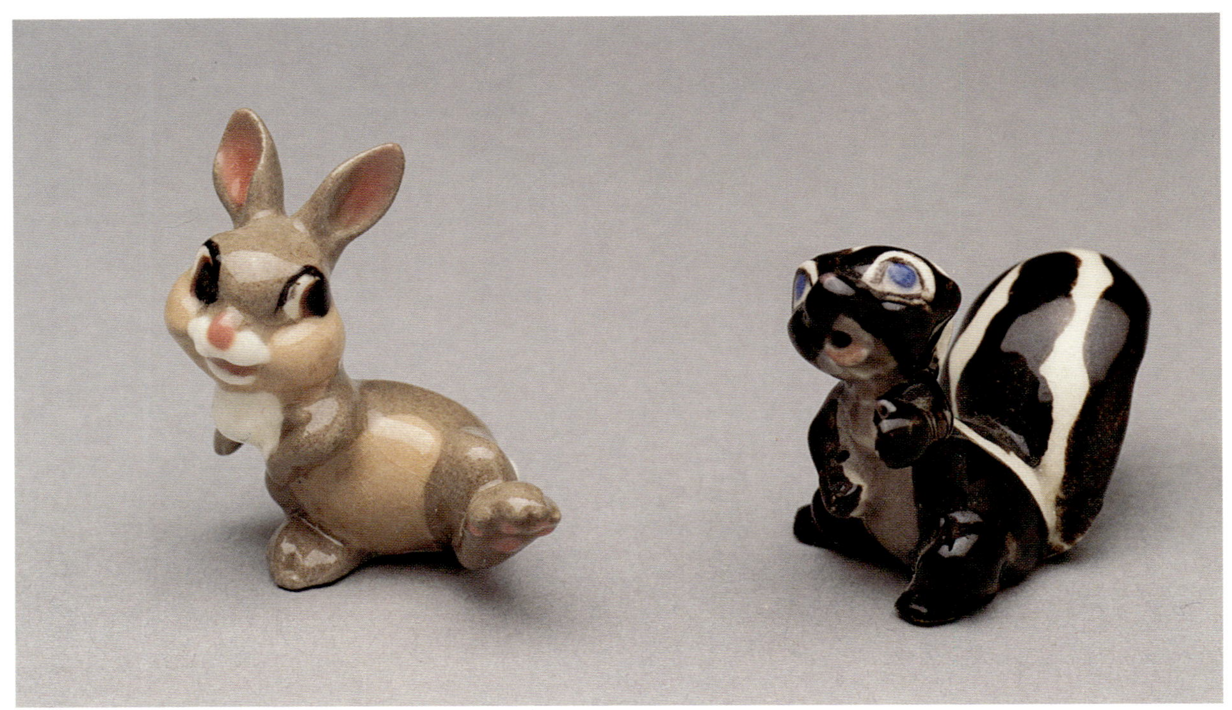

Thumper 1 1/4" and Flower 1" $85-125 each Flower originally sold holding a flower

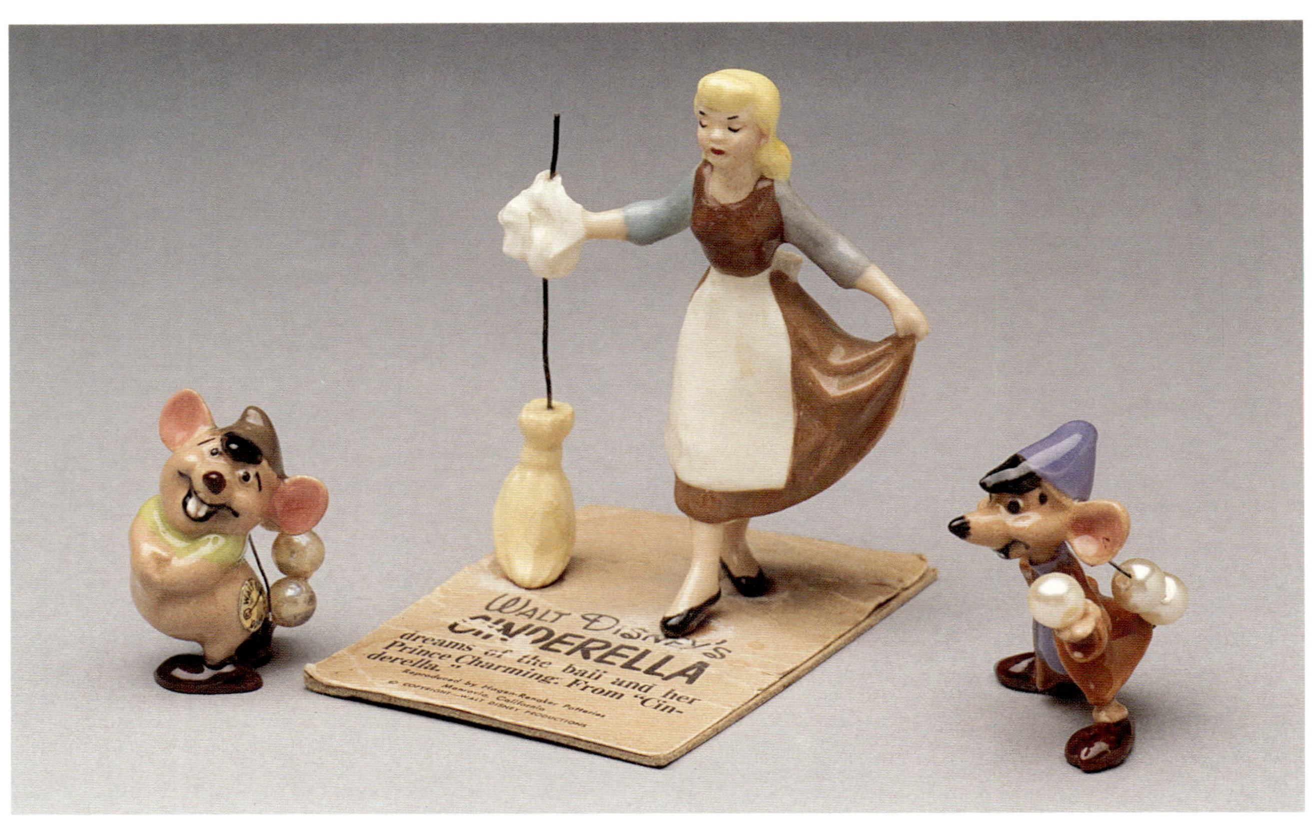

Gus 1 1/4" $250-450, Cinderella 2 1/2" $375-500, Jaq 1 1/4" $250-450.

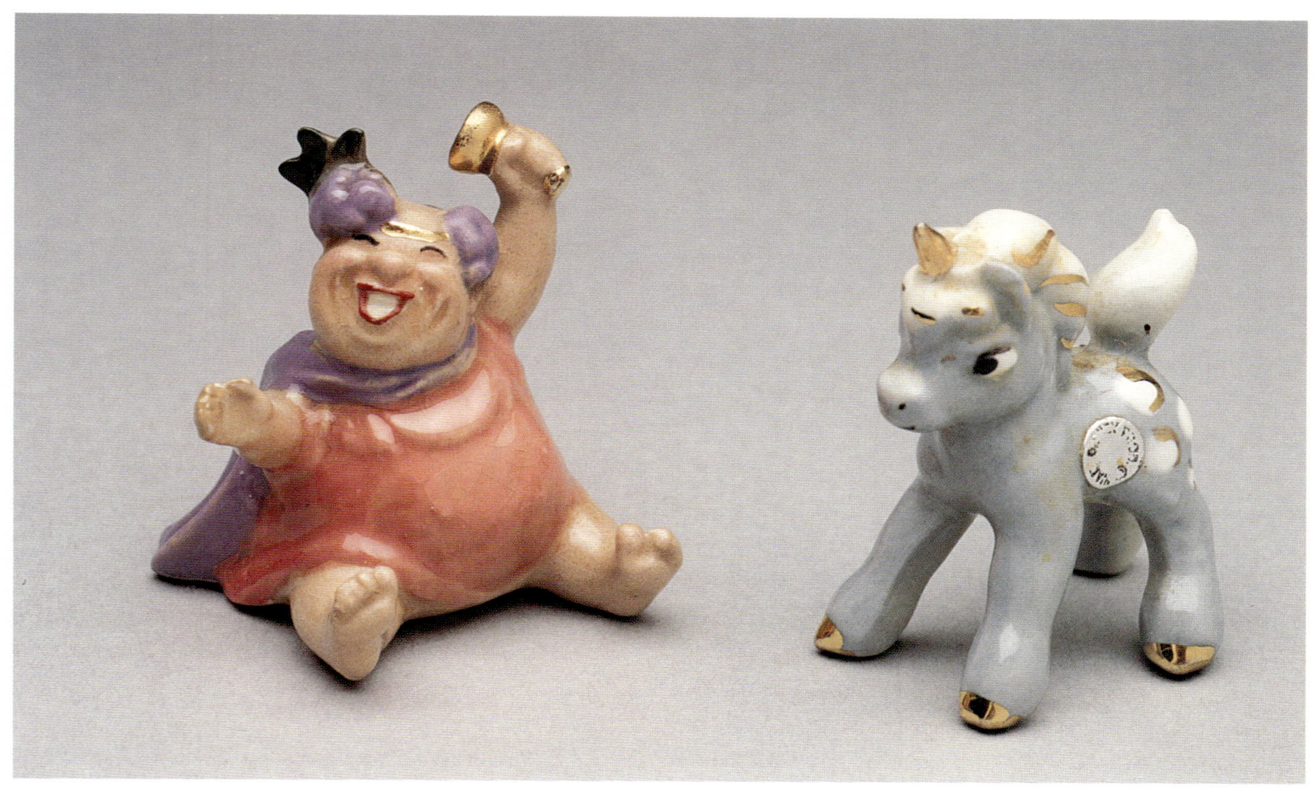

Bacchus 1 3/4" $175-350, Baby Unicorn 1 3/4" $125-250. Not Pictured Unicorn $150-275 or Baby Pegasus

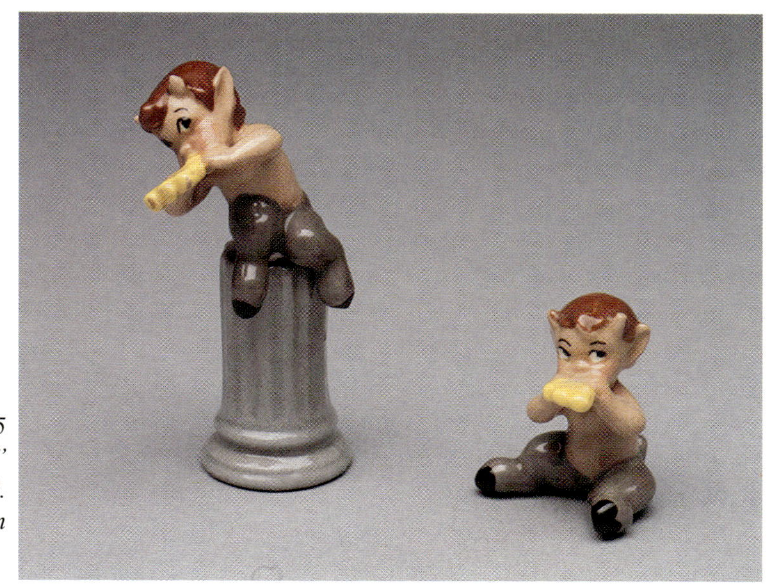

Fauns 1 1/4"each $175-275 each, Greek Column 1 3/4" $40-80.
Not Pictured: Third Faun

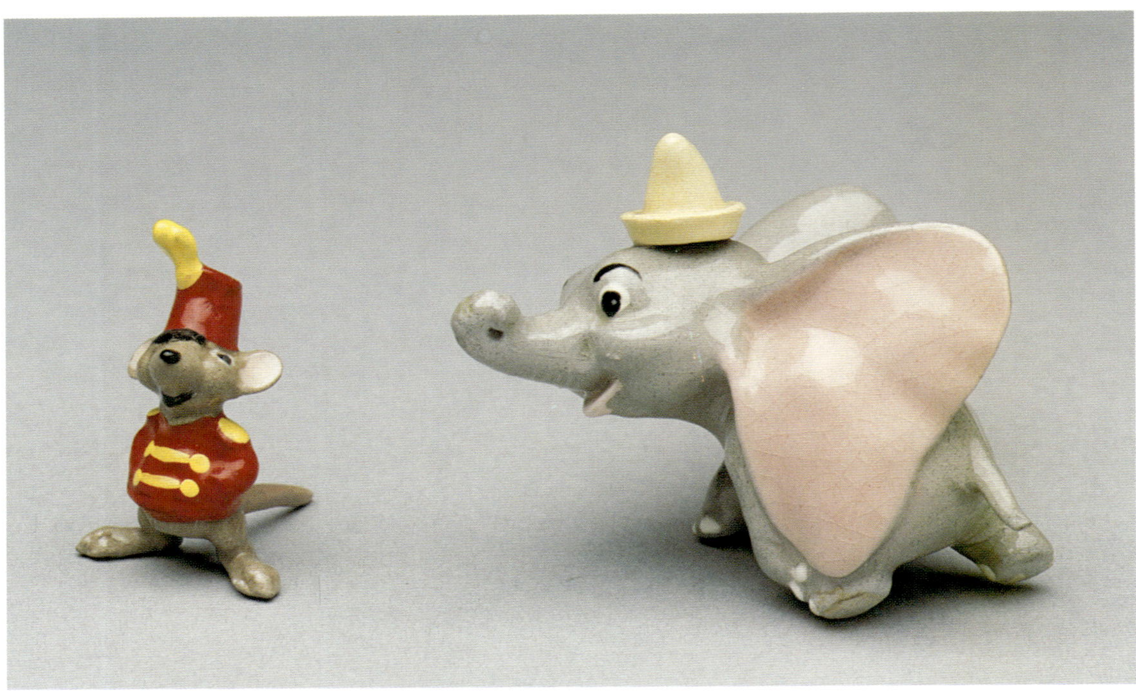

Timothy Mouse 1 1/4" $150-200, Dumbo 1 1/2" $150-275. Dumbo originally sold holding a tiny feather.

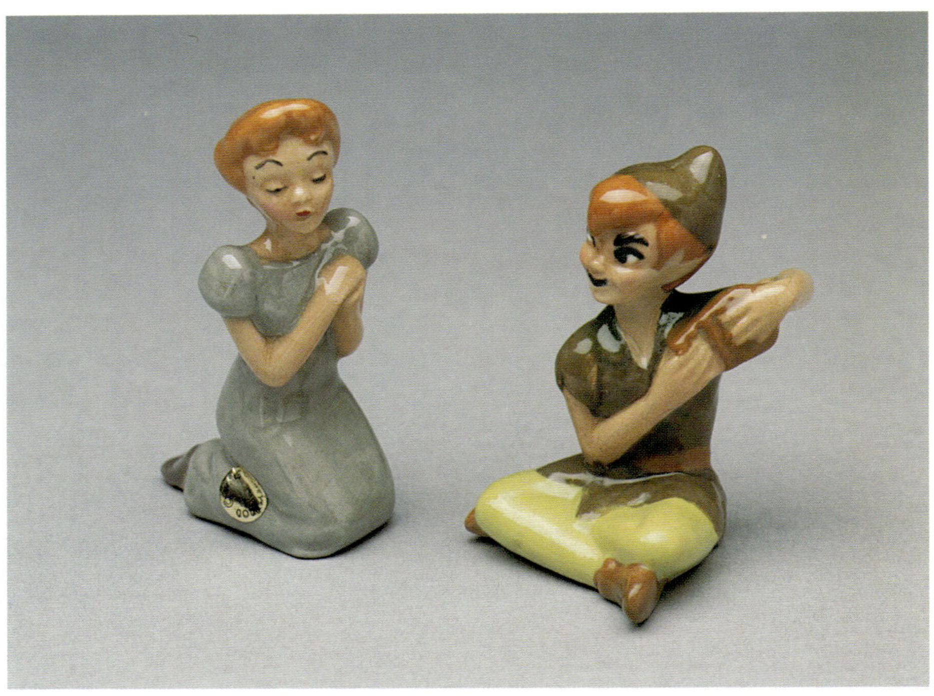

Wendy 2" $250-375, Peter Pan 1 3/4" $200-375.

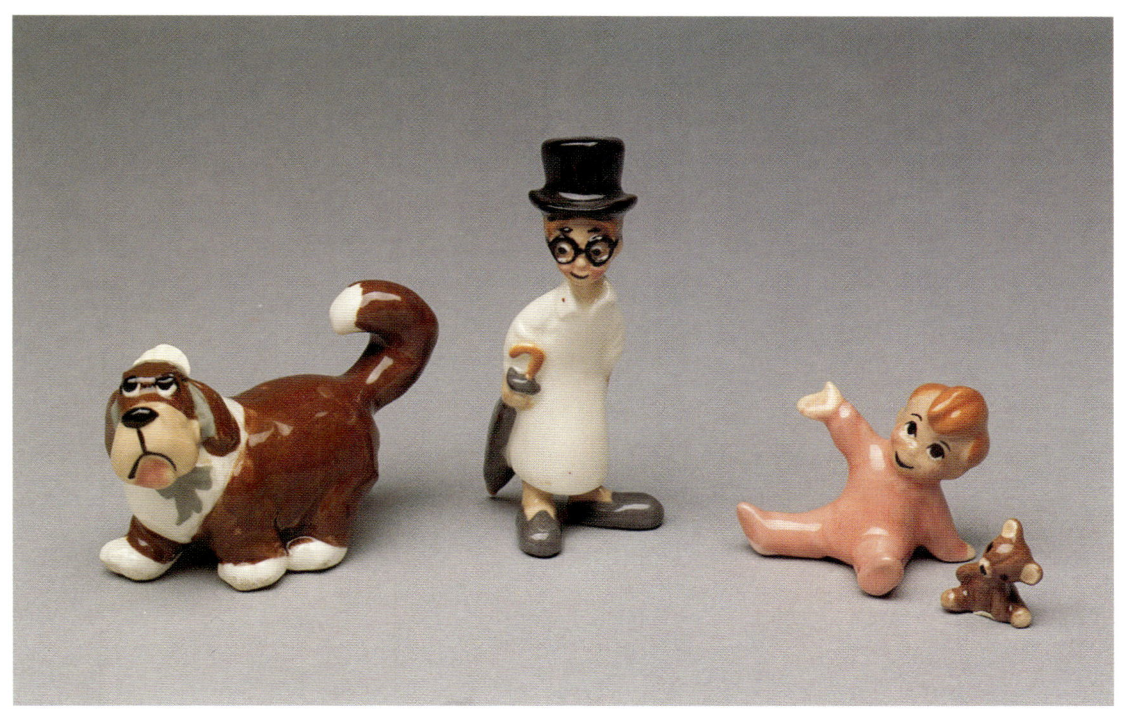

Nana 1 1/2" $175-275, John 2 1/4" $450-550, Michael 1" $125-190, Teddy 1/2" $50-100.

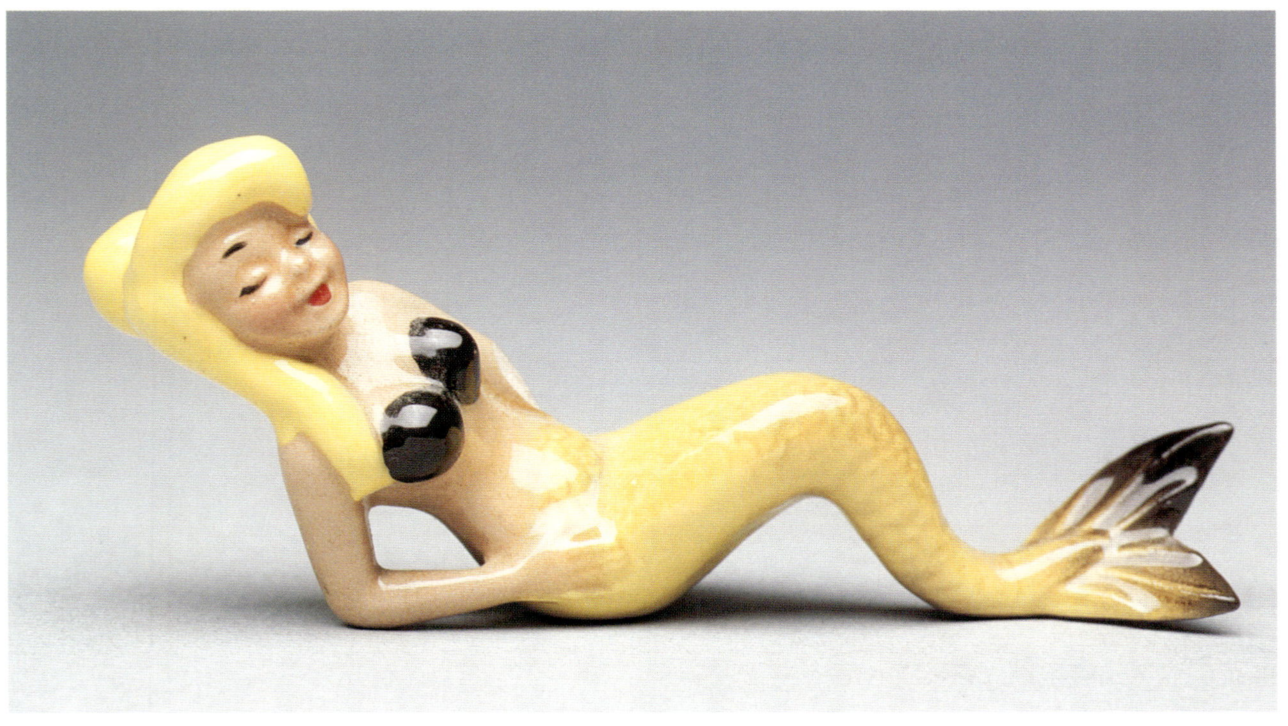

Reclining Mermaid (blonde) 1 1/4" $200-375. Not pictured, kneeling Mermaid (blonde or redhead) $200-375.

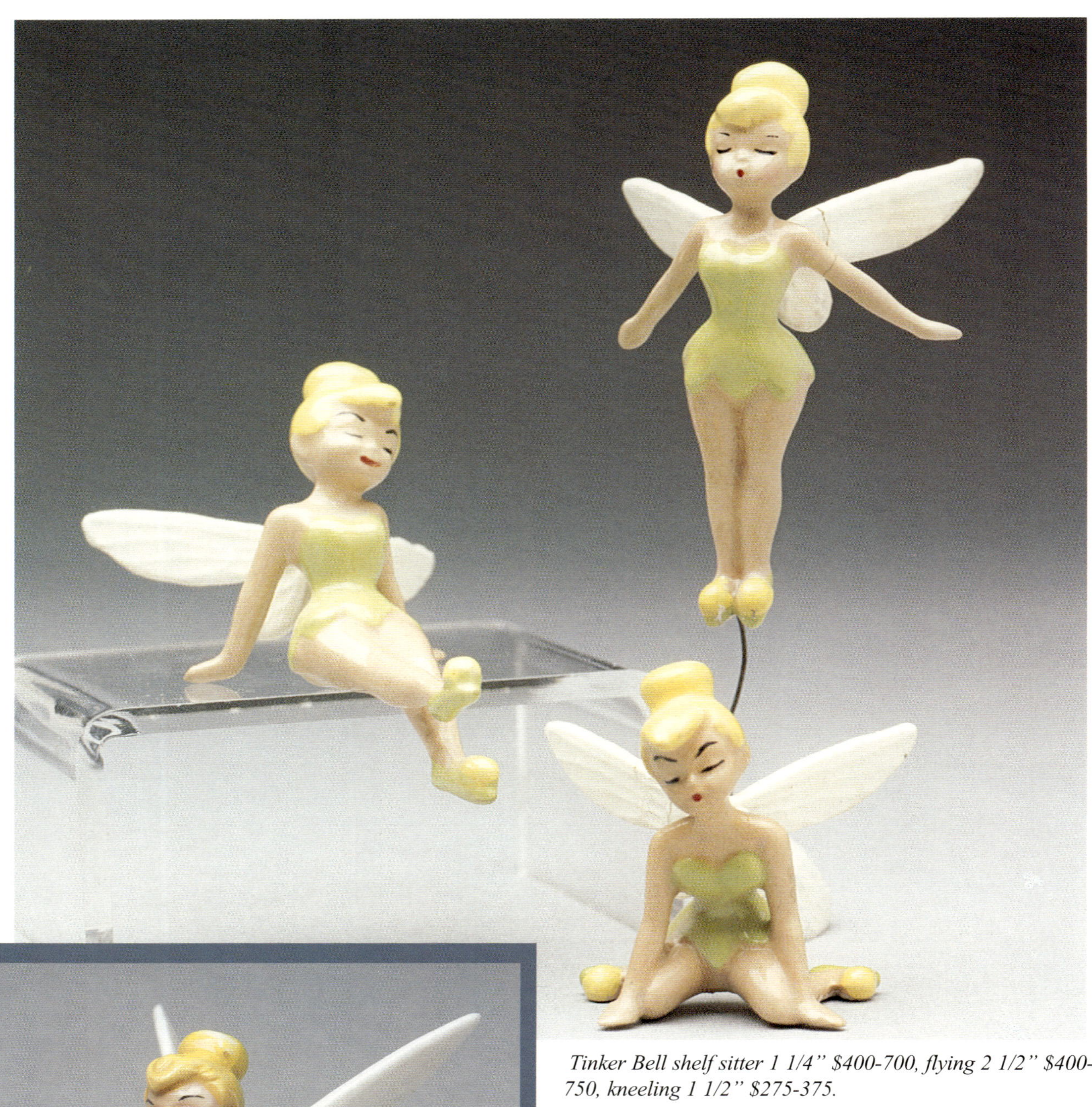

Tinker Bell shelf sitter 1 1/4" $400-700, flying 2 1/2" $400-750, kneeling 1 1/2" $275-375.

Tinker Bell kneeling was later made by Enesco with slight differences.

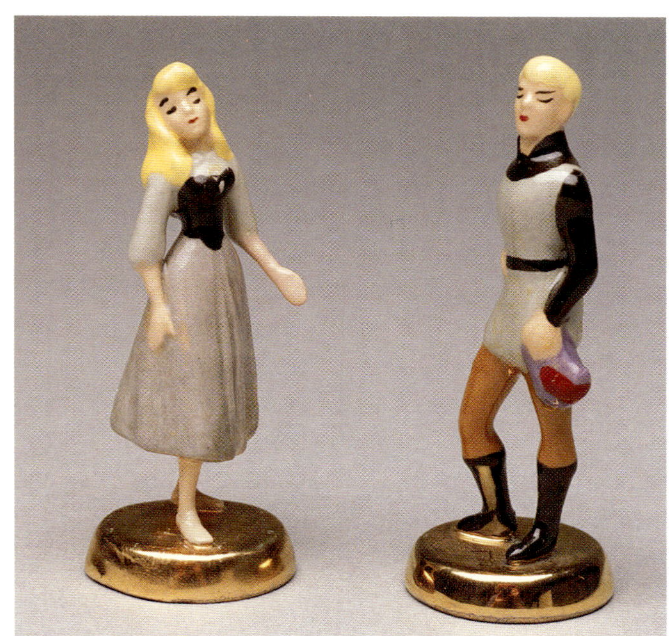

*Briar Rose 2 3/4" $300-450,
Prince Phillip 2 3/4" $250-350.*

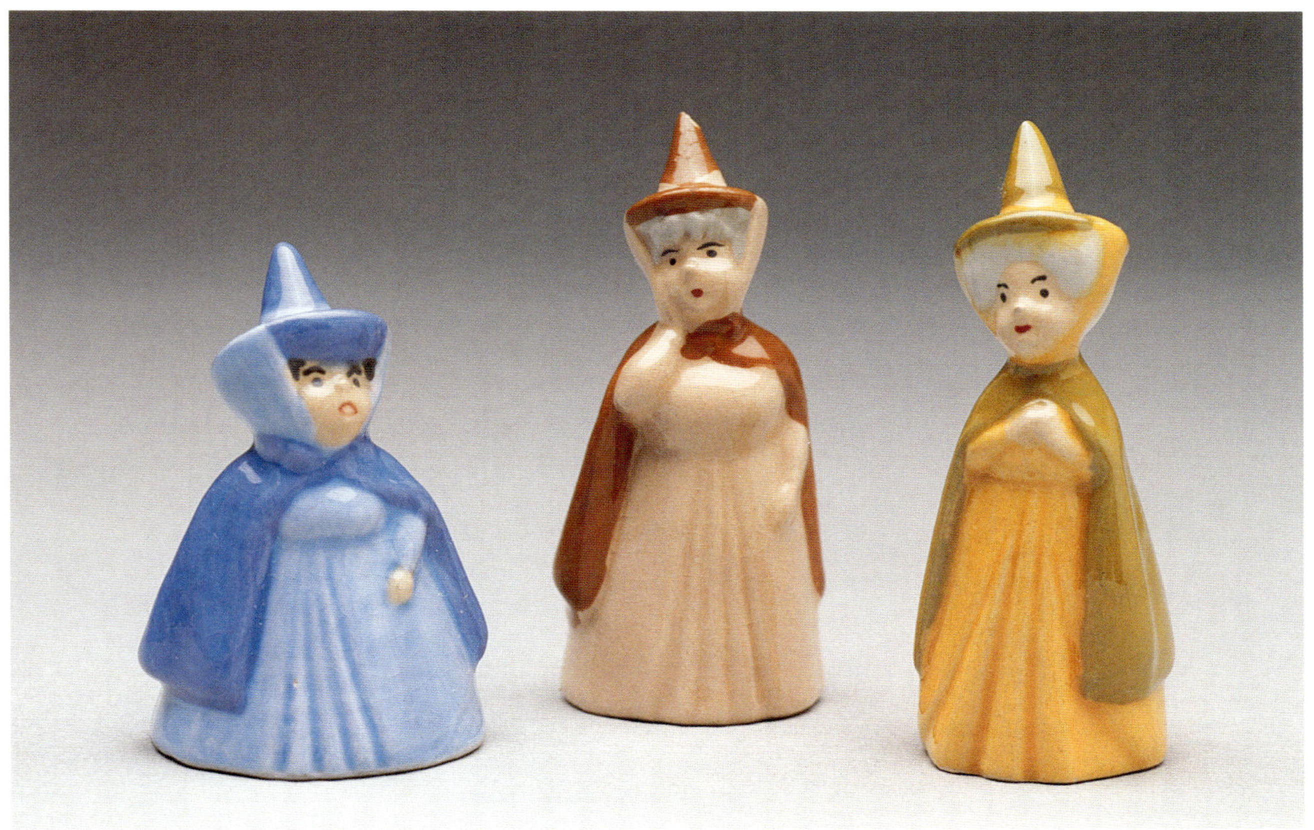

Merriweather 1 3/4" Flora 2 1/4" and Fauna 2 1/4" $180-300 each

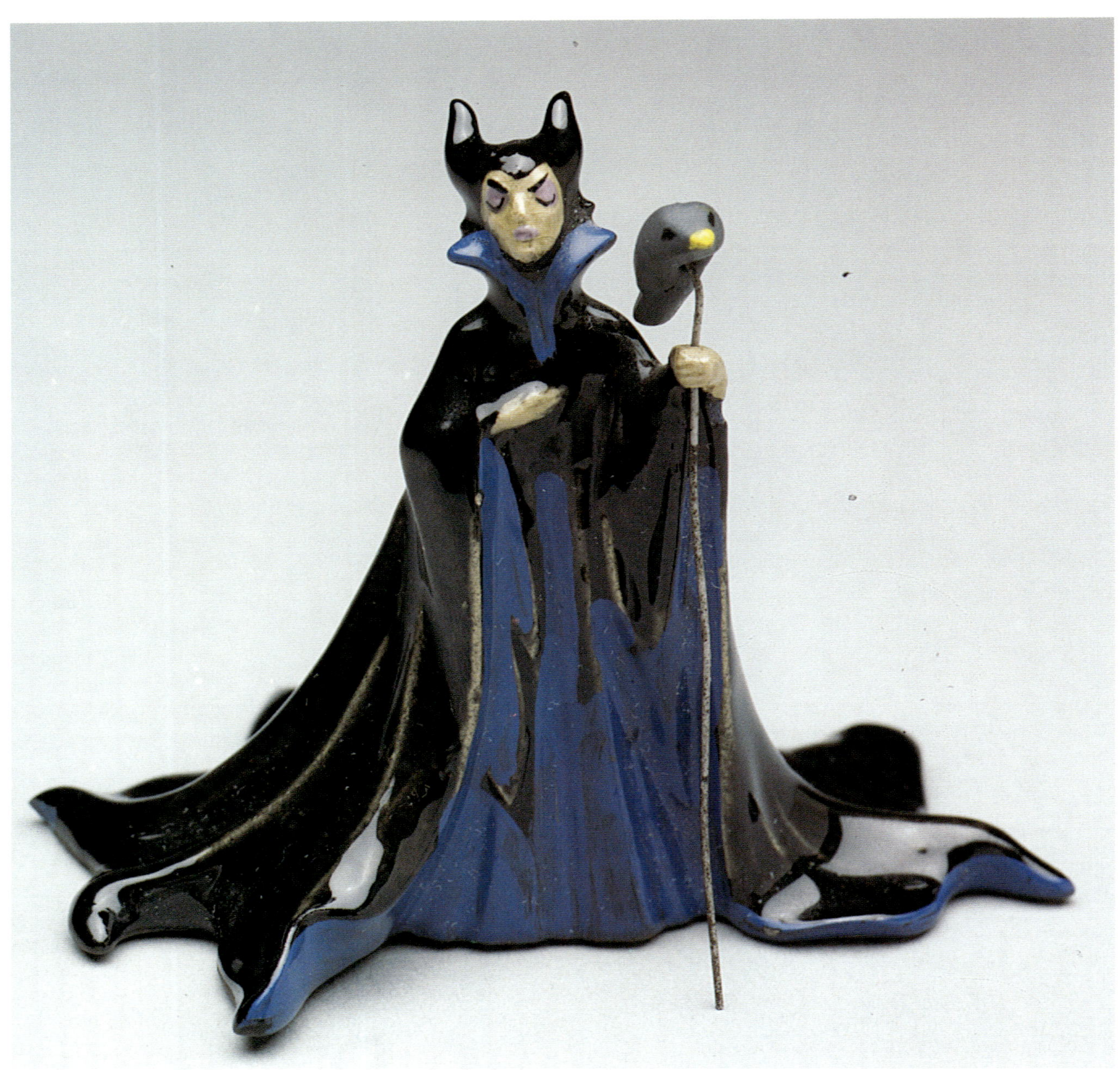

Maleficient and Raven 2" $800-1300.

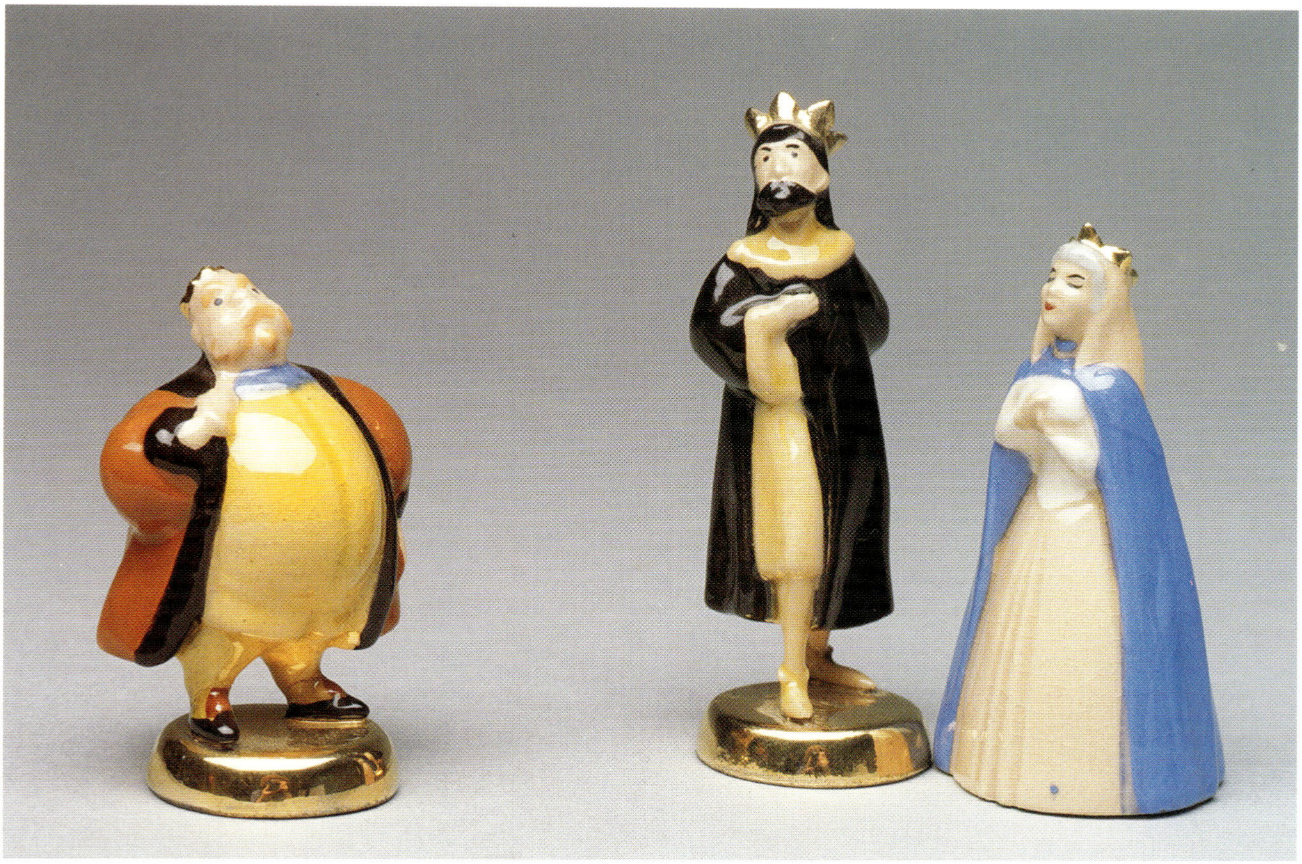

King Hubert 2 1/4" $350-450, King Stefan 3" $350-450, Queen 2 1/2" $250-350

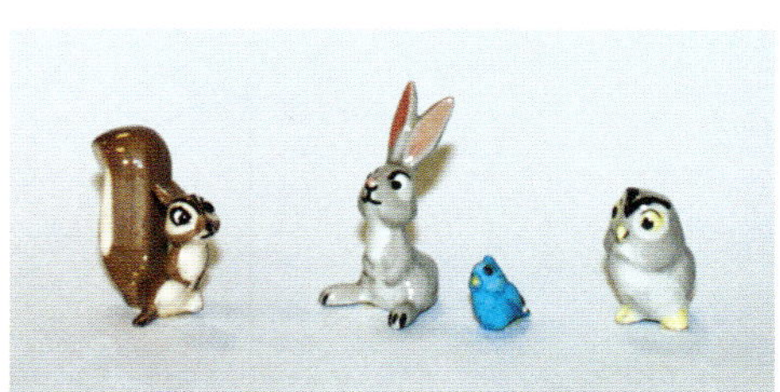

Squirrel 1 1/4", Rabbit 1 1/2" and bluebird 1/2" $60-80 each. Owl 1" $90-150
Not pictured: Cardinal.

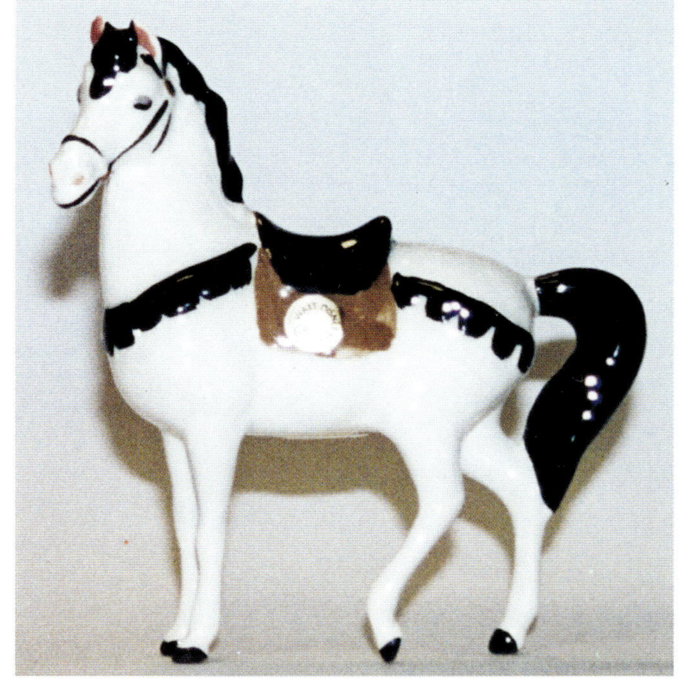

Samson 2 1/2" $900-1500.

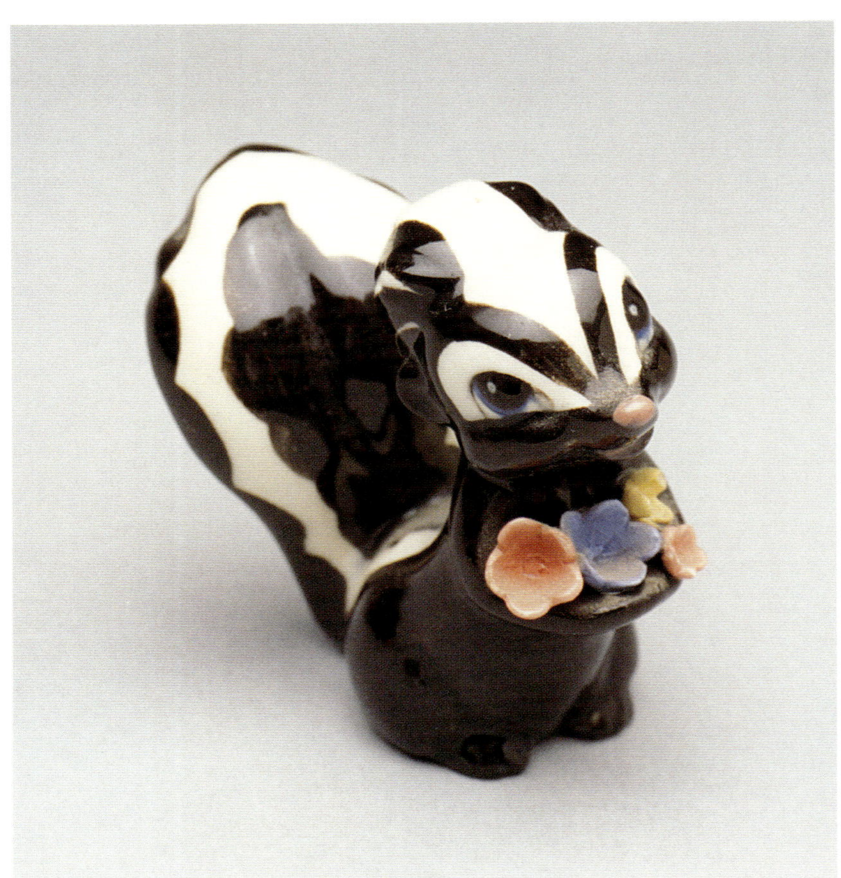

Designer Workshop Flower 3 1/2" $175-250. Not pictured, Designer Workshop's Bambi $300-450.

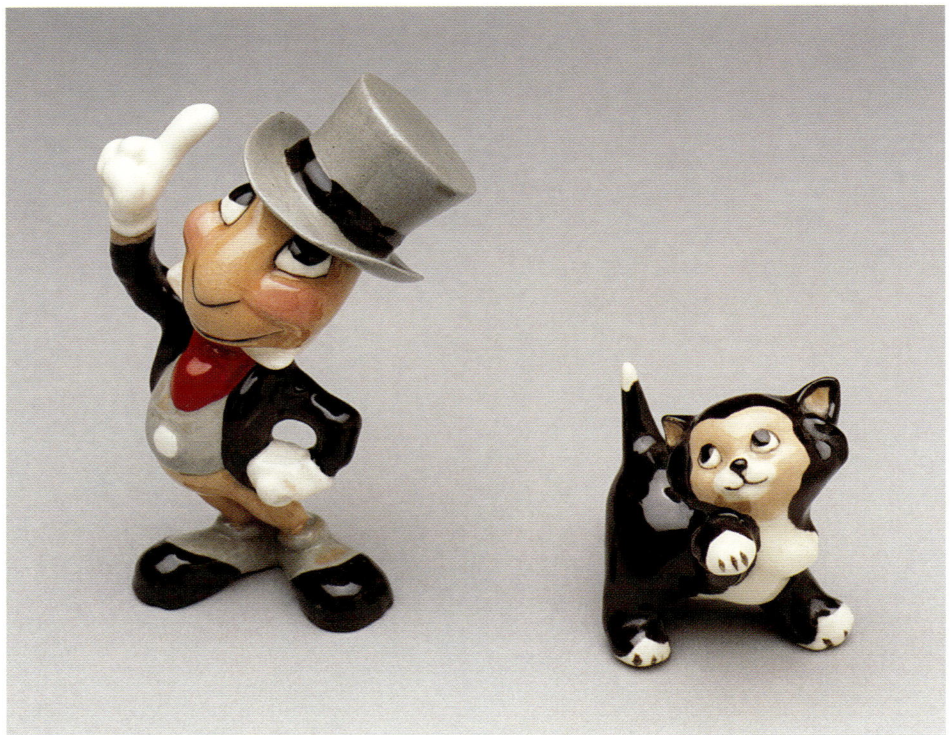

Jiminy Cricket 3 1/2" $450-650, Figaro 1 3/4" $175-350

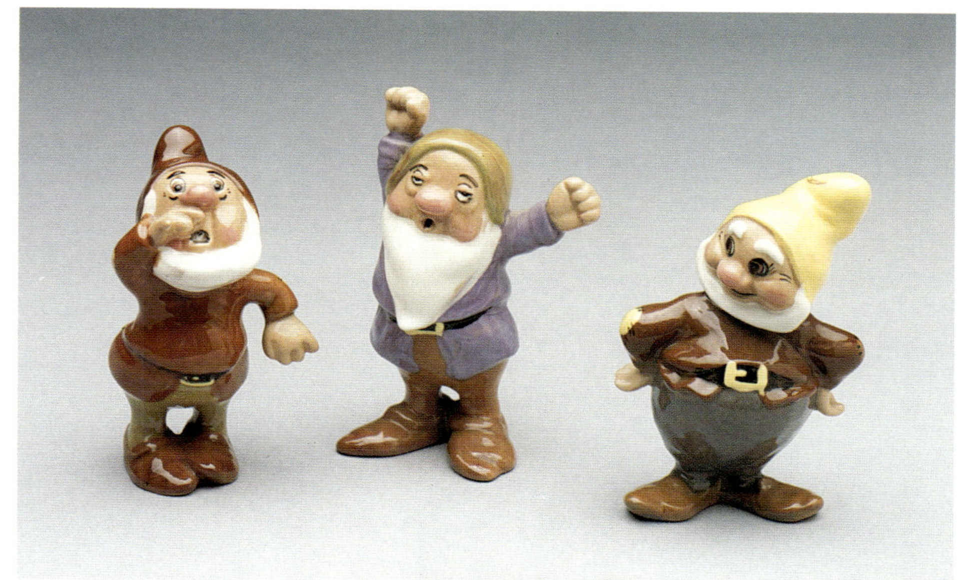

Sneezy 3 1/2", Sleepy 3 3/4", Happy 3 1/2" $175-275 each.

Grumpy 3 1/2" and Doc 3 3/4" $175-275 each.

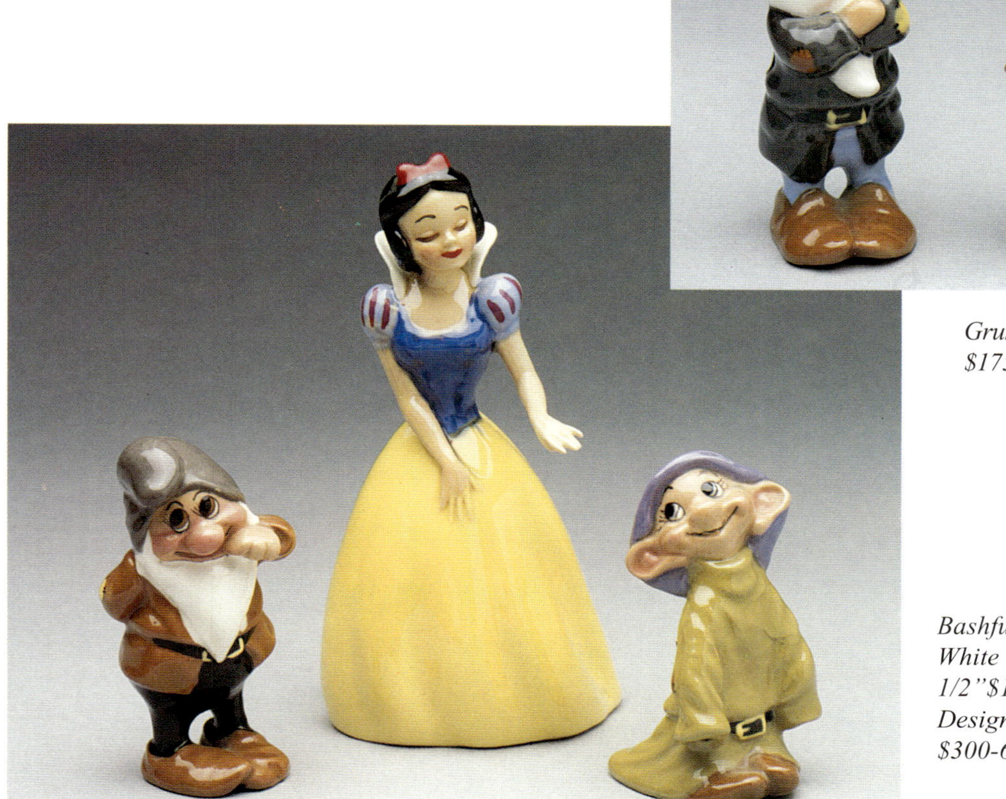

Bashful 3 3/4" $175-275, Snow White 6" $400-650, Dopey 3 1/2"$175-275. Not pictured; Designer Workshop's Dumbo $300-600

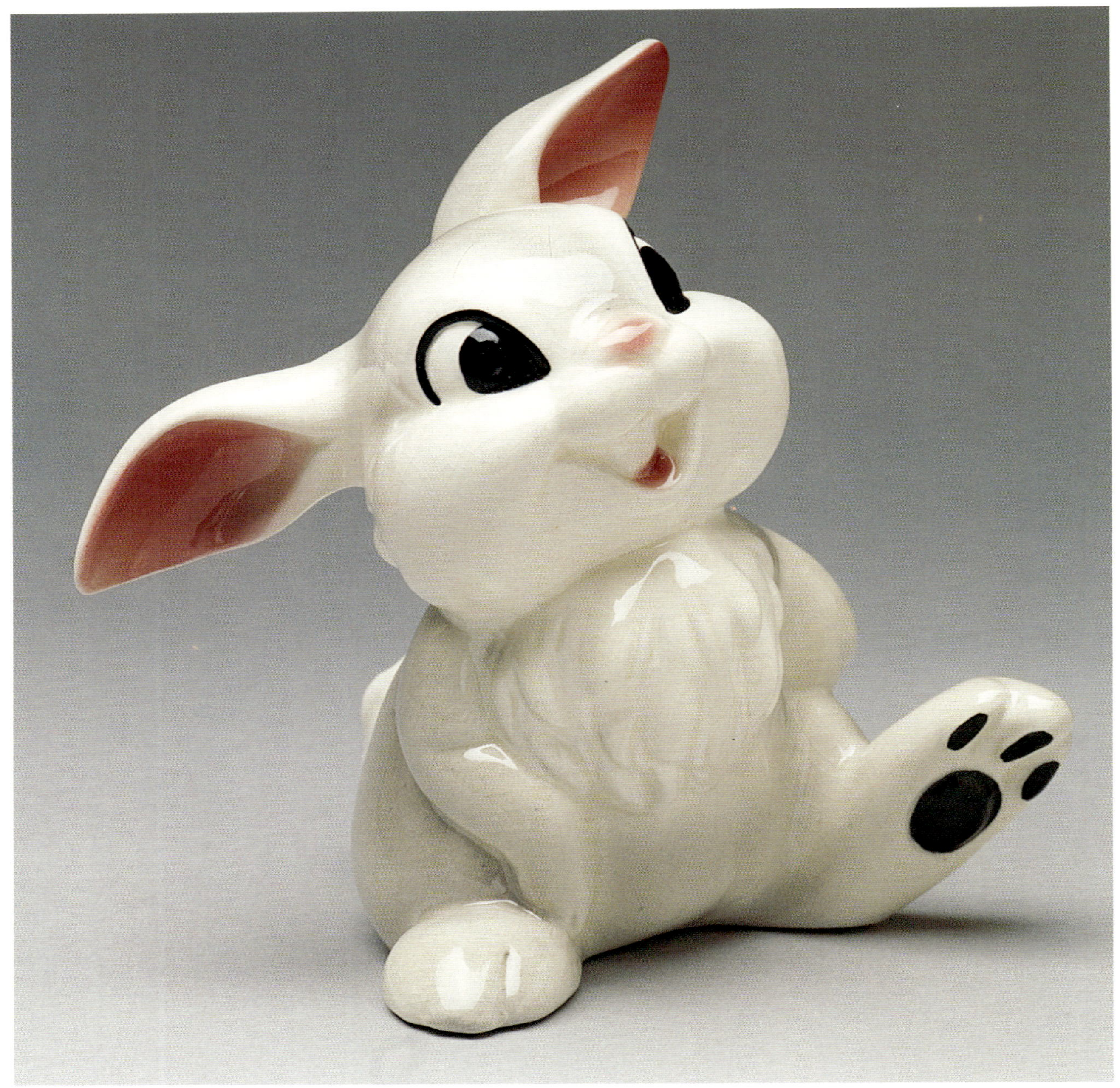

Thumper bank 5 3/4" $400+

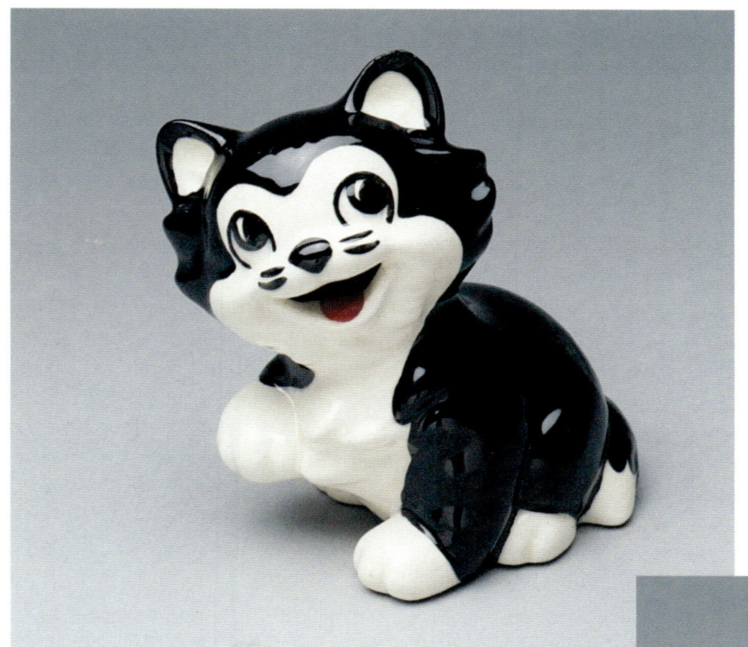

Figaro bank 5 1/2" $300+

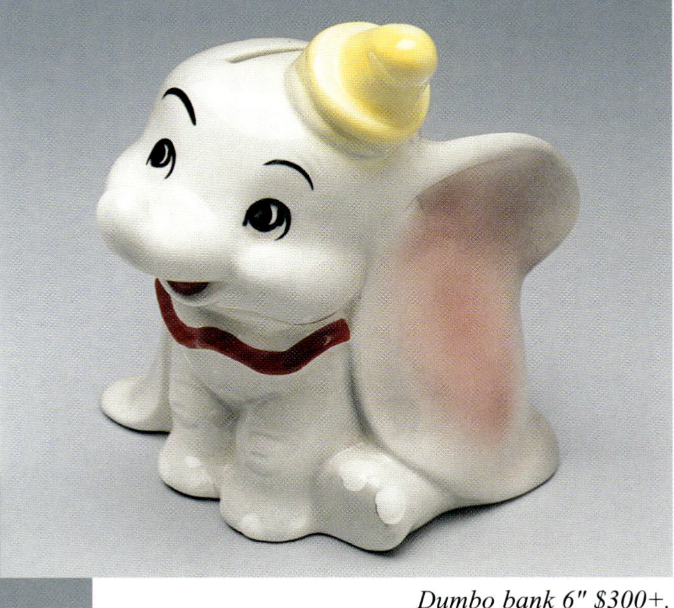

Dumbo bank 6" $300+.

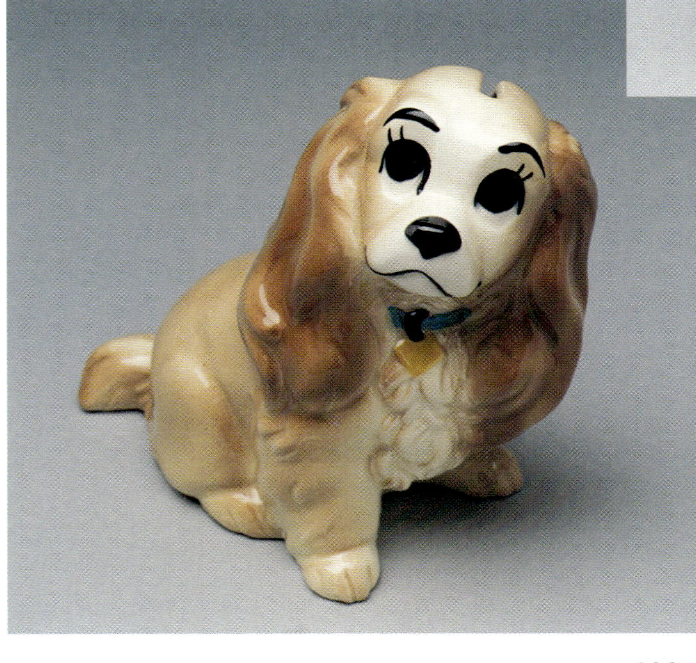

Lady bank 5 1/4" $400+.
Not pictured, Practical Pig bank $400+.

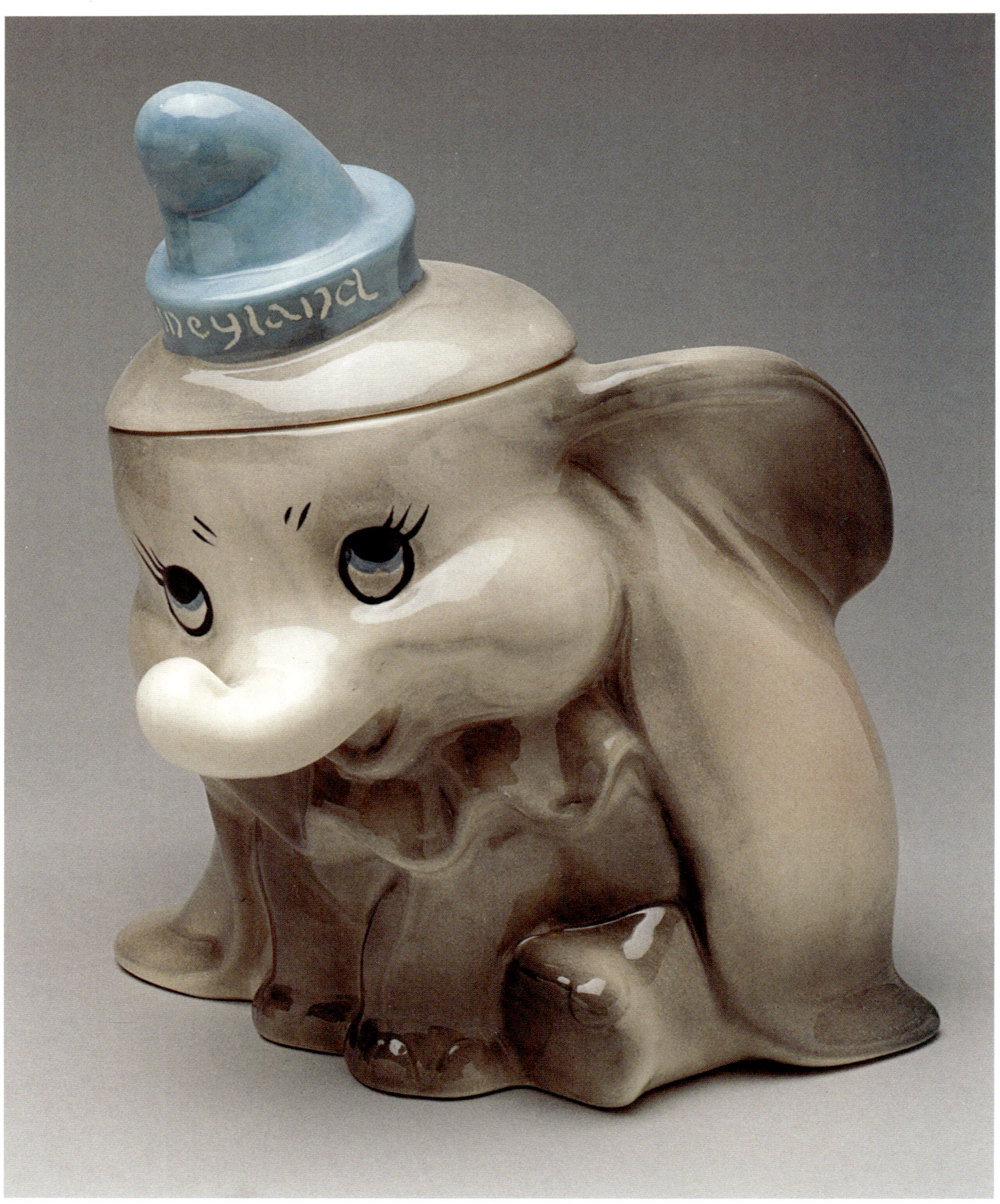

Dumbo cookie jar 10" $1500+. Hat reads "Disneyland".

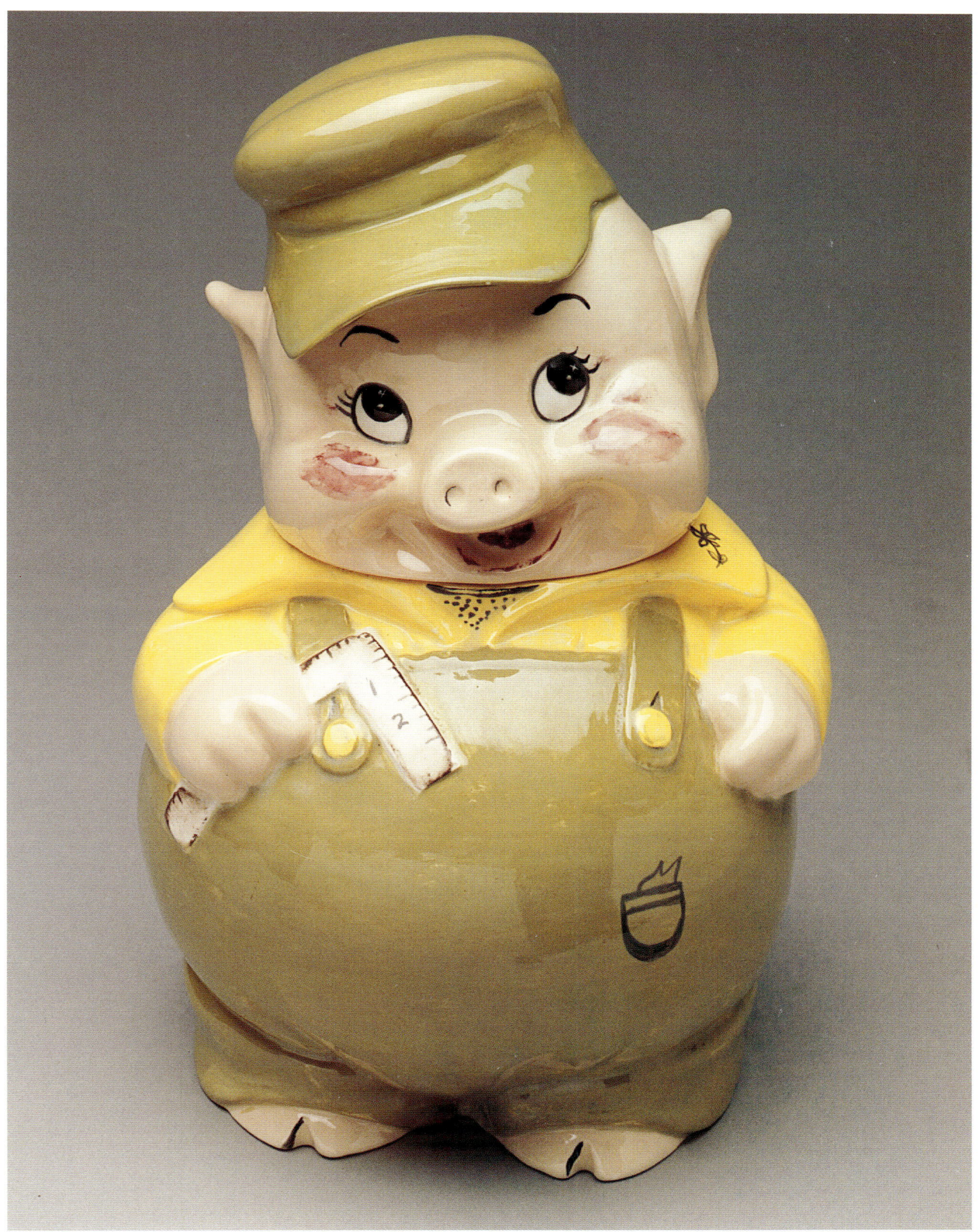

Practical Pig cookie jar 12 1/2" $1500+. Not pictured; Figaro cookie jar and Thumper cookie jar $1500+ each

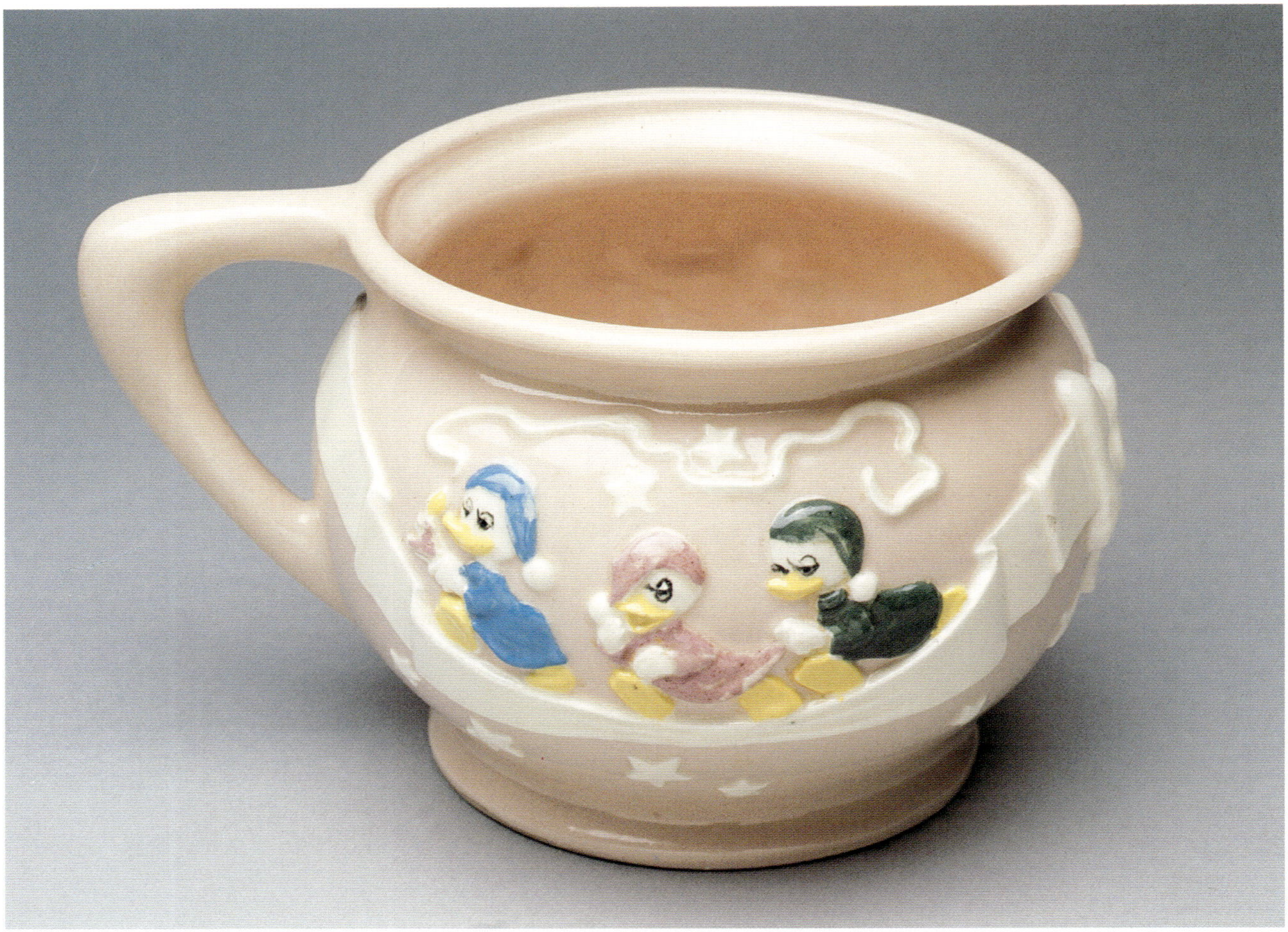

Designer Workshop pottie, pink or blue, $1800+.

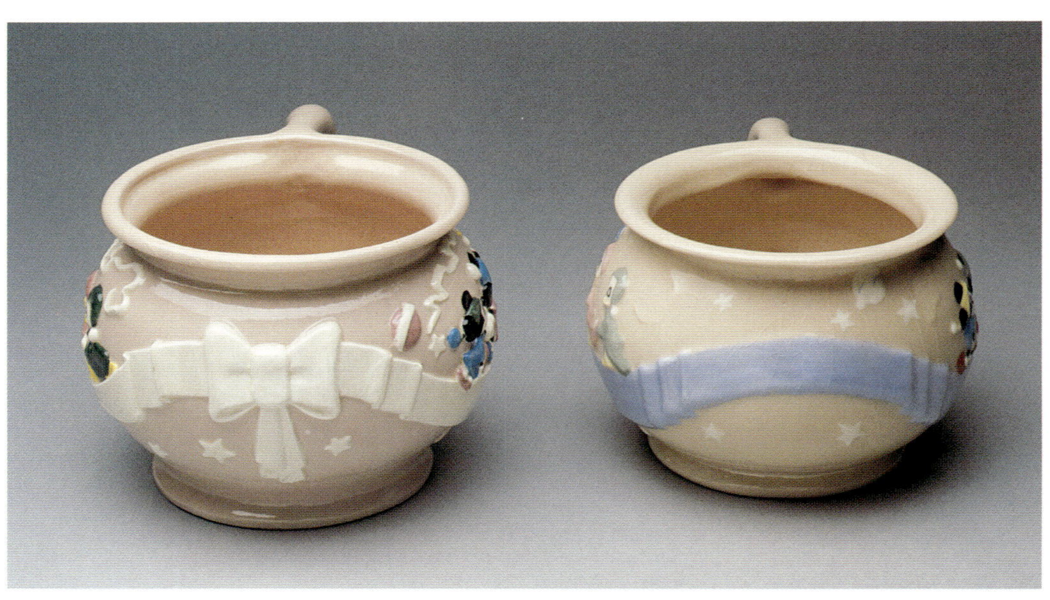

Comparison between Designer Workshop's pottie 4 1/2" (left) and American Pottery Pottie 4 1/4" (right).

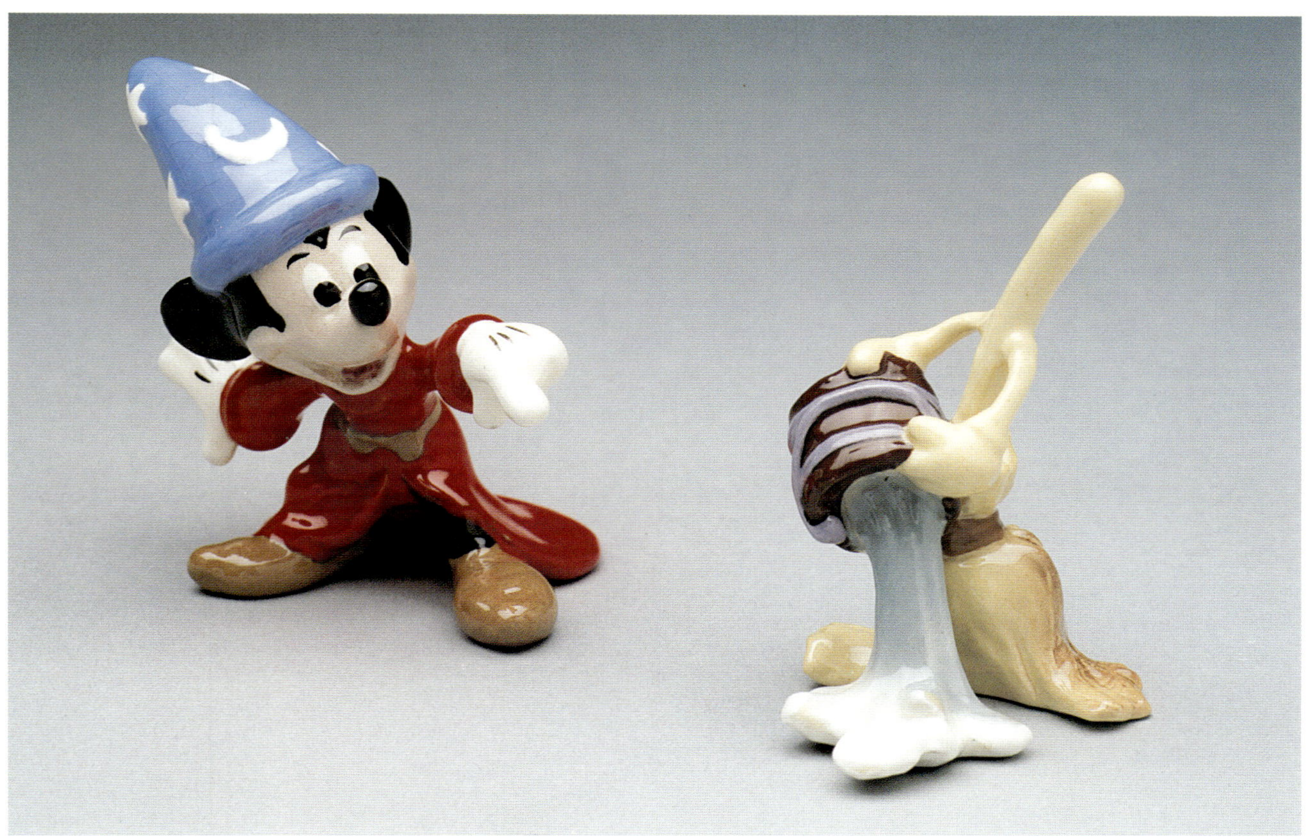

1985 Fantasia set Mickey Sorcerer 2 1/2" $95-200, Broom 2 1/2" $60-80.

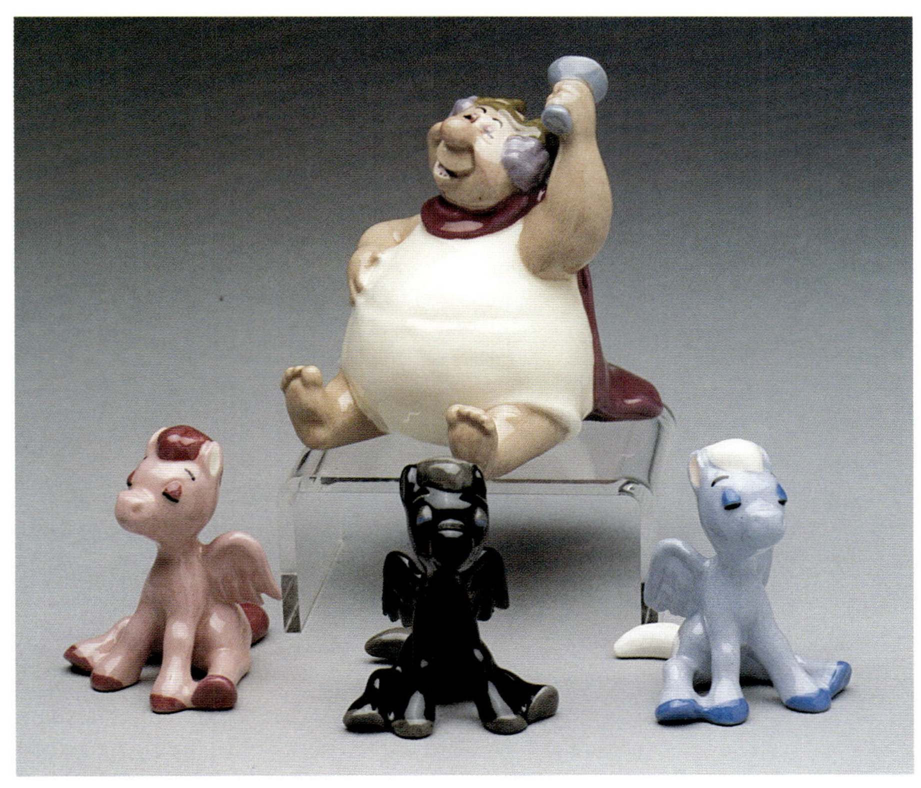

Bacchus 3" $75-125, Pegasus pink, blue or black 1 3/4" $50-90 each

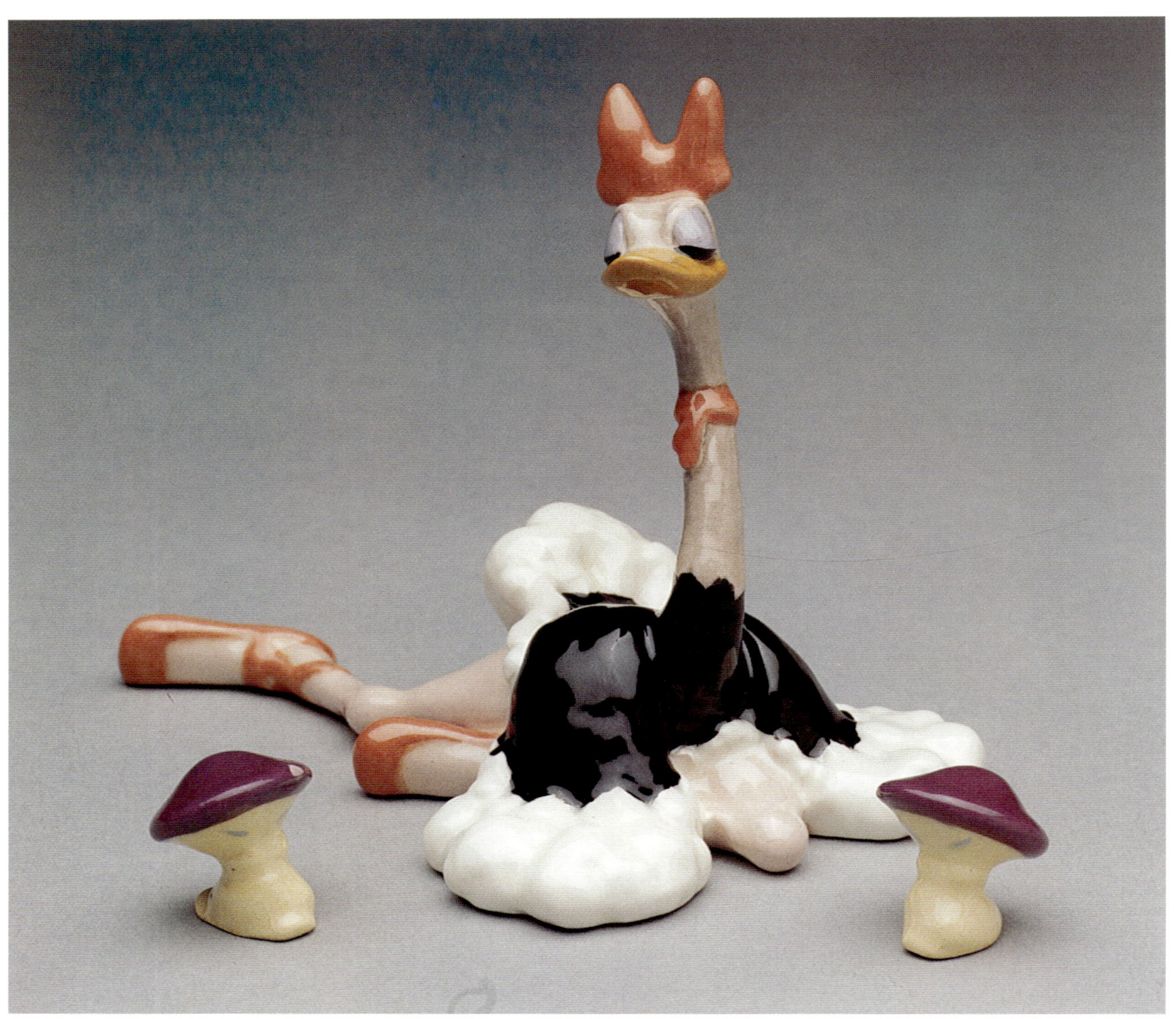

Ostrich 3" $95-250, Mushrooms 3/4" each $20-40 each.

Glossary

This is to assist the many pottery collectors, who are unfamiliar with much of the art terminology used in the ceramic world. It will give the collector a better understanding of how ceramics are created.

Airbrush Decoration- This is the process in which an atomizer is used by employing compressed air and paint in a very fine mist to the fired piece before glazing.

Bisque-pottery that has been fired for the first time but not glazed.

Body-The consistency, structure of the ceramic piece.

Ceramic-Any object made of clay that is fired with other minerals.

Clay-Can be a fine-grained, firm natural material, plastic when wet, becomes hard when fired.

Crackle Glaze- Is the process in which a ceramic object has been fired at a higher and faster temperature in the kiln causing a fine network of cracks throughout the glaze.

Engobe-This is a layer of slip which is applied to alter body color.

Finishing-Is the process of removing all mold lines, rough edges from cast ceramic before the first firing. If the finishing is not done properly, mold lines will appear in the firing.

Glaze-A smooth, glassy coating on a clay surface. Can be made of silica.

Green-Unfired pottery that is dried by natural air.

Kiln furniture- The shelves, cranks, and props used for supporting ware in the kiln

Leather-hard-The state of clay between plastic and dry.

Luster- A metallic quality produced by the reduction of oxides.

Luting-Joining leather-hard clay by slip.

Master mold-The original mold made from the model called the block.

Modeling- This is the process of sculpting the original art from which the molds are made for production of ceramic objects.

Mold- The second process; a hollow plaster of Paris form into which liquid or plastic clay is poured.

On-glaze- Decoration applied on the glaze, usually ceramic colors and enamels.

Oxidation-Firing with enough oxygen to ensure complete combustion of all carbonaceous matter, either in the fuel or in the clay.

Periodic Kiln- This is where pottery is fired/heated in gradual cycles and then allowed to cool before removal from the kiln.

Plasticity- The essential quality of clay, enabling it to be molded.

Relief decoration-Raised modeled decoration.

Resist- A decoration technique in which selected areas of clay, biscuit, or glaze are treated so that they reject the application of slip, color, or glaze.

Sgraffito-The decorative process which employs a scratched line through a layer of slip to expose the clay body beneath.

Slip-A form of liquid clay used for decorating. It can be used to act as a binder (luting) to join clay pieces to an unfired figure.

Slip Decoration-Underglaze decorative process in which colored liquid clay is used as a painting form. Can be tinted many colors.

Talc-A fine-grained mineral which is used as a mixture with clay to give it body and a more plastic form.

Tunnel Kiln-This is a continuous moving conveyor in which ceramic ware is moved through at a very slow pace at varying heat temperatures. May take up to 24 hours for the full process.